AIRLIFT TO AMERICA

ALSO BY TOM SHACHTMAN

NONFICTION
Rumspringa: To Be or Not to Be Amish
Terrors and Marvels
I Seek My Brethren
Absolute Zero and the Conquest of Cold
Around the Block
The Most Beautiful Villages of New England
The Inarticulate Society
Skyscraper Dreams
Decade of Shocks, 1963–1974
The Phony War, 1939–1940
Edith and Woodrow
The Day America Crashed

FICTION
Driftwhistler
Wavebender
Beachmaster

COLLABORATIVE WORKS
Dead Center, with Shiya Ribowsky
Torpedoed, with Edmund D. Pope
Justice Is Served, with Robert K. Ressler
I Have Lived in the Monster, with Robert K. Ressler
Whoever Fights Monsters, with Robert K. Ressler
The Gilded Leaf, with Patrick Reynolds
Image by Design, with Clive Chajet
Straight to the Top, with Paul G. Stern
The FBI-KGB War, with Robert J. Lamphere

AIRLIFT TO AMERICA

HOW BARACK OBAMA, SR., JOHN F. KENNEDY,

TOM MBOYA, *and* 800 EAST AFRICAN STUDENTS

CHANGED THEIR WORLD *and* OURS

Tom Shachtman

St. Martin's Press ➤ New York

To the airlift students

AIRLIFT TO AMERICA. Copyright © 2009 by Tom Shachtman. Foreword copyright © 2009 by Harry Belafonte. All rights reserved. Printed in the United States of America. For information, address St. Martin's Press, 175 Fifth Avenue, New York, N.Y. 10010.

www.stmartins.com

Library of Congress Cataloging-in-Publication Data

Shachtman, Tom, 1942–
    Airlift to America : how Barack Obama, Sr., John F. Kennedy, Tom Mboya, and 800 East African students changed their world and ours / Tom Shachtman.— 1st ed.
        p. cm.
    ISBN 978-0-312-57075-0
    1. African-American Students Federation.   2. College students—Africa, East—History—20th century.   3. United States—Relations—East Africa. 4. East Africa—Relations—United States.   I. Title.

LA1503.7.S53 2010
378.1'98299676073—dc22

2009013186

First Edition: September 2009

10   9   8   7   6   5   4   3   2   1

Contents

Foreword

During World War II, millions of Africans, Asians, Caribbeans, and Latin Americans fought bravely alongside Allied forces to crush Hitler and his fascist allies. Not much has been written about them. Their commitment was to put an end to not only fascism but also to the concept of race supremacy, and to invest their hopes in promises of democracy and social equality. When the war ended, those promises of a more humane and compassionate world were not fulfilled. Throughout the world, colonialism continued to thrive

and, in America, the unjust laws of legal segregation and racial oppression grew with a vengeance.

I volunteered and served in the armed forces of the United States
during World War II, and recall how painful it was for me, and for
hundreds of thousands of African-American men and women who
served the country, to return home only to find that there was no
reward for us. It was a bitter time because in the wake of this great
victory, America showed no generosity toward its citizens of color.
We returned to intensified conditions of racial, political, and social
oppression. The same was true for millions of people of color around
the world. The British, French, Dutch, and Portuguese, who had
colonized more than two-thirds of the world's population, subjected
their victims to the same harsh, inhumane conditions being experienced in the United States by black Americans. But, like black Americans, the colonial peoples refused to return to "business as usual."
Together, they began a great global rebellion.

In 1956 I met a remarkable young man my age with a revolutionary vision that would change the course of history. His name was
Tom Mboya, and he was a labor leader with a passionate dedication
to rid his country, Kenya, of the shackles of colonialism. He detailed
for me a view of Africa that inspired my commitment to its struggle
for liberation.

Airlift to America tells the story of Tom's vision and the courage
of hundreds of young people who dared to venture forth to unknown
destinations that were far from the heretofore "acceptable" places
for higher education, such as London and Moscow.

It also tells the story of a group of white and black Americans who
understood that in postcolonial, independent Africa, without education there could be no government, no democracy, and no justice.
This group became as active in supporting the liberation struggle in
Africa as it was in its commitment to the civil rights movement and
erasing the brutality of racism in our country. It was a very, very tiny
but valiant group of people who accomplished remarkable things.

Tom sought me out and through his eyes I saw the harsh ugliness of colonialism. I met extraordinary young people determined to live life free of the prison of colonialism. Kenya, like Tanganyika (now part of Tanzania) and other East African countries, then had no universities. There was only one college, Makerere, in Uganda, and it was a technical school. The fear was that when *uhuru*—freedom—came to Kenya in 1963, there would not be enough people prepared to take over the many civil service, diplomatic, and teaching positions that would be vacated by the British.

The year 1959 saw the rise of anticolonial support movements around the world as well as of the civil rights movement in our country led by Reverend Martin Luther King, Jr.—he, too, was just thirty years old—and of a young senator with presidential aspirations, John F. Kennedy, chair of the Senate Subcommittee on Africa.

The period and spirit of the airlift were connected to, and in line and rhythm with, the whole landscape of America on the issues of race and civil rights. I knew firsthand, and through the eyes of Dr. King, of the boycotts and turmoil in the South. It was perfectly natural for us to want to be part of both of these creative struggles for freedom. Largely as a result of Mboya's meeting with John F. Kennedy and the senator's meeting with Dr. King, he, too, learned to appreciate the historic significance and moral imperative of the liberation struggle in Africa and the civil rights movement in America. Kennedy's role in supporting the 1960 airlift and Dr. King's movement proved equally important.

I, along with Jackie Robinson and fellow artist Sidney Poitier, agreed to help implement Tom's vision. I wrote letters and gave concerts to raise funds to charter airplanes that would bring young people from East Africa who had successfully applied for scholarships at many of our colleges and universities. The concerts did well and the response to the mailing was extraordinary. Postal workers from the Bronx sent one- and two-dollar contributions with letters explaining how important they realized the airlift would be for the future of a free Africa. Many people from across America sent their precious contributions, few exceeding twenty-five dollars. It was an amazing outpouring of belief in a dream.

Today, Professor Wangari Maathai, who came on the 1960 airlift, is the first African woman to become a Nobel Peace laureate. Perez Olindo, a 1959 airlift alumnus, became one of Kenya and Africa's greatest conservationists. Professor Mahmood Mamdani of Columbia University, the brilliant "public intellectual" from Uganda, came on the 1963 airlift. Their stories and many others are recounted in these pages. One that readers will find of great interest is that of Barack Hussein Obama, Sr. Imagine—perhaps if not for support from the African American Students Foundation, he might not have come to America. Then who would be in the White House today?

We had no idea how many ripple effects this effort, the vision of young Tom Mboya, would have both in East Africa and in our own country. Tragically, the men who took the risks, who had the passion to insist on equality, justice, and freedom, all met similar fates. Tom Mboya might one day have been president of Kenya, but he was assassinated in 1969. Dr. King, who met with Mboya and also helped a number of airlift students, was felled by an assassin in 1968. John F. Kennedy, who was so impressed with Tom at their first meeting in 1959 that he persuaded his father's family foundation to support the 1960 airlift, was gunned down in 1963.

This book about the airlift and its impact is also a testament to the continued need for young people with courageous visions to take risks for social change. And for the rest of us to support them.

—Harry Belafonte

Cast thy bread upon the waters;
for thou shalt find it after many days.

—Ecclesiastes 11:1

AIRLIFT TO AMERICA

Prologue

IOWA *and* KOGELO

In December of 2007, before the Iowa caucuses—the first tests of the 2008 presidential primary season—Senator Barack Hussein Obama of Illinois was not thought by most Americans to have much of a chance of winning his party's nomination or the presidency. He was not well known in the rest of the country, and the media for the most part treated his candidacy as a novelty because he was African-American. That he was truly an African-American, the son of a Kenyan father of the same name and of a white mother from Kansas, was not well understood despite the growing popularity of his memoir *Dreams from My Father*, in which he explored his unusual combination of African and American heritage.

Prior to Obama's 2004 election to the Senate he had been an Illinois state senator, and before that a community organizer, civil rights attorney, and law school professor. His curriculum vitae also included having been elected editor in chief of the *Harvard Law Review*, the first black to hold that position. Prior to declaring his candidacy for the presidency he had come to intense national attention only briefly, during the 2004 Democratic National Convention, when he gave a rousing, well-received keynote address that marked him as an up-and-coming national figure. In that speech he mentioned that his father, the son of a cook, had herded goats in Kenya and attended a school with a tin roof, and then had received "a scholarship to study in a magical place, America," but this aspect of his story did not attract much attention.

Though a *60 Minutes* profile in early 2007 raised his visibility, for most of 2007 his chances to become the Democratic nominee were considered slim. New York Senator Hillary Clinton, wife of former president Bill Clinton, was the front-runner, and she and the pundits predicted that she would wrap up the nomination in advance of the February 5, 2008, Super Tuesday primaries. But Obama kept on giving speeches and meeting people and touching bases. Although his campaign was relentlessly forward-looking, he frequently acknowledged the past. Speaking in Selma, Alabama, site of the 1965 civil rights confrontation known as Bloody Sunday, he told an audience, "I'm here because somebody marched. I'm here because you-all sacrificed for me. I stand on the shoulders of giants."

By December 2007 opinion polls in Iowa, portions of which adjoin Illinois, showed a definite shift to Obama. His message of change and his friendly appeal, coupled with superior organizing, drew him even with Clinton. The polls showed that white voters were not afraid to vote for this particular African-American candidate. *Time* magazine commented, though, that Iowa "isn't always a good match for Obama's strengths. The graveyards of political campaigns are littered with candidates who excel at forging connections with individual voters but who can't give a big speech to save their lives. Obama may be that rare politician with the opposite problem. Before a crowd of 4,000, he can be magnetic and compelling. But before a crowd of several hundred, he can sometimes fall flat."

Predictions were for a virtual three-way tie in the Iowa caucuses among Obama, Clinton, and former senator John Edwards, the 2004 vice-presidential nominee. It was expected that after Iowa, primaries in New Hampshire and other New England states would put Clinton in position to clinch the nomination. Obama, like other supposedly attractive candidates before him, was expected to fold his campaign within a month or so.

And so on January 4, 2008, when Obama unexpectedly won the Iowa Democratic presidential caucuses, handily defeating Clinton even among women voters, the effect was stunning. Overnight he became a leading contender for his party's presidential nomination. David Brooks, conservative columnist for *The New York Times* and commentator for PBS, in his *Times* column called Obama's primary victory a political "earthquake."

> You'd have to have a heart of stone not to feel moved by this. An African-American man wins a closely fought campaign in a pivotal state. He beats two strong opponents, including the mighty Clinton machine. He does it in a system that favors rural voters. He does it by getting young voters to come out to the caucuses.
>
> This is a huge moment. It's one of those times when a movement that seemed ethereal and idealistic became a reality and took on political substance.... Obama is changing the tone of American liberalism, and maybe American politics, too.

Obama was being propelled to prominence and potential victory by a tide of youthful voters who saw in him the promise of a society whose politics would no longer turn on racial images and stereotypes. His apparent ease with his unusual background contributed to that perception. But he was also the embodiment of the hopes of several generations of Americans, black and white, who had fought for civil rights. They perceived his candidacy, and the possibility that he might actually be elected president, as the chance to break a barrier that they had been trying to cross for fifty years, in pursuit of social justice and a color-blind society. Obama encapsulated the aspirations of both groups in his oft-repeated line, "We are the ones we have been waiting for."

The history of Barack Obama's rise is a version of the American dream story, but not the one that most Americans were used to hearing. In most previous iterations of the dream saga—rags to riches, anonymity to glory, victim to victor—the protagonist was white and from a European background. Few who achieved the promise of the dream had been men or women of color, and almost none had a parent who came from Africa.

As the campaign wore on, the public was intrigued to learn, from Obama's now-bestselling books and from interviews with him and capsule bios on television and on the Internet, that his father, Barack Obama, Sr., had come to the United States in 1959, supposedly with several dozen other East Africans, mainly from Kenya, in an "airlift." Some reportage called it the Kennedy airlift, for John F. Kennedy; others the Mboya airlift, for Kenyan politician Tom Mboya; and still others, the East African airlift. The term "airlift" was shorthand, a reference to planes chartered to bring dozens and then hundreds of East African students to the United States between 1959 and 1963.

As interest in Obama grew, so did curiosity about his Kenyan roots. Some articles included the information that Obama Sr. had been a friend of fellow Luo tribesman Mboya, the visionary who conceived the airlifts and was able to get them airborne through the efforts of American friends. Others cited the tale that a generation earlier, Obama's grandfather had been the first person in his tribal area—Alego Kogelo, the home of the Olego people, near Lake Victoria in western Kenya—to have exchanged his native garb for Western clothes.

The facts bore out much, though not all, of this story. Grandfather Onyango Obama was a Luo of considerable personal force and integrity. Born in 1898, he had fought in various parts of Africa in the Great War, then returned to Kogelo to clear land for a farm near Lake Victoria; but to earn money for his family he had also worked as a cook in Nairobi and on safari. An herbalist, he had fought against the confidence schemes of shamans and witch doctors. When a first wife was unable to bear children he took a second and later a third, who did. Despite many obstacles, he learned to read and write some English, a rare thing among rural Africans then. Initially subjected to suspicion from the other villagers for this, he eventually earned their respect because he was one of the few who could speak with the Europeans in their own language. He was the first to adopt Western ways, such as putting food on plates and eating with utensils. Converted to Protestantism when young, he later converted again to the Muslim religion, which accounts for the name that he gave to his eldest son, born in 1936. He also added "Hussein" to his own name. Later, Onyango drifted away from the Muslim religion, did not raise his children in that faith, and was not known by the Hussein name. He served again with the British in Burma in World War II, and then returned home. According to his widow, Onyango was arrested in 1949, imprisoned, and tortured by the British for supposedly consorting with other former soldiers who were beginning the revolt that would become known as the Mau Mau uprising. Never convicted, upon his release he became bitterly anti-British.

Barack Obama, Sr., was brilliant, rebellious, charming from an early age, and always difficult to handle. He would take many days off from classes, then cram for exams and come out with the highest marks. Eventually, his antics got him expelled from high school. Onyango then sent his son to the port city of Mombasa to work as a clerk for an Asian friend; Barack left that job and found another, at a lower salary. He drifted into the orbit of the Kenyatta-led political party at around the time that emergency regulations were promulgated in 1952 in reaction to the Mau Mau rebellion, and was briefly jailed. He married, fathered two children, and made a connection with Mboya, then a rising union official, and with another aspiring political Luo, Oginga Odinga, who was known as a committed socialist. Obama also came to the attention of two American women working in Kenya, Mrs. Helen Roberts of Palo Alto and Miss Elizabeth Mooney of Maryland, a literacy specialist. They recognized his intellect and thirst for further education and helped him take correspondence courses, to which—for the first time—he applied his full efforts and skills.

According to Olara Otunnu, an advocate for children in armed conflicts and a former undersecretary-general of the UN, who as president of the student body at Makerere University in Uganda met Obama then, the Kenyan was "brilliant, well read, brimming with confidence." Obama Sr., Otunnu remembers, gushed with enthusiasm for going to the United States, inspired by Tom Mboya's efforts to garner the first students and scholarships for the 1959 airlift. Prior to this most of the few Kenyans who had gone out of the country for their higher education had attended Makerere or a school in Great Britain. Attending colleges in the United States had not been a goal because, Otunnu recalls, "all roads led to the U.K., and if you received a degree in the U.S. you had to be recertified in Kenya. That was the level of prejudice against the U.S., the British colonial mentality. What was good and serious was the U.K., what was frivolous, fluffy, was the U.S."

But Mboya thought differently about U.S. colleges, especially for the purpose of educating Kenyans for independence from Great

Britain, and had been working since 1956 with a white American industrialist, William X. Scheinman, and with a few other Americans, white and black, to send Kenyan students to the United States. By privately transporting promising students who on their own or through Mboya's intervention had won scholarships to American universities, the Scheinman-Mboya group was doing several radical things. They were circumventing the British colonial education system, which rewarded only a handful of Kenyans each year with scholarships to study in Great Britain; they were finessing the U.S. foreign-student establishment, which only accepted Africans from already-independent nations; and they were attempting to bring over large groups rather than a few "elite" students. Scheinman had formed a nonprofit entity, the African American Students Foundation (AASF), for this purpose. The goal was to create a cadre of well-trained young people who would be available to staff the government and the educational system when Kenya gained its independence.

Between 1959 and 1963, the AASF "airlifts" would bring to the United States nearly eight hundred East African students, mostly Kenyans but also some from Tanganyika (now Tanzania), Uganda, and Northern and Southern Rhodesia, to take up scholarships at dozens of colleges and some high schools. The "airlift generation" would achieve a remarkable record of accomplishment. Upon returning home, they would become the founding brothers and sisters of their countries. For the next quarter century they would make up half of Kenya's parliaments and account for many of its cabinet ministers and even more of its high-level civil servants, in addition to staffing the professorships and deanships of its nascent universities, starting medical clinics and schools, growing multimillion-dollar businesses, and leading international environmental programs. Among the airlift graduates would be Wangari Maathai, winner of the 2004 Nobel Peace Prize.

Professor of medical physiology Dr. Owino Okong'o, another of the airlift students, succinctly summed up the airlift's impact on

Kenya in an e-mail to Mboya's widow, Pamela: "The airlifts provided manpower at the time of independence, demonstrated the inadequate nature of the then Kenyan education system, changed perceptions which the British were spreading about the quality of American education . . . and transformed the elite culture of Kenyans from the British model to the American model in which performance is more important than where you went to school."

In 1959, all of this lay in the future as a bright promise. Since 1956, the Mboya-Scheinman program had brought to the United States a handful of individuals at a time. But for the academic year that would begin in September 1959, the Kenyan community knew, Mboya and his associates in Nairobi were expanding the program to assist eighty-one individuals—the number of passengers that could fit on a single chartered plane.

This information electrified Obama Sr., and he applied to more than thirty U.S. colleges, many of which were historically black or were those in the San Francisco area that were recommended by Mrs. Roberts. Most were unable to accept him. The reasons remain unclear, but it may have been because he did not complete his secondary education at a school, although he had taken correspondence courses, or because he did not yet have a Cambridge A-Level certificate, the British diploma that could only be obtained after passing a rigid national examination, although according to Otunnu he did have a lesser O-Level certificate, as did most of the other candidates for airlift seats in 1959. Obama appears not to have applied for any advanced schooling in the USSR or in the Communist satellite countries; Oginga Odinga, also a patron of his, was recruiting for such schools in 1959.

The University of Hawaii was willing to accept Obama Sr. for reasons that also remain unclear but that were likely connected to Hawaii's just becoming a state in 1959. He was an otherwise-attractive, well-recommended candidate who would be Hawaii's first-ever African student, a circumstance that intrigued him. As far as can be determined from incomplete records, Mrs. Roberts and Miss Mooney paid his fare to Hawaii and provided a partial scholarship. Mboya, while unable to transport the twenty-three-year-old, did put him on the AASF list to receive one of the handful of scholarships contributed by the former baseball star Jackie Robinson, which the Scheinman foundation was administering, and encouraged him to look to the AASF for further help if needed, which he later did.

As the University of Hawaii's first-ever African student, Obama Sr. received more than the usual freshman's share of attention from the campus press. He pursued courses in economics and world affairs, became the leader of the International Student Association, and graduated at the top of his class in three years. U.S. Representative Neil Abercrombie knew him at the university, and described him in those years as "self-involved, egotistical, vivid" but entirely "dedicated to Africa, to freedom and justice." Obama Sr. was "brilliant" and "always had an opinion," Abercrombie said in a recent interview, and "always had the information to back it up."

Early during Obama Sr.'s Hawaii years, he met, in a Russian class, the seventeen-year-old Ann Dunham, an anthropology student, daughter of a local family originally from Kansas. They married in 1961, and the couple's only child, Barack Hussein Obama, Jr., was born later that year.

Onyango threatened his son, by mail, with revocation of his student visa for marrying a white woman who, Onyango predicted, would not want to return to Kenya with Barack, but the threat was not carried out. Obama Sr. continued at the University of Hawaii, and the AASF continued to send him checks, in increments of $50 or $150 for expenses, $243 for tuition. He was mostly supported by Mooney, who in 1960 had married an expatriate American, Elmer Kirk, and shortly moved with her husband back to the United States. Mboya forwarded letters written by Obama Sr.'s Kenyan wife, which she had handed to Mboya in Nairobi, along with his own notes urging Obama to get back in touch with his Kenyan family.

As Obama Jr. would later write in *Dreams from My Father*, his father was a complicated man; the son gleaned a sense of that complexity from the *Honolulu Star-Bulletin* interview with his father published upon his graduation in 1962.

> He appears guarded and responsible, the model student, the ambassador for his continent. He mildly scolds the university for herding visiting students into dormitories and forcing them to attend programs designed to promote cultural understanding—a distraction, he says, from the practical training he seeks. Although he hasn't experienced any problems himself, he detects self-segregation and overt discrimination taking place between the various ethnic groups and expresses wry amusement at the fact that "Caucasians" in Hawaii are occasionally on the receiving end of prejudice.

Because of Obama Sr.'s good record at Hawaii, he received scholarship offers to work toward a doctorate in economics, a full one from the New School in New York City and a partial one from Harvard University; he chose the latter, which did not have enough money attached for him to bring his wife and son. He moved to Cambridge alone, and, except for the occasional letter, mostly disappeared from his young son's life for the next decade. He suddenly reappeared when Barack Jr. was ten years old, and the two had an intense reunion for a month, after which the father and son never saw one another again. Barack Jr. knew that his father had remarried, and had a new family in Kenya and worked for the government, but he had few other details about his father's life.

Barack Jr. was twenty-one and living in New York City when he received the news of his father's death in a car accident in Kenya. It hit him hard. He then embarked on a journey of discovery—of himself and of his father—that took him a decade, reunited him with his Kenyan half-brothers and half-sisters, brought him to Kogelo and the site of his grandfather's land—which he was taught to revere as "Home Squared," the "center of the center" of his Kenyan family's existence—and culminated in *Dreams from My Father,* his autobiographical exploration of the complex relationships between father and son, whiteness and blackness, and being American and Kenyan.

As the 2008 Massachusetts primary approached, Senator Obama's candidacy was endorsed by several members of the Kennedy family, including Senator Ted Kennedy of Massachusetts, surviving patriarch of the clan, and Caroline Kennedy, daughter of the late president. They said that Obama and his candidacy, with their expressions of great promise and hope, reminded the family forcefully of John F. Kennedy and his 1960 campaign for the presidency. The Kennedy endorsement was a very important matter for Obama, since Hillary Clinton was still the choice of Democratic Party leaders.

In trying to make the connection between himself and President Kennedy more direct, candidate Obama, based on incomplete information, made a mistake about his own history, saying that his father's journey to America in 1959 had been aided by the Joseph P. Kennedy Jr. Foundation. Not exactly, fact-checkers soon found out. The Kennedy Foundation had not underwritten the airlift until 1960, although Obama Sr. had been aided earlier by the AASF, and some Kennedy money was later used to assist him in Hawaii. Glossed over by news reporters in 2008 was that John F. Kennedy's support for the 1960 airlift had created a political uproar that affected the African-American vote in a very close election—a story long overlooked by historians and popular culture. The Kennedy Foundation's underwriting of the airlift had trumped Vice President Richard Nixon's attempt to force the State Department to fund the airlift so that Nixon rather than Kennedy could reap the political benefit of African-American votes.

Obama lost the 2008 Massachusetts primary to Clinton but won many other primaries in the late winter and early spring, and amassed significant numbers of delegates even in states where he came in second. His delegate total continued to rise until June 4, 2008, when it became obvious even to die-hard Clinton supporters that Barack Obama would win the Democratic nomination.

In a speech announcing the delegate total that put him over the top, he called his victory a "defining moment for our nation," the nominating of an African-American as the presidential candidate of a major political party. "[T]onight we mark the end of one historic journey with the beginning of another—a journey that will bring a new and better day to America."

Five months later, in the general election, Obama was elected as the nation's forty-fourth president. His new prominence as a result of his victory emphasized that much more needed to be known about the East African airlifts, which had started his ball rolling.

Like the story of Obama's rise, the airlifts were an expression of a quintessentially American trait, an aspect of what America had so consistently offered to the peoples of the rest of the world: an open, helping hand, and the experience and understanding of what it means to be free, to be educated, and to conceive personal dreams that have a substantial chance of being realized.

This book tells that story, recounting the creation, execution, and achievements of those airlifts, including their important effects on the presidential elections of 1960 and 2008, as well as on the integration of American campuses, on the way that foreign students were recruited for the United States and treated once here, and on the health and survival of the independent nations of East Africa in their most formative years.

1

COLD WAR *and* MORAL CRUSADES

The years immediately following World War II saw a tremendous upwelling of hope in the world and initiated a period in which change once again seemed achievable. After fifteen years of Depression and war, Americans took to the tasks of bettering their own economic health and future and at the same time preventing the Communist powers, the Union of Soviet Socialist Republics and the People's Republic of China, from expanding their influence and territory in ways that would push the United States into a third world war. The Cold War battles against Communism waged by the United

States ranged from funding and operating the Marshall Plan—the generous economic recovery program for Europe undertaken in large measure to halt the leftward drift of nations severely damaged by World War II—to the shooting war on the Korean Peninsula. Even Eleanor Roosevelt, whom President Harry S. Truman called "the first lady of the world" for her championing of civil rights, women's rights, and dignity for oppressed peoples, wrote that "in this period, we have wanted above all else to keep the world from falling into Communist hands."

Americans also began to focus on the need to look for solutions to some of the ills of society that had been festering for decades, prime among them ridding the United States of segregation and helping subject peoples abroad to obtain their freedom. Anti-Communism interfered with these objectives, deflecting the drive against segregation at home while placing America internationally on the side of the colonial powers because they were our anti-Communist allies in Europe.

Just as most white Americans still acted toward the black 10 percent of the U.S. population, then called "Negroes," as though they were "invisible" (to borrow the term from novelist Ralph Ellison), most whites similarly gave little thought to Africa, referred to as "the dark continent" not only because its 200 million people were dark-skinned but also because it was so unknown.

Battles were raging throughout Africa, but most Americans, white and black, had little knowledge of them and no sense of why they should feel connected to them. In Algeria, rebels threatened French control. In the Gold Coast, American-educated Kwame Nkrumah and his party were agitating for independence from Great Britain. In Kenya, Jomo Kenyatta, educated in the USSR as well as in America, was calling for an end to whites-only rule. In South Africa, the African National Congress (ANC) was pressing for full citizenship for blacks. Many of these conflicts were painted for Americans as Cold War battles—the South African government and the U.S. government charged that the ANC was Communist-influenced—but that label obscured what was actually going on. For these clashes, one and all, featured African nationalists struggling against their British, French, Belgian, and Portuguese colonial rulers.

Because the colonial powers were our allies in NATO (the North Atlantic Treaty Organization), the U.S. government was constrained from being too sympathetic to African independence movements in which blacks were attempting to throw off the shackles of white rule. Furthermore, institutionalized racism was the way of life in the American South, as was de facto segregation in the North. "Anyone who has worked in the international field," Mrs. Roosevelt wrote, "knows well that our failure in race relations . . . and our open discrimination against various groups, injures our leadership in the world. It is the one point which can be attacked and to which the representatives of the United States have no answer."

In 1947, when the President's Committee on Civil Rights attempted to address discrimination forthrightly by declaring that our national goal was "the elimination of segregation based on race, color, creed, or national origin from American life," to be achieved by outlawing attempts to base voting rights on race, enacting a federal law against lynching, and ending segregation in education and in employment, it felt the need to do so by wrapping these goals in the mantle of protecting the United States' moral position in the world:

> Throughout the Pacific, Latin America, Africa, the Near, Middle, and Far East, the treatment which our Negroes receive is taken as a reflection of our attitude toward all dark-skinned peoples [and this] plays into the hands of Communist propagandists. . . . The United States is not so strong, the final triumph of the democratic ideal is not so inevitable that we can ignore what the world thinks of our record.

Reactionaries in Congress, Southern Democrats and their Republican allies, blocked the report's most important proposal, the establishment of a Fair Employment Practices Commission, which might have helped African-Americans gain more meaningful employment. Truman integrated the armed forces with a stroke of his pen in 1948, but Washington, D.C., still remained a segregated city. Soviet propaganda seized on the many incidents of overt racism in the United States as providing reason for other countries to reject American military, economic, and moral leadership.

Given this set of circumstances, how was a small group of Kenyans and Americans able to successfully challenge these obstacles and take actions that benefited an entire generation in East Africa, as well as race relations in the United States?

The short answer is that empathy for independence movements lies deep in the American grain. George Washington declared that he felt "irresistibly excited whenever in any country I see an oppressed people unfurl the banner of freedom." The notion that Americans should applaud and support attempts to overthrow oppressive governments, whether tyrannies or colonial regimes, had continued unabated in the twentieth century.

It surfaced, memorably, in the Atlantic Charter, drawn up by President Franklin D. Roosevelt and Britain's Prime Minister Winston Churchill in August 1941. Roosevelt knew that there had been independence movements in Africa during the 1930s, engendered in part by starvation and shortages due to the worldwide Depression, but that they had fizzled out. Having in mind these independence struggles, as well as the seizure of many previously sovereign nations by the Nazis and Imperial Japan, Roosevelt attempted to insert a bold promise into the Atlantic Charter. Along with a pledge by both powers to seek no territorial gains from the ongoing world war (which the United States had not yet entered), Roosevelt wanted to obligate all colonial powers to free their colonies, in part to force the USSR to allow free elections in its captive Baltic and Balkan nations. Churchill objected to this pledge since Great Britain had no intention of relinquishing its colonies, which comprised the Indian subcontinent, parts of the Middle East, Malaysia, and large swaths of Africa. He was able to compel a more bland promise, for the United States and Great Britain to respect peoples' inherent right to self-determination.

But when World War II was in its final stages, at an Allied meeting in Tehran in April 1945, a day after the death of Roosevelt, Churchill vehemently stated that the United Kingdom would not be bound by the Atlantic Charter's principles. Nonetheless African, Asian, and Indian nationalists took sustenance from its self-determination tenet, shortly to be reinforced in the charter of the United Nations; they drew upon these documents' moral certification of the right of all peoples to self-government to assert their own right to self-rule. In 1947 India and Pakistan gained independence from Great Britain, a positive example for other colonial peoples.

Truman tried to reach out to aspiring Third World countries through the Point Four Program. Blocked in Congress for a year and then underfunded, it was further resisted by State Department bureaucrats intent on having the United States concentrate on assisting European and Asian allies. Despite these roadblocks, Truman later wrote, Point Four became "a symbol of hope to those nations which were being fed Communist propaganda that the free nations were incapable of providing a decent standard of living for the millions of people in the underdeveloped areas of the earth. . . . Point Four provided the strongest antidote to Communism that has so far been put into practice."

But it didn't do very much for independence-minded Africans. Overly cautious, Point Four sent American technological expertise only to already-independent Iran, Paraguay, Liberia, Saudi Arabia, Mexico, and India. Areas still under colonial rule received only token help. Moreover, as the Cold War heated up on the Korean

Peninsula—and in the United States, in Senator Joseph McCarthy's hunt for Communists—the vast majority of the American people focused on those matters.

A few Americans looked beyond anti-Communism, focusing on matters of social justice at home and abroad. If they were just a handful, they had the satisfaction of occupying the moral high ground, their zeal for social equality embracing not only the cause of civil rights in the United States but also the cause of anticolonialism in Africa. Asked today what stirred them to work so hard for African independence, they cannot point to a lone motivating incident or cause, but there was one time period during which they began to focus their energies on Africa—during 1952 and 1953, when two localized problems on the continent burst their boundaries and were featured on the world stage: the putting down of antiapartheid protests in South Africa, and the similar repression of the Mau Mau "uprising" in Kenya.

A two-races system had long been in operation in South Africa, but the 1948 election of a rightist, autocratic, white supremacist, Christians-only government codified apartheid into law and exacerbated it. South African blacks were declared not to be citizens of South Africa, only of one of ten tribal homelands within South Africa's borders. Their education, medical care, movement around the country, and ability to work for pay were more severely restricted than before. Mixed marriages were prohibited, identity cards with racial categories were issued, and the Communist Party was declared illegal, along with all political parties whose aims were in sympathy with the Communists. This last legislation was used to try to dismantle the African National Congress, which the government accused of having ties to the Communists. ANC leaders Walter Sisulu and his protégé Nelson Mandela determined to resist apartheid by a nonviolent "Programme of Action" that included strikes, boycotts, and protests.

George M. Houser, an American minister long in the forefront of pacifism and of antisegregation efforts in the United States, began an organization to support the ANC in its nonviolent campaign. Houser was no armchair moralist. Son of Methodist missionaries in the Philippines, he had attended college in California and spent a year in China before becoming a minister, a pacifist, and a socialist. His claim of conscientious-objector status during World War II had resulted in his imprisonment for a year. "The Social Gospel, putting the Christian ethic into practice on the social scene, was the credo that moved me," he later wrote. "I was a pacifist as well as a supporter of organized labor and all the efforts to challenge racial discrimination and segregation." Emerging from prison, he joined the pacifist Fellowship of Reconciliation, which led him to become a founder of CORE (the Committee of Racial Equality); he and other CORE members went on "freedom rides" with African-Americans and whites in the South in 1947, a full generation before that tactic crested in the 1960s. However, Houser writes, until the close of the 1940s, "my knowledge and concern about Africa was minuscule," although he did find it "easy and natural" to transfer his social justice concerns and preference for nonviolent protest into support for the ANC's Gandhian campaign of resistance.

The committee that Houser convened to assist the South African resistance was a who's who of prominent liberals, pacifists, and anti-segregationists, including A. Philip Randolph, the head of the Sleeping Car Porters union; Bayard Rustin, a civil rights organizer and establishment gadfly of long standing; Norman Thomas, perennial Socialist candidate for president; James Farmer, cofounder of CORE; Reverend Donald Harrington, activist minister of a Unitarian church in Manhattan; and Roger Baldwin, founder of the American Civil Liberties Union (ACLU). Some CORE board members questioned whether CORE monies and energies should be diverted to an overseas struggle, but the majority thought it a good idea. Soon, what became the American Committee on Africa (ACOA) separated from CORE and thereafter functioned independently.

The big names on the new committee's board were not the ones who became the leaders of the airlifts project. That leadership came from two board members who joined the organization a few years later, William X. Scheinman and Frank Montero. Their aspirations were aided by one of the founding ACOA board members, Peter Weiss, an Austrian-born Holocaust survivor, international intellectual property lawyer, and constitutional rights expert who had done work in Africa as executive director of the International Development Placement Association.

The group's main constituents were those Northern white liberals who contributed regularly to the ACLU and responded to civil rights appeals. The tenor of ACOA was determinedly not too far to the left, because it had become very important for Americans with liberal views to be perceived as patriotic members of what historian Arthur Schlesinger, Jr., identifies as the "non-Communist left." "We were living in the midst of the Joseph McCarthy 'red scare,'" Houser recalled of the time of ACOA's founding. "Although all our supporters were unalterably opposed to McCarthyism, we were not interested in joining forces with the Communists in a united front." Houser could readily empathize with the ANC's problems in fighting the Suppression of Communism Act in South Africa because, he remembered, "We knew that in our own country the red label was sometimes put on our own activities in CORE simply because we actively opposed racism."

For Houser and his associates, supporting the ANC was working against colonialism, or, as it was practiced in South Africa, neocolonialism, the persistence of colonial exploitative practices in a successor regime after independence had been achieved. The ANC's 1952 Defiance Campaign Against Unjust Laws did raise international consciousness about apartheid, but South Africa arrested many of the campaigners and quickly convicted them. At their sentencing, the magistrate accused the defendants of furthering Communist goals "to break down race barriers and strive for equal rights for all sections of the people." The South African government imprisoned eight thousand people and passed a new Whipping Post Law, under which anyone who received funds for resistance could be publicly whipped.

Houser's alarm that a South African to whom he might send money could be whipped as well as jailed discouraged him from forwarding more donated funds to South Africa, even for church-building activities. Instead, he aimed his support at other African resistance movements, especially those pledged to nonviolence, in territories that had remained more directly under European colonial control. This broadening of the committee's focus allowed it to become known as the American Committee on Africa.

This was when Scheinman joined the cause. Young, tough, idealistic, and—for the moment—wealthy, he was willing to put his money in the service of his ideals. William X. Scheinman, Bill to his friends, was then in his midtwenties. Like Senator John F. Kennedy of Massachusetts, he had been a navy skipper of a World War II landing craft, and had once brought down a Japanese airplane with the boat's machine gun. After the war, he attended college for a short spell, then drifted through the Midwest with a group of professional poker players. "Bill was always a gambler," Houser would recall. Scheinman moved to New York, became a publicist for the Count Basie Orchestra, and was very involved in jazz. He supplemented his publicity activities by working as a salesman for an airplane-parts manufacturer; in short order he learned enough about that business to start his own company, Arnav Aircraft Associates, in 1950, on "a shoestring and plenty of nerve," as he later characterized it to a reporter. Arnav had factories in New Jersey and in California, and won government and private aviation-industry contracts for hydraulic fittings for planes and missiles. By the mid-1950s Arnav was a steady $1 million-a-year business. Parlaying his Arnav profits into larger sums by investing in the stock market, Scheinman was on his way to a small fortune; in later years, he would make and lose that fortune several times, and become a market analyst and the author of a bestselling book on investing. He was known as an iconoclast. "Bill always wore an open collar and a loose tie—a messy appearance," his AASF colleague Cora Weiss recalled. "But he always said, 'Why not?' It went with his view of himself as a risk-taker." Scheinman's interest in jazz had led him to a general interest in African-Americans and in race relations, and to a profoundly liberal outlook.

Frank Montero, another ACOA board recruit who became a stalwart of the AASF, was a civil rights pioneer who by the mid-1950s had made enough money in business to no longer need a salary. He was in his forties, an African-American with an outsized, booming voice and an ingratiating personality who in addition to serving as the assistant executive director of the National Urban League had also spent some time in Liberia and was generally interested in African affairs. "Frank knew everybody," Houser recalled—everyone in the forefront of the civil rights movement, as well as many white corporate chieftains and government bureaucrats. "He was incredibly connected." Montero was the son of an unusual couple, his father a black baseball player who had toured in South America at a time when blacks were not allowed in major league baseball and his mother one of the first black women to teach in the New York City public school system. As a child Montero was beaten regularly by his public school classmates. His family, fearing that he might become a juvenile delinquent if he stayed in that school, sent him to Mount Hermon, a New England prep school, where he became a basketball star. Although offered a scholarship at an Ivy League college, he chose to attend Howard University in Washington, D.C., where he became a protégé of Ralph Bunche. Montero studied for two master's degrees, one from Columbia in social work and a second from New York University in public administration, and worked as a sociologist and real estate developer until he joined the Urban League. His first marriage ended in divorce, and in 1950 he remarried, to a volunteer at the Urban League, a white socialite who could trace her descent from Cotton Mather, the colonial New England fire-and-brimstone preacher. By the 1950s he was devoting his time and energies to various philanthropic and civic endeavors. Cora Weiss recalls Montero as a man bubbling over with ideas for fundraising and continually on the telephone. In civil rights circles he was known as a fixer, a man who solved problems and did so by negotiation rather than confrontation: for instance, demonstrating to a Southern baked-goods manufacturer that it made more economic sense to hire additional African-American workers and allow them to unionize than to let his operation be the object of a previously threatened boycott.

The need to do something about oppression in South Africa had also become the focus of college students such as Cora Rubin, a University of Wisconsin anthropology undergraduate, daughter of a civic-minded industrialist and a well-known Caribbean basin anthropologist. "While in college I was attracted to African and other international students because of their stories and their evident needs," she recalls. Principal among those needs was "pin money . . . so I organized speaking engagements for them; they had remarkable stories to tell." She became progressively more involved in their respective home countries' problems. Serious and articulate, she was able to hold her own in interactions with older and more experienced civil rights and African-independence activists. A few years later, she would marry Peter Weiss and be recruited by Montero to serve as student adviser and executive director of the airlifts for the AASF.

What tied together this core group of future AASF leaders—Houser, Scheinman, Montero, and Cora and Peter Weiss—was their shared rejection of colonialism and their desire to help Africans shape their own destinies. All it took to spur them into action was the opportunity to do something quite specific to further that cause.

K enya, the British colony that would be the group's eventual focus, thrust itself into the American consciousness in 1952 because bloodshed had finally roused the international press to pay attention. The Western media hastened to report the Mau Mau uprising, with its tales of natives running amok with machetes, but failed to balance their reports with adequate recognition that the African participants believed themselves to be involved in a nationalist, anticolonial peasant revolt.

The Mau Mau crisis had actually been building in Kenya for years. The underlying economic source of the revolt was the displacement and impoverishment of the Kikuyu, the most numerous tribe in Kenya, who had been steadily pushed off their farms since the area had been colonized in the nineteenth century. By 1952 many Kikuyu worked either as low-wage laborers on white settlers' farms or in cities at equally low-paying jobs. Kenyan servicemen who had returned from World War II and a few Kikuyu local chieftains had begun an "oathing" campaign, encouraging and sometimes forcing fellow Kikuyu to take oaths of solidarity to all other Kikuyu, as well as of resistance to the colonial government and of refusal to cede any more land to whites; the more fervent and radical oath makers constituted a secret society known as Mau Mau. Senator Barack Obama's grandfather Onyango, a World War II veteran, had been arrested because, his widow later said, "His job as cook to a British army officer made him a useful informer for the secret oathing movement."

The Mau Mau movement in some ways ran parallel to and in some ways clashed with the more mainstream political activities of Jomo Kenyatta and his associates, who were attempting to change the colonial government with an eye toward having it eventually become an African-oriented, African-led entity.

Across the continent, in the Gold Coast, was an example of

what Kenyatta and his partisans hoped for. In 1951, after years of resistance, Kwame Nkrumah's party won a national election that gave them an overwhelming legislative majority, and Nkrumah became the first prime minister of a country that would be called Ghana, whose full independence was to evolve over the next five years. Similar liberation struggles, expected to result in independence, were going on throughout the continent from Mozambique to Guinea-Bissau, Tanganyika, and Angola.

But in Kenya there was little progress toward independence.

The existence of the Mau Mau gave the British reason to slow down the independence process, and this reasoning was understood by the three high chiefs of the Kikuyu, two of whom opposed the Mau Mau, and by Kenyatta, who saw the growth of the Mau Mau as inimical to the progress he sought. This was the situation on September 19, 1952, when the new governor, Sir Evelyn Baring, took office, determined to keep Kenya as a British colony. More violence flared up immediately, both by the Mau Mau—who killed cattle belonging to white settlers, and one of the senior Kikuyu chiefs who opposed their oaths—and by police and military units, who took reprisals.

"After these two shocking occurrences," the American consul general in Nairobi, Edmund J. Dorsz, wrote to his superiors, "it is not possible to ignore the growing boldness and defiance of the Mau Mau, and the inability of the Police so far to effectively deal with its anti-European campaign." Dorsz noted that the "arbitrary methods" of the police were "playing into the hands of the Mau Mau by alienating the goodwill of the law-abiding Africans." He attributed the uprising to the bad underlying economic conditions, in which the "racial division of wealth" had been exacerbated by an "inflationary spiral, which only serves to make the division of wealth (European) and poverty (African) more extreme."

After the assassination of a second of the three senior chiefs, the Baring government issued emergency regulations and rounded up thousands of Africans, among them Kenyatta. The regulations of the Emergency, as it became known, were draconian, akin to martial law with its suspension of most civil liberties. Later comparisons of Kenya under the Emergency to life under Stalin in the Soviet Union were not too overstated. There was no indication of when or if the Emergency would ever be lifted. The Emergency and the suspension of parts of the colony's guiding constitution, Dorsz wrote home, were a "calculated gamble" by the Kenyan colonial government, because if "the Mau Mau continues to be an efficient subversive force, the government will be in a very embarrassing position." He was certain that the measures would "make martyrs" out of Kenyatta and his associates, and that the Kenyan government had no "tangible evidence" to support its allegation of Kenyatta's "Moscow connections." Put on trial in a venue twenty-five miles from the nearest large city by a judge imported from Great Britain just for this trial, Kenyatta was quickly convicted and sentenced to seven years' hard labor. Years later, it would be discovered that the trial had been rigged—the key witness against Kenyatta would recant, and the government's payoffs to the judge would be exposed.

The Kenyan colonial government's campaign to suppress the Mau Mau and their sympathizers featured battles in which machine guns and air-dropped bombs were arrayed against spears and rifles, and Kikuyu residents of Nairobi were restricted to what amounted to a guarded ghetto. By mid-December 1952, despite the presence of colonial troops from a half-dozen other areas to reinforce local troops, it was clear to the dozen newspaper reporters from Europe, Asia, and the United States who had been assigned to Nairobi that the colonial government would not easily suppress the Mau Mau or halt the Kenyan peoples' thrust toward independence. In that sense, the Mau Mau had won.

In 1960, when the Emergency finally ended, the official tolls of the total cost in blood were that the Mau Mau had killed two thousand black Africans, two hundred police officers and soldiers, and thirty-two white settlers. But the colonial government had killed twelve thousand Kenyans in combat, hanged one thousand more, and detained three hundred thousand, of whom tens of thousands died in the prison camps. Details unearthed by historian Caroline Elkins have established that the British-run Emergency was a culture of violence in which the Kikuyu were subjected to horrific torture on a regular basis, starvation, and random killings of the sort that had previously only been associated with the Nazi and Soviet regimes. That was one reason why, when the British left Kenya in 1963, they burned all records of the Emergency.

In 1953, those who sympathized with the anticolonialists in Kenya found an individual on whom to focus their hopes and their desire for action: Tom Mboya.

The declaration of Emergency in Kenya, continuing with no end in sight, had led to the outlawing of political parties and a suspicion of all things Kikuyu. This set the stage for Kenyans to rely for leadership on the still-extant labor unions and on the non-Kikuyu, such as members of the second most numerous tribe, the Luo. The rise of young Tom Mboya, Luo and labor leader, was accelerated by these Emergency prohibitions to the point where, within four years, he could begin the collaboration with Houser and Scheinman that would blossom as the airlifts.

Firstborn son of an overseer at a white-owned sisal plantation, Mboya attended a Catholic catechism academy; he noted in *Freedom and After* that the fee for his year's study there was more than his father earned in a month of hard labor. Since literacy was not taught at the academy, he transferred to another school and lived with a tutor in a mud hut that lacked sanitary facilities and light to read by in the evenings. Unwilling to burden his father with additional school fees— he knew the money was needed to educate his younger siblings— Mboya dropped out of boarding school and studied to become a sanitary inspector. "Eager to do something about the bad health conditions in many parts of Kenya," he later wrote in *Freedom and After*, once he had completed his training he became an inspector for the Nairobi city council in 1951, at age twenty-one. He was soon elected secretary of the African Staff Association, which "began my interest in the trade union movement."

His work as a sanitary inspector, he wrote, "brought me face to face with racial prejudice in a way I had not known before." When he was alone in a laboratory, testing milk samples—a procedure required before dairy farmers could be issued a license to sell their milk in Nairobi—a white woman walked in and asked, "Is there anybody here?"

"Is there something wrong with your eyes?" he replied. The woman thought he was cheeky; she complained and also generated a petition signed by other dairy farmers saying they wanted a European, not an African, to judge the quality of their milk. The chief sanitary inspector refused to knuckle under, and backed Mboya, a lesson that Mboya never forgot. But he also did not forget that the African sanitary inspectors were paid one-fifth the salary garnered by European inspectors for doing the same work.

Articulate, intense, careful, and fluent in five African languages in addition to English, Mboya worked to further labor interests while cultivating the men in the government's labor ministry to ensure that gains made for union members would not be taken away. In eight months as secretary of the Staff Association, he tripled its unionized membership. By 1953, when he was just twenty-three, he was already in the upper hierarchy of the Kenya Federation of Registered Trade Unions (KFRTU), and, although a Luo, was readily accepted as a leader by the mostly Kikuyu membership. An admirer of certain "positive virtues of tribalism," as he had experienced them during his life to date, he was also cognizant of the "dangers of negative tribalism," having "learned clearly how harmful to Kenya was the man who saw only good in his own people and only evil in those of other tribes." As was Kenyatta, Mboya was willing to reach across tribal and racial lines, one reason why the colonial government liked him. Mboya shared this attitude with other men he admired, Nkrumah of Ghana and Julius Nyerere of Tanganyika, and he dreamed of following their example by helping to lead his country as it emerged to independence.

Acutely aware of his own shortcomings, Mboya borrowed law and statute books to acquaint himself with the regulations covering unions, and took a correspondence course with a South African university to fill in the gaps of what he deemed his lack of knowledge about subjects important to his own development and to his country's future.

Mboya understood that the British colonial education system made it all but impossible to achieve a full education past high school in Kenya. As American educator Albert Sims would put it after a visit to Kenya, "The British system of [colonial] education is by design a sharply tapering pyramid for the production of elites at the university level. . . . The financial capacity and educational policies of the governments in East Africa [provide] educational opportunities . . . at a rate that falls far short of the surging aspirations of the African people." Mboya yearned to go "overseas" and complete his education; he did not know what course of study he would pursue but, as he wrote, "I only felt I should go away and come back a learned man."

It was Mboya's feeling about what he personally needed—and what his compatriots would need as Kenya gained independence— that gave rise to the airlifts.

As the Truman administration yielded to the Dwight D. Eisenhower administration, the president-elect wrote in his diary, two weeks before taking office,

> Nationalism is on the march, and world communism is taking advantage of [it] to cause dissension. . . . Moscow leads many misguided people to believe they can count on Communist

help. . . . The free world's hope of defeating the Communists
does not include objecting to national aspirations. We must . . .
convince dependent peoples that their only hope of maintaining independence, once attained, is through cooperation with
the free world.

Both Eisenhower and his secretary of state, John Foster Dulles,
believed that colonialism was wrong and morally repulsive, and said
so many times, in public and in private. However, on this issue, as on
race relations at home, Eisenhower's rhetoric was well in advance of
what he was prepared to commit the U.S. government to support.
Dulles held a Manichean view of the world: A nation was either in
the vanguard of the Western powers or it was fatally compromised
by being in the Communist orbit. To Dulles, there was no third way,
no true neutrality; he suspected all attempts at "non-alignment."

That was why the United States agreed to pay one-third of the
cost for France to fight the nationalist/Communist attempts by Ho
Chi Minh to overthrow the colonial establishment in an ongoing war
in Vietnam. At that time, the United States envisioned the potential
loss of Vietnam to the Communists as a disaster that could start the
dominoes toppling, affecting British control of Malaysia with its rub-
ber and tin, the stability of the nonsocialist French government, and
thus France's willingness to participate militarily in NATO, which
would adversely affect the balance of power in the world.

The implications for what might be required of the colonial powers in order to maintain their colonies elsewhere—military action in
which the United States might have to participate—nudged Eisenhower toward advocating freedom for all colonies, though with a ca-
veat. He wanted them independent only if they would continue to be
oriented toward the West and to give the United States access to
their natural resources. Eisenhower wrote to Churchill in July 1954,
pleading with him to promise self-government to all British colonies

within five years as a way of defusing the debate in which "we [in the West] are falsely pictured as exploiters of people, the Soviets as their champion." Churchill refused, writing that he was "skeptical about universal suffrage for the Hottentots even if refined by proportional representation."

Simultaneously with the fall of Dien Bien Phu in Vietnam, in the spring of 1954 the U.S. Supreme Court handed down its unanimous decision in *Brown v. Board of Education of Topeka*, ruling that "separate educational facilities are inherently unequal," and, therefore, that segregation must end. However, the Court said that integration should be introduced "with all deliberate speed," and suggested that plans for implementation be drawn up over the next year—a schedule that many African-Americans deemed painfully slow and an encouragement to states and segregationist groups to put up serious roadblocks. The administration's response to *Brown* was to uphold the decision but not to actively enforce its provisions. This at best ambivalent attitude toward matters involving nonwhites' rights was also reflected in the administration's lackadaisical response to the first conference of nonaligned nations, in Bandung, Indonesia, in 1955, a conference that pledged its African, Asian, and Indian subcontinent participants to solidarity against "colonialism in all its manifestations."

Only after Dien Bien Phu, Bandung, and *Brown* did the administration finally formulate a new policy toward the African independence struggles. A West Point colonel wrote a position paper that became the core of that policy: "Premature independence [of any African country] would be as harmful to our interests . . . as a continuation of nineteenth century colonialism, and we must tailor our policies to the capabilities and needs of each particular area as well as to our overall relations with the metropolitan [European] powers concerned." Eisenhower agreed. He recognized the "flood force" of nationalism, but worried that "[t]he determination of the peoples for self-rule, their own flag, and their own vote in the United Nations resembled a torrent overrunning everything in its path, including, frequently, the best interests of those concerned."

Had the stalwarts of the future AASF believed that pessimistic estimate, the East African airlifts, which evolved over the next several years, would never have been begun, and people such as Mark and Josephine Ofwona of Uganda and Kenya might never have realized their dreams.

In the mid-1950s Mark Ofwona wanted to be a civil engineer, to have a hand in the building of big projects, but there were no certified African civil engineers in Kenya or Uganda; there were only European ones. Africans, no matter what their skill level, were not hired by the governmental entities that oversaw large infrastructure projects. Mark was Kenyan but from a Ugandan background; his grandfather had amassed a substantial amount of land near the common border of the two areas. After graduating from Catholic primary and secondary schools Mark attended the one "college" in East Africa, Makerere in Uganda. The technical training he received from Makerere would not lead to a professional-grade engineering degree on a par with that offered by British universities, but it would likely help him get a technical job in an engineer's office. That was the most he could aspire to at that point because he had not qualified for inclusion in the very small program that sent a few Ugandans and Kenyans each year to study in the British Isles. While at Makerere he married Josephine Ogalla, a Kenyan Catholic, daughter of a sergeant major. Against the odds, she was also a school graduate, though only through intermediate school. It was uncommon for a Kenyan girl to attend school in the 1940s and early 1950s, their daughter Diana later recalled. She remembered her mother telling how she had faced harassment and bullying for even trying to attend school. While Mark attended Makerere, Josephine ran a grocery store and a hostel for visiting Kenyans, and discovered she had a natural talent for business. Their first child was born before Mark graduated, and after graduation the Ofwonas moved to Nyeri, Kenya, where Mark had a technical job and Josephine ran a transportation service between Nyeri and Embu, two midsize towns 150 miles northeast of Nairobi, on the slopes of Mount Kenya.

In 1959 Mark heard of the Tom Mboya airlift program and decided to try to get into it. Of the American schools to which he applied, one in Akron, Ohio, offered the best possibility, a relatively low-cost engineering degree. According to his family, America also offered him the opportunity to worship freely as a Catholic. By the time Mark took his seat on the airlift, the couple had three children, and he had to leave them and Josephine behind. At Akron, he did well in his courses, and his professors and classmates liked him, but he worried about the family that remained in Kenya.

In response to a request from an AASF board member, Firestone Tire executive Robert Boyajian and his wife, Martha, looked up Mark Ofwona at the school. They recalled in a 1999 letter that they first asked him to come for dinner, and were delighted to find that they could discuss, among other subjects, the work of Charles Dickens, a favorite of Mark's. Ofwona was also befriended by the campus ROTC officer and his wife.

He did well enough academically to be awarded a partial scholarship from the Kenyan government, which the two American couples supplemented, as did the AASF. Then Mark's worry about his family became acute, because the government scholarship demanded that he work for the government for four years after receiving his American degree, and the government might send him anywhere in the world. "I do not think that after 5 years [away] I would live in harmony with my wife because of the obvious reason that I shall have different outlook in life. . . . I have certain basic principles of living which I want my wife and children to follow, and this cannot be done unless we are together," he wrote to the AASF, pleading for assistance in bringing over Josephine and the children. "Any knowledge which Mrs. Ofwona may acquire here will be just as important to our people as any other person's." Such funds were regretfully beyond the scope of the AASF, executive director Cora Weiss wrote back.

Mark turned to his Akron friends, and they came through. Boyajian obtained a supplemental scholarship for him from Firestone, and the ROTC couple paid for Josephine and the children to travel to the United States. The following year Josephine enrolled at a community college in Akron, and a year after that the Ofwonas moved to Cincinnati to continue their education. Josephine's business acumen and skills as a hostess were attractive to the University of Cincinnati college community, and she and Mark had two more children.

Mark could have had a career in the United States, but he yearned for Kenya; when he fell ill, he told his wife and children that even if he died in the United States, they should bring him back to Kenya, and if they could not manage to transport his whole body they should at least take his heart, to be buried there.

He recovered, and in 1965, two years after Kenya became independent, Mark was recruited to return home and become the first African civil engineer employed by the Ministry of Public Works. On the side, he opened a consulting business, and he and his partners obtained some government contracts. He was matched in his initiative by Josephine, who, with college degrees to her credit, revived her entrepreneurial career, restarting her taxi and transportation business and from these edging over into construction. Even as she juggled several businesses, another daughter later recalled, "She was a strict disciplinarian and kept close watch over [us children] despite her busy schedule. She would hold Friday evening meetings where the family would discuss individual problems and collectively we would help one another to solve them. It was her vision that we, her children, remain united and use our talents for the benefit and name of the family."

Mark Ofwona prospered, and the land that his grandfather had assembled devolved to his generation. Yearly, they would convene gatherings of the several generations of the Ofwona family at the ancestral tract.

In 1974 he stood for parliament and lost. At around the same time, he was forced to give up control of his consulting business and found himself blocked from rising further in the federal Ministry of Public Works. He accepted appointment as chief municipal engineer of the port city of Mombasa, on the Indian Ocean near the Tanzanian border. Built on islands connected to the mainland, Mombasa presented many challenges to interest a civil engineer. Mark helped the city become the most important port in that area of Africa, the second most populous city in Kenya, and a center for coastal tourism.

In Mombasa, he opened a real estate business and Josephine Ofwona continued as an entrepreneur, but her main work came to be with the YWCA, which she joined in an administrative capacity and in which she rose to the position of warden, or supervisor. In the course of her twenty-two years at the YWCA she would become known as Mama Ofwona to the thousands of women who passed through its doors, comforting and assisting them as she did her eleven children. Her strong faith was fulfilled in this YWCA work. Mark became less religious, but never vindictive, willing to let things go; when he lost his consulting company, he did not look back but formed a new one in a new city. "Poppa liked to laugh a lot, and was never angry for more than a few moments at a time," Diana recalled. He told his daughter that wealth and good fortune might come and go, but that he was giving to her and to her ten brothers and sisters something that no one could ever take away from them: education. He also importuned them never to sell or divide the ancestral land, to hold it in common, and to take care of one another, which, according to Diana Ofwona, they have done. The eleven Ofwona children grew up to achieve positions as lawyers, accountants, entrepreneurs, and stalwarts of ministries both for the Kenyan government and for the United Nations.

Mark Ofwona died in 1994, and Josephine in 2004.

2

AMERICAN LABOR *and the* RISE *of* TOM MBOYA

Money, political clout, and institutions pledged to doing the right thing are all necessary in order for a daring venture such as the East African airlifts to succeed. Two strands relevant to that effort converged in 1955: a quickening in the pace of civil rights activism and an enabling merger in the labor movement.

A year after the Supreme Court's unanimous *Brown v. Board of Education* decision, although a few individual schools and school districts in the South had begun to implement desegregation, the vast majority had not; moreover, White Citizens' Councils, Southern governors, legislatures, and their supporters had organized to resist desegregation in every way possible. Interstate commerce and transportation also remained segregated in the South. That year, three African-Americans were murdered in the South: Emmett Till, a Chicago teenager, George Lee, and Lamar Smith; the murders were ascribed to Southern resentment against the *Brown* decision. So on a December afternoon, when seamstress and local NAACP executive Rosa Parks refused to move to the back of the bus in Montgomery, the city's black churches, led by Martin Luther King, Jr., and others, decided to uphold her and their rights by beginning a boycott of the city's bus system, an effort whose effectiveness and nonviolent character soon made headlines around the world. That boycott continued, unresolved, through much of 1956.

It was also a critical time for American labor. The American Federation of Labor (AFL) and the Congress of Industrial Organizations (CIO), after twenty years apart, were about to merge. The split of the two organizations in 1935 had been logical. The AFL was primarily made up of craft unions in which each member worked at the same craft as every other member, though in various shops or factories; the CIO unions were organized on a different basis, consisting of all the hourly employees in one particular factory or workplace, from sweepers to automated line technicians.

Although the more than one million unionized African-American workers were almost equally divided between the AFL and CIO unions, leadership on civil rights issues had mostly been taken by CIO unions. And not by all of them; rather, civil rights had been mainly championed by unions and locals that were either run by Communists or significantly influenced by far-left notions of the purpose and character of union activity. "During the 1930s and 1940s," labor historian Ellen Schrecker writes, "the Communist Party was the only political organization not specifically part of the civil rights movement that was dedicated to racial equality."

The leftward tilt of the American union movement was halted in

1947 when Congress overrode Truman's veto of the Taft-Hartley Act, which decreed that unions must purge themselves of Communists or lose their certification as accepted bargaining units. Taft-Hartley deeply affected nearly one-third of the CIO's entire membership, as the parent organization expelled eleven unions over the next several years. This elimination, Schrecker comments, "also kept the labor movement from reaching beyond its traditional white male constituency to bring in new types of workers." It was also a big setback for civil rights and racial equality, causes whose main labor proponents had been the eleven expelled unions.

The AFL and CIO began to edge toward each other when George Meany and Walter Reuther, both staunch anti-Communists, moved into the leadership of their respective organizations. As they pursued the merger in the early 1950s, these two chose not to continue the union movement's momentum for social activism, feeling instead the need to devote their energies to fighting automation and to contending with the probusiness Eisenhower, whose antipathy to unions was acute. By 1955 Meany, Reuther, and their allies in Congress had succeeded in having the minimum wage raised from seventy-five cents to one dollar an hour, and in lowering the number of hours lost to strikes. With these gains in hand, the newly merged AFL-CIO could then allow its more liberal elements to once again put social justice at the forefront of the union movement's agenda.

Theodore W. Kheel, a nationally known labor lawyer and mediator, embodied the emerging consciousness that melded civil rights and unionization in 1955 as he accepted the presidency of the New York chapter of a venerable civil rights organization, the National Urban League. Kheel had been head of the National War Labor Board during the war, and then had served as chief of New York City's labor relations division and as unpaid mediator for large-scale labor disputes in the transit industry. In 1955 he was considered a Manhattan power broker; although lacking previous experience in civil rights or race relations, he was sympathetic to the cause. "I took my philosophic cue from what Ralph Ingersoll [publisher of the newspaper *PM*] said, 'We're against people who push other people around.' My attitude also reflected what Adlai Stevenson later said about Eleanor Roosevelt, 'She would rather light candles than curse the darkness.'" Unlike the NAACP, which concentrated on desegregating public facilities, the National Urban League, founded in 1910, concentrated on obtaining jobs for minorities in mainstream companies.

The airline industry employed no blacks on its plane crews, and Kheel decided to work on that problem with the New York division of the National Urban League, focusing on American Airlines; he told the airline that the League had a "bank" of one hundred qualified African-American personnel including pilots, copilots, stewardesses, flight engineers, navigators, and radio operators who were available to work for it. The stumbling block for the airline was its belief that such employees would not be able to find facilities in which to stay overnight at various destinations. The League would take care of that, Kheel promised. Working with his longtime friend William Rogers, then the chief assistant attorney general in the Eisenhower administration, Kheel successfully pressured eighteen airlines with landing rights at New York airports to break the color barrier. On the strength of that, he was appointed as president of the National Urban League. This brought him into contact with people interested in the independence movements in Africa.

Jay Lovestone, a former head of the Communist Party of the United States who had long since become a leading anti-Communist, took another route to becoming interested in those independence movements. Since the war he had served as an aide to George Meany of the AFL; one of Lovestone's tasks was to combat Communist influence on labor unions abroad, particularly in Europe. This entailed AFL support for the 1949 establishment and continued underwriting of the International Confederation of Free Trade Unions (ICFTU), based in Brussels, whose brief included attempting to

resist or limit Communist influence in the labor movement. The
Kenyan labor federation was affiliated with the ICFTU. Many of
Lovestone's anti-Communist activities involving overseas labor
unions were funded by the U.S. Central Intelligence Agency; some
are detailed in a recent book on CIA influence in the United States,
in a chapter entitled "AFL-CIA."

Lovestone also created AFL scholarships for African-Americans
affiliated with the labor movement, such as Maida Springer, who was
an associate of A. Philip Randolph of the Sleeping Car Porters union
and other African-American union leaders as well as an advocate for
women and minorities. Springer had begun working in the garment
industry in the 1930s and had joined its major union, the International Ladies Garment Workers Union (ILGWU). She used her
scholarship to attend Ruskin College, based in Oxford, an institution
known as the "workers' college" because of its close ties to British
unions. In 1955 she began traveling to Africa as an AFL observer, reporting back to Lovestone, Randolph, and Meany on the opportunities and challenges of the continent for American labor. Lovestone
and Springer advocated that the AFL separately support indigenous
African federations, such as Mboya's in Kenya, as a way of keeping
those union movements independent of the European-controlled
ICFTU. This enabled the African unions to better assist their peoples
in seeking political independence for their countries.

Maida Springer characterized her work with African labor unions
at this time as "dancing on the end of a needle" whose point was
spurring social change. The ICFTU tried to keep African unions
out of politics, but Springer and her African colleagues agreed, biographer Yevette Richards writes,

> that the problems many [African] labor unions faced neces-
> sitated a political solution leading to the end of colonialism.
> After all, the colonial governments, which were also the
> largest employers in most African countries, passed labor leg-

islation designed to shape, contain, and constrain the labor movements. . . . The insistence of European labor leaders on complete separation of political and labor issues was a constant source of tension in both labor and political organizations. . . . Moreover, in places where political organizations were banned people looked to labor unions to help advance human rights and fight against colonialism.

All sorts of Kenyans, Mboya later recalled, turned to unions to achieve a modicum of power over their lives. "Suddenly," he wrote, "everyone was coming to us. There was nowhere else they could go." They would come for help in resolving problems having nothing to do with union activity—disputes involving farms, evictions from housing, and the like. During a sweep by the government in 1954, Mboya narrowly avoided arrest and was saved from incarceration only by the intervention of friends in the labor ministry, grateful to him for having led the Kenya Federation of Registered Trade Unions (KFRTU) in staving off a Mau Mau–inspired general strike. When his employer warned that continued union activity would jeopardize his job, Mboya resigned his Sanitary Department position and devoted himself full-time to his largely unpaid union activities.

Mboya's big moment came in March 1955. He had been organizing a small independent union on the docks in the port city of Mombasa. In an incident mirroring what had happened in the United States after the Taft-Hartley Act, Mboya and his associates had demanded that certain unions in the Kenya Federation must make payments to the national organization or be expelled, and five of eleven had walked out. Another consequence was a strike called by a rival Mombasa dockworkers' union that initially crippled the city. Mboya and an associate from the ICFTU had been scheduled to begin giving classes in that city, and so were available and on site. Mboya persuaded the authorities to allow him to address the strikers and others, without police present, in a soccer stadium. It was,

Mboya later wrote, "one of the ugliest scenes I have ever faced," but he convinced the strikers to agree to arbitration. A session with the employers was held while soldiers with fixed bayonets stood guard outside. Eventually, through representing the workers during the arbitration proceeding, Mboya won a significant increase in pay for the striking workers while preserving order and current ownership on the docks and avoiding a shutdown. In May, he similarly settled another potentially explosive strike situation, this one against his former employer, the city of Nairobi. Shortly thereafter, the unions that had walked away from the Federation opted to accept Mboya's conditions for reaffiliation; in the wake of this victory, Mboya biographer David Goldsworthy writes, Mboya's leadership of all of Kenya's unions "was beyond challenge."

Mboya was thus brought to national prominence and international attention; a *New York Times* article would soon appear under the headline AFRICAN LEADER LOOMS IN KENYA, asserting that "Mr. Mboya is regarded as a man who may easily become the political leader of the Africans in a land where since the imprisonment of Jomo Kenyatta . . . no important African leader has appeared." *Life* magazine would shortly characterize Mboya as "[a] superb political speaker with an actor's sense of drama . . . Intellectually quick, courageous, dedicated."

The government saw Mboya as a more acceptable African leader than others in the Kenya labor movement or among exiled former political chieftains. He was not a Kikuyu, nor was he associated with the Mau Mau uprising, as was Mbiyu Koinange, the Kikuyu who had established a school system for Kenyans and was currently in exile, and Mboya provided a centrist contrast to his fellow Luo, Oginga Odinga, the socialist who was viewed by the colonial government as the Communists' man.

Mboya decided to accept an offered scholarship to Ruskin College for 1955–56. Just then he had no desire or opportunity to attend college in the United States, even though the school in Kenya at which he had trained as a sanitary inspector had been founded and was still run by an American church organization.

Prior to 1955, while hundreds of West Africans, primarily Liberians, had been schooled in the United States, only a handful of Kenyans had sought higher education there. Moreover, Africans from various territories who had been educated in the United States and who then returned home to move their colonies toward independence were a significant problem for Great Britain and the other colonial powers; these problem men included Nkrumah of the Gold Coast, Nnamdi Azikiwe in Nigeria, Julius Nyerere in Tanganyika, and Mbiyu Koinange of Kenya, who had started a private school system in the colony but had wisely remained in Great Britain once the Emergency had been declared, certain that if he returned home he would be arrested.

The experiences of the few Kenyans at colleges in the United States were mixed. Njoroge Mungai was completing his medical degree at Stanford; Gikonyo (Julius) Kiano, at Oberlin and then at Berkeley, had compiled a brilliant academic record, including an article written for the literary magazine *Saturday Review*, in which he explained the Mau Mau revolt as a consequence of prior decades of British injustice toward the Kikuyu. But Mugo Gatheru, an equally talented Kenyan writer and philosophy and political science student believed by the British to be part of the Mau Mau apparatus, was targeted by the Kenyan colonial government. Nairobi asked Washington to expel Gatheru as a subversive. He was then in his junior year at Lincoln University, a historically black college near Philadelphia that counted Nkrumah among its graduates; Gatheru's fellow Africans at Lincoln included two friends from Kenya, the mathematician Mbugua Kimani and the sociologist Kariuki Njiiri, son of a senior Kikuyu chief. Kimani and Njiiri were not pursued by the British but Gatheru was, in part because he had come to the United States by a roundabout route from India.

"I had just finished my English class and was walking over to another class," Gatheru later wrote, when "the shadow of Mau Mau" fell upon him, in the form of a U.S. immigration agent who took him to a secluded place and interrogated him for hours. During the interrogation he realized, from the content of the questions, that the queries had to have originated in Nairobi. Deportation proceedings were begun against him. Gatheru refused to go quietly, and his friends, such as Roosevelt University professor St. Clair Drake, rallied the American liberal establishment to his cause. Eventually, the proceedings against Gatheru were dropped. He went on to graduate school at New York University. But his application for a permanent visa to remain in the United States was denied; fighting that case took him another five years. So when it came time for him to attend law school, he opted to do so in London.

Mboya also showed no interest in attending school in Moscow. The Soviet Union had begun actively recruiting students from all over Africa for a new Moscow university, named as a college for "peace and friendship." Generous travel and living allowances were being given, including money for annual trips back home. Similar programs of assistance to African students would shortly be offered by Bulgaria and other satellite countries. These Warsaw Pact countries also expanded their programs of technical assistance, subsidies for sales of equipment, and monetary support to various African governments and, behind the scenes, to pro-independence groups in areas under colonial control.

Even though Mboya had an invitation to attend Ruskin, he found it difficult to get out of Kenya because he would not be going to Great Britain on a government scholarship, and the Kenyan government felt no obligation to give him an exit visa. While dealing with that inconvenience, Mboya also was attempting to solve a larger organizational problem, finding a sponsor to underwrite a Kenya Federation of Registered Trade Unions headquarters in Nairobi that he had envisioned. To obtain an exit visa from Kenya, he cadged an invitation from the Moral Re-Armament Society in Caux, France, and the Nairobi government accepted that as a reason to issue the visa. He did spend a few days at Caux but quickly went on to Brussels, where he importuned the ICFTU for money to build the KFRTU headquarters. The ICFTU turned down his request.

Mboya then proceeded to Oxford, arriving in the fall of 1955. His sojourn there, he later wrote, was an "eye-opener . . . my first opportunity to taste something of the atmosphere of an academic institution, to meet intellectuals and to read books." He spent much of his time at the Bodleian Library.

Had he been in attendance there a few years earlier, he would have found a few more Kenyans at Oxford and Cambridge, but in 1955, according to Bethwell A. Ogot, an Alliance high school math teacher and Makerere graduate who thought he had won a scholarship to Cambridge that year, none of Kenya's "government scholars was to be placed in Oxford, Cambridge, or London, because it was feared, there was too much Communist influence in that area." Instead, they were shunted to less prestigious Welsh and Scottish universities. Ogot went to St. Andrews. Mboya, having arranged his own scholarship, could not be kept out of the Oxford area.

In 1956 Kenya's future was still quite uncertain: A constitution proposed by the British government was unacceptable to Kenyans. While in Great Britain, Mboya worked with the Labour Party on a substitute constitutional configuration that would more readily lead to majority rule, and on a "Plan for a Socialist Party in Kenya." For years, Mboya wrote, he had been "a Socialist at heart and a believer in democracy," working to alleviate poverty by various means but holding no brief for Marxist analysis or ideology. At a press conference in London, called to issue his screed based on that plan, retitled "What Needs to Be Done in Kenya," the twenty-five-year-old was so impressive, a reporter wrote, that "he has more aplomb than some British trade union leaders and can politely turn away an awkward question with an adroitness that a Cabinet Minister might envy." Mboya had tried out his program in speeches and debates in front of different audiences across the British Isles, nearly every weekend, until he had it ready to present at the press conference. The plan called for an immediate end to the Emergency, a release of political prisoners, and expanded African participation in the political process. He made it plain that he was not agitating for immediate independence but rather for concrete steps to be taken toward eventual independence and majority rule. This paper became the basis for his sixteen-thousand-word pamphlet, *The Kenya Question: An African Answer*, published in Great Britain by the Fabian Colonial Bureau. In it, Mboya addressed the roots of the Mau Mau revolt, the role of labor in Kenya, the current government's overly repressive stances, and how best to have Kenya evolve toward majority rule and true representative democracy. A Fabian Colonial Bureau insider carped before publication that "[t]here is no real analysis of the factors inhibiting the development and working of the institutions of mass democracy in a plural society," but the pamphlet was intended as a political big-picture document, not a scholarly analysis or a detailed prescriptive document, and was published without alteration.

It was a hit in Great Britain but in Nairobi the government-friendly newspapers, led by the *East African Standard*, refused to review it in either English or Swahili and also would not carry it in their bookstores. *The Kenya Question* and Mboya's growing stature as a public speaker did, however, bring him to the attention of George Houser and the American Committee on Africa. Houser invited Mboya to come to the United States on an ACOA-sponsored speaking tour of American colleges in August and September 1956. ACOA would distribute his book in the United States and publish an excerpt in its well-circulated magazine, *Africa Today*.

At that moment in time, the struggle over civil rights in the United States was symbolized on the one hand by Martin Luther King, Jr., leading the successful bus boycott in Montgomery, Alabama, despite his home being bombed, and on the other by a presentation made to Eisenhower's cabinet by FBI chief J. Edgar Hoover.

The presentation linked King through an associate with Communist influences, and also asserted that the White Citizens' Councils could be reasonable agents for change. Both claims were later proved untrue, but just then the cabinet believed them, and so did archconservative William F. Buckley, who wrote, "The central question that emerges . . . is whether the White community in the South is entitled to take such measures as are necessary to prevail, politically and culturally, in areas where it does not predominate numerically? The sobering answer is Yes—the White community is so entitled because, for the time being, it is the advanced race."

Attorney General Herbert Brownell, Jr., put together a civil rights bill. It was blocked in Congress by the Dixiecrats, authors of the Southern Manifesto, which equated integration with undermining the Constitution. For the 1956 presidential election, Democratic candidate Adlai Stevenson wanted to keep civil rights out of the campaign so that his party could hold the South, while Eisenhower attempted to gloss over his unwillingness to enforce *Brown* by going to a baseball game with his one black aide, E. Frederick Morrow, and by soliciting the endorsement of Harlem Democrat Adam Clayton Powell, Jr., through promises of federal money for Powell's projects.

Houser had been uncertain whether ACOA would be able to provide large enough audiences for Mboya, but American interest in Africa had been growing, piqued by such bestselling books as John Gunther's *Inside Africa* and Alan Paton's novel about South Africa, *Cry, the Beloved Country,* which had also been made into a Hollywood film starring Sidney Poitier. Mboya's campus appearances were a smash hit, love at first sight; Americans embraced him as Kenyan audiences had, as the promise of a bright and democratic African future.

Traveling with Mboya all across America and at his side as Mboya spoke, several times a day, to college and civic-group audiences, Houser was, he recalled in a recent interview, "deeply impressed" by Mboya's maturity and interpersonal abilities. After all, Mboya had just turned twenty-six on the day he landed in New York City. What "amazed" American audiences during Mboya's appearances, Houser added, was that "this young fellow would stand up and without notes would speak so clearly." And wittily. Asked by an American reporter where he had learned English, Mboya replied, "Coming over on the plane." The tour was so successful that it was extended and included ten days in Canada. So many copies of *The Kenya Question* were sold at these lectures that Houser was continually alerting the publisher to ship more to later stops on the tour.

Intelligent and knowledgeable, Mboya was also able to hold his own in meetings arranged by Maida Springer with the leaders of the American labor movement—George Meany, Philip Randolph, David Dubinsky of the ILGWU, David McDonald of the United Steel Workers of America, and others such as Jay Lovestone. In New York, he stayed at Springer's Brooklyn home, becoming close to her son, who was near his age. These meetings with labor leaders allowed Mboya to solve his second problem: He successfully petitioned Meany for AFL-CIO funds to build the union headquarters in Nairobi. Biographer Goldsworthy thinks it likely that Meany knew a similar request to the ICFTU had been turned down, and believed that by assisting Mboya, American labor and solid anti-Communism would prevail in Kenya over the influence of the Europeans and the Communists. Mboya was not interested in the Cold War, but he knew that American labor leaders were, and knew how to appeal to them on that basis in the service of furthering his own ends and those of his country. Meany promised $35,000 for the Nairobi headquarters; Randolph would hand-deliver it to Mboya in Africa. This donation, and the erecting of the building, helped cement Mboya's status as the leader of all the unions in Kenya.

At every U.S. college venue, Mboya would talk privately with the college president about scholarships for East Africans, as he also did in his meetings with labor leaders; for instance, he obtained commitments from the Meat Packers Union in Chicago to support students who had earned tuition scholarships but had no additional funds to live on in the United States. He also extracted similar promises of assistance from such African-American leaders as journalist P. L. Prattis, editor of *The Pittsburgh Courier*, the country's highest-circulation black newspaper. Prattis personally went to the University of Pittsburgh and made arrangements for scholarships, and brought in Tom Murray of the Steel Workers to work on providing room, board, books, and spending money.

A main theme in Mboya's speeches was the lambasting of the European powers' attempts at continuing their domination in Africa through denying Africans access to higher education, which, he contended, prevented the training of the sort of educated leaders who could take new African nations through independence and to stability. As a former government bureaucrat, Mboya could speak knowledgeably about the extent to which a government requires subcabinet-rank people with expertise and skills as much as it requires political leaders. One example that Mboya gave in his speeches was that in Tanganyika there were only eighteen Africans with college degrees, and no medical doctors and no lawyers, even after eighty years of European rule. The situation was equally as dire in Kenya, Uganda, Rhodesia, and other places long under British rule. To help an African student, then, he said, was to assist very directly in the present and future growth of that student's country.

Some colleges that agreed to extend scholarships to Kenyans had never had an African-American student. But they had little hesitation in accepting Africans because they were foreigners. Moreover, extending tuition scholarships in this era was a less costly matter than it is today; most tuitions were around one thousand dollars per year, so a college's commitment to provide a tuition scholarship was not particularly burdensome to the institution. Still, the majority of the colleges and universities that were willing to offer scholarships and places to Kenyan students were those affiliated with churches and religious groups, who believed it their duty to assist fellow worshippers who had attended church-run schools in East Africa.

On this trip to the United States, Mboya also made the acquaintance of several men who would be crucial to the airlifts: Harry Belafonte, William X. Scheinman, Frank Montero, and Peter Weiss.

Belafonte was at the height of his popularity as a singer of Caribbean folk songs. His breakthrough album, *Calypso*, released in 1956, was the first long-playing record to sell more than a million copies. Widely popular everywhere, Belafonte refused to appear onstage in the South because of its segregated policies and institutions. He had long been an activist, a protégé and defender of Paul Robeson, and during McCarthy's heyday had been blacklisted. He had also already become a friend and monetary supporter of Martin Luther King, Jr.

When Belafonte, then twenty-nine, met Mboya, then twenty-six, he was thunderstruck by "this wonderful moon-faced person" who told "remarkable stories of Kenyatta, and the struggle, and what was really going on in Kenya. . . . His blackness was so completely evident, not just in his physiology but in his passion for his homeland, and the continent, and the liberation of the whole of Africa," Belafonte said in a recent interview. Of all the African leaders that he met, "Tom Mboya gave me my richest sense and deeper sense of the conflict that was going on," and did so "with a remarkable absence of race."

Belafonte and other Americans who met Mboya at this time had anticipated someone who was antiwhite or at least very bitter about white European domination of Africa, as many black Americans were angry about Americans who practiced white supremacy and continuing segregation. For Mboya the issue was not which race would dominate his country's political discourse, but the democratic nature of that discourse and the extension of voting rights to all citizens. He had adopted a resolutely aracial stance, asserting that Kenya should be open to all, regardless of their race, and that white residents of Kenya ought to continue to participate in the political process. Only once, during his American tour in 1956, did Mboya fail to uphold this stance; asked by a college audience member to describe in a word or two how he envisioned the future of Africa, he answered, "Black." As he had expected, the audience chortled along with him.

It was an era when American whites were still in the forefront of the fight for racial justice, though less so for freedom in Africa, and when they had not yet been shouldered aside by the insistence of some African-Americans on fighting their own battles and excluding whites from leadership positions.

Early in 1956, Houser had been the host of a public reception at a midtown Manhattan church for a crusading cleric from South Africa, and afterward received a note from one of the attendees, William Scheinman, requesting a meeting. Scheinman offered his services, his enthusiasm, and his willingness to donate to the American Committee on Africa, and was elected to the ACOA board.

Later, Scheinman remembered ACOA in those days as an organization struggling to make certain the American public understood that despite having a board full of peace activists and civil rights partisans, "We're for racial justice, we're for freedom in Africa, but we're not Communists."

Among the first ACOA projects Houser was able to interest Scheinman in was support for Mboya's speaking tour. Since all the lectures were going to be free of charge, they would produce no income. Scheinman was asked to help cover some transportation and lodging costs, which he did, and he also made some arrangements to put Mboya on television and radio—all without having met the Kenyan. They did meet on Mboya's last evening in the country, when he spoke at the Carnegie Endowment for International Peace. Later Scheinman recalled not being very impressed with Mboya's speech that evening, but understanding that the Kenyan was exhausted and it might not have been his best effort. After the speech, Mugo Gatheru introduced him to Mboya, and Scheinman asked whether Mboya had ever been to Harlem. He had not, so Scheinman took him to a small restaurant in Harlem and they talked into the early hours of the morning.

A week later, Scheinman received a long handwritten letter from Mboya, postmarked from Cairo; Mboya wrote that he had just come from meeting Gamal Abdel Nasser, and detailed some of his plans for the future. Scheinman responded, but before the American's letter reached Kenya, Scheinman received a second one from Mboya, also long and handwritten, postmarked from the Sudan. Thus began a correspondence that grew and grew. Mboya was "meticulous" about writing letters, Scheinman recalled, answering every letter even if it took him months to get around to it. Scheinman, too, liked writing letters, according to Cora Weiss. Tom and Bill's friendship grew through their long-distance communications. Both were articulate, passionate, self-made, fond of women—Mboya had a slew of girlfriends—and ambitious. In addition, George Houser recalls, "Bill was just fascinated by Tom, and Tom knew how to play into that."

Scheinman understood that in becoming friends with Mboya, Gatheru, Kiano, and other Kenyans, he was availing himself of a once-in-a-lifetime opportunity to have an insider's view of and some influence on important players as Kenya marched toward independence. His letters to and from these men reveal Scheinman's exhilaration at being involved in lofty philosophic and political exchanges.

During Mboya's 1956 trip to the United States, Houser also introduced him to Frank Montero, and through him and other ACOA people Mboya was put in touch with virtually all of the important African-American and civil rights leaders in the United States during this visit. These included Congressman Charles Diggs, newspapermen, entertainers, the president of Roosevelt University, and the deans of Howard and other historically black colleges. One leader whom he was unable to meet on this visit was Martin Luther King, Jr., who was extremely busy with the Montgomery boycott and with

moving his family back to Atlanta so he could assume the chairmanship of the new Southern Christian Leadership Conference. But Kiano
met and spoke with King during this period; Kiano and Coretta
King had been classmates at Oberlin, and their association led to the
Kings agreeing to sponsor several Kenyan students at Alabama State,
a historically black college in Montgomery where two female professors had generated the idea for the Montgomery bus boycott.

Mboya's main find was Scheinman. The Kenyan knew that Scheinman was underwriting Gatheru's law studies in London, and so, a
few months after the Mboya-Scheinman correspondence commenced,
Mboya asked him to donate or ask others for the money for a ticket
to the United States for another Kenyan who had won a scholarship
to an American university but was unable to get to the States. Scheinman decided that rather than solicit his friends it was easier to just
buy a ticket for the young man, and he did. Shortly there were more
requests from Mboya—and then more—totaling, over the next three
years, approximately three dozen. At one point Scheinman's accountant suggested that he form a foundation so that he would be able to
deduct these mounting expenses from his tax bill as charitable donations. He did so, and named it the African American Students Foundation. The early, one-by-one instances of Scheinman and Mboya
helping individual Kenyans come across the Atlantic for schooling—
outside the bounds of the Kenyan and U.S. governments—established
the pattern.

Lots of potential candidates for such assistance waited in the
wings.

Cyrus Karuga, a young Kikuyu teacher who lusted after more
education, was then in prison, where he had been since shortly
after the Emergency had been declared. His crime was having been
an instructor at the Kenya African Teachers College, a training institute for which Kenyatta had been the principal; when the college
was shut down, Karuga and some other teachers had been put in

detention. At times he was given no food for five or six days at a stretch, and in other ways was routinely mistreated. He wondered whether he would ever again see his wife, or have children with her. Still, he dreamed of getting out of prison and going to America to study liberal arts and then law.

Dorcas Boit was the daughter of a minor government official; bright, she had graduated from one of only three all-girls secondary schools in Kenya. She had not dreamed of going abroad for schooling until she was chosen to attend the Windsor World Camp in England one summer. She had a good experience there but upon her return learned that almost no Kenyan young women were considered eligible for further study in Great Britain. She was uninterested in attending Makerere—what she wanted to do was teach, and so she found a teaching job in Kenya and put her further education dreams on hold.

During Geoffrey ole Maloiy's youth with the nomadic Maasai tribe, in between his studies he had killed a rhinoceros, two antelopes, and four cobras, but as he grew older his father did not want him to participate in the rite of passage into the older band of warriors, the *moran,* and so he did not take part in killing a lion. Instead, his father sent him to a school in a nearby town; he had to walk back and forth from the *boma* every day, spending nearly as many hours in transit as he did in classes. He developed an interest in science, particularly biology, and thought about becoming a doctor. He fixated on Harvard University: Someday he would go there and become a physician, like Njoroge Mungai, who had studied at Stanford.

Isabelle Muthagi was a well-known woman in her area. In her midtwenties she had become the headmistress of a home economics school while also getting married and having three children. Her fame came partly from her work at the school but mostly because she was the host of a weekly radio program about home economics that was a favorite of women in rural communities for miles around. She wanted to teach the women in her area more than home economics, but felt she needed more education in order to do so. The notion of going to America to obtain that education was hardly a glimmer in her mind until a professor from Howard University in Washington, D.C., visited Muthagi's school on a swing through Africa and broached the idea. Soon Muthagi was informed that a scholarship to Howard would be waiting for her. She was even offered a job teaching Swahili at the university, so she could earn money for her keep. Now all she had to do was find a way to go to Washington, D.C., to accept these offers.

Evanson Gichuchi had been a standout student at Alliance, Kenya's most prestigious secondary school, and had gone on to graduate from Kagumo Teachers Training College. For several years he had been teaching science at Kagumo, but had been incensed that the European teachers there were given access to indoor bathrooms with toilets that flushed, while the African teachers were forced to use outhouses. Through an acquaintance he was introduced to Kariuki Njiiri, a recent graduate of Lincoln University in Pennsylvania; Njiiri was impressed enough with Gichuchi to agree to arrange a scholarship for him at Lincoln. That might take a while, but at least now Gichuchi had hope.

When Kamuti Kiteme was born in 1935, in what he described as the "arid backwater" Mwingi district of Kenya, Europeans had not yet penetrated the area. Shortly, they did, and while his mother converted to Christianity and Western ways, his father did not; they divorced, and Kiteme was raised by his mother and stepfather. He developed a passion for education, completing secondary school and the teachers college at Kagumo in 1957. After teaching for two years at another secondary school, he became headmaster at Kyuso Intermediate School, near the largest town in the Mwingi. He wanted more training as an educator—a master's and a doctorate—and realized he would have to go out of the country to obtain those. But despite his teachers college training and his competence as a teacher and administrator, he was unable to find a venue or a scholarship in

Great Britain or in the larger colleges of the United States. Then he learned that some historically black colleges in the American South were offering partial scholarships. The education there might be well below his knowledge and abilities, but such a college would be a place from which to begin a higher-level educational career.

Miriam Khamadi thought she might become a poet or some sort of writer. The seventh child of a Quaker family in western Kenya, she was a dutiful scholar. When the Butere girls' school opened its high school in 1957, she was in its first class, and every year since then, she had received the top prize—a book. Butere was one of the few schools that taught pure science, and Miriam was always interested in natural things; she also wanted to become a scientist or a science teacher. There was a Quaker college named after the famous William Penn in the United States, she learned, but it was not in Pennsylvania—it was in a town of ten thousand people called Oskaloosa, Iowa.

Another would-be writer was Maina wa Kinyatti, a Kikuyu whose father and brother had been imprisoned. Kinyatti was an unrepentant supporter of the Mau Mau and others who rebelled against the colonial government, as well as being something of a Marxist—though at the time he kept these beliefs to himself so that he could continue in the educational system and be eligible to be sent abroad. There were rumors that an African studies program was being established at Michigan State University; that was a likely place for him to pursue a degree in history.

Perez Olindo wanted to be at Michigan State University because that was the home of a man with whom he had been corresponding, Dr. George Petrides. Olindo, the son of a government health inspector in western Kenya, had been attending the Kakamega African Secondary School for several years. In his first year there, he had excelled in science and math, and wanted to be a medical doctor—until he came under the influence of a University of Chicago–trained biologist at Kakemega, Hezekiah Openda. In a recent e-mail Olindo recalled that Openda "was very close to the students, friendly, and welcomed us to talk to him very freely about his academic studies and experiences in America." Openda found Olindo a pen pal in the United States, George Petrides, a well-known wildlife management biologist who had visited Kenya and was an expert on the impala. Olindo had no idea what a "wildlife biologist" did, but soon learned. Petrides asked him, by mail, if he had ever visited Nairobi National Park or if he knew the director of the national parks. Olindo recalled his reaction to such questions:

> How could a rural African boy have visited a National Park hundreds of miles away from his home area? And who would have bothered to notice and introduce a young African boy to the Director of the National Parks of Kenya! Even if I had someone to introduce me to such a Senior, and White Government Official, would he have the time to grant me an Appointment!

Petrides soon made a connection for the young man to the founder and secretary general of the East African Wildlife Society, Noel Simon, who entertained him at his farm in the Rift Valley and gave him some wildlife magazines. "I became obsessed with studying wild animals that appeared in the magazines I had acquired," Olindo recalls, but "in those days, no one knew the need for studying wildlife or if it was of any practical use for me or for any other African to study." His schoolwork soon reflected his avidness for new learning, however, and he was appointed a school captain for science; one of the perks was that the electricity in his dorm was not turned off at 9:30 P.M. but remained on until 11:30, giving him two extra hours to read. He easily passed his final exams in 1959 but "had no desire to go to Britain or to Russia for further studies." He also discovered that attending MSU right away was out of the question, financially and otherwise. He would have to begin, in the United

States, at another school that cost less and that would give him a partial scholarship, and hope that he would prove to be a good enough student to earn his way thereafter. For the moment, joining Dr. Petrides at Michigan State University was still a dream.

In order to make their educational journeys, these young people and hundreds of others in similar circumstances—whole phalanxes of qualified potential students—would have to wait for Mboya and a handful of other well-placed individuals in Kenya and in the United States to shoulder the burden of helping them to help themselves.

3

ALLIANCE FORMED

The March 1957 ceremonies in Accra marking the independence of Ghana were epochal. After five years under the leadership of Kwame Nkrumah, the former Gold Coast was declaring full independence and taking its new, African name. To emphasize the change, when Nkrumah and his associates arrived for the public ceremony, they wore the prisoner garb that they had been forced to don years earlier by the colonial administration. The sight transfixed Tom Mboya and was equally significant to Martin Luther King, Jr., and to Vice President Richard Nixon, who led the American delegation.

A. Philip Randolph, Maida Springer, Adam Clayton Powell, Jr., Ralph Bunche, and Ted Kheel, among many other Americans, also attended the ceremonies and were similarly affected by them. Kheel and Randolph later wrote about the size and attitude of the delegation from the Soviet Union, which spent money lavishly during the week. "There was little doubt as to [the Soviets'] intentions," Randolph observed. "Africa is Communism's major target." Africa seemed more up for grabs by the warring Cold War combatants than in prior years because of the tremendous blow to colonialism struck by the Suez Canal crisis of late 1956, in which the British and French had been humiliated. The fiasco toppled the British government and impaired London's ability to maintain tight control over its African colonies struggling to emerge from domination.

Martin Luther King, Jr., had just become a celebrated figure; the successful conclusion of the Montgomery bus boycott had put him on the cover of *Time* a few weeks before Accra, and he took advantage of his new celebrity to tell a radio interviewer:

> [T]he birth of this new nation will give impetus to oppressed peoples all over the world. I think it will have worldwide implications and repercussions—not only for Asia and Africa, but also for America. As you well know, we have a problem in the Southland in America, and I think this freedom—the freedom in the birth of a new nation—will influence the situation there.

His assertion echoed what King had heard from Nkrumah over a private lunch, that Africans "would never be able to accept the American ideology of freedom and democracy fully until America settles its own internal racial strife."

Richard Nixon was the highest-ranked American official ever to visit sub-Saharan Africa. One evening he was seated next to a black couple at a table, and asked the man, "How does it feel to be free?" "I wouldn't know, I'm from Alabama," his tablemate responded. Nixon was further tweaked by King's remarks to an interviewer suggesting that the vice president had been able to come halfway across the world to this ceremony but would not come to the American South.

Then Nixon and King met, by chance, on the campus of the Ghana national university. Nixon's Quaker background had fused with his college friendship with a black football teammate and with his having had to argue for desegregation while at Duke Law School to make him a quiet supporter of civil rights, despite his public reputation as a nasty politician. A King biographer writes that in Accra, "Nixon treated his Negro countryman [King] with the courtesy due to an ambassador." Nixon suggested that King visit him in Washington upon their return to the United States so they could discuss civil rights more fully. King was agreeable, and at Accra made no further anti-Nixon statements to the press.

Ted Kheel and National Urban League executive director Lester Granger, who knew both Nixon and King—Kheel would later serve as an officer of the Gandhi Society, a fundraising organization for King's work—then met separately with them in Accra to urge further dialogue. "We mentioned to the vice-president the advisability of his using his report to the nation on his trip to Ghana as an occasion to speak specifically on the racial problems we now face and their new significance in the light of our relations with Ghana," Kheel later said at his press conference in New York.

Nixon, scholar James Meriwether suggests, had been looking for ways to "beef up his foreign policy resumé for a presidential run, and Africa offered a non-controversial opening that neither Eisenhower nor Dulles opposed." When the vice president returned to Washington he filed a report that established his sympathies for the emerging African nations and his belief that Africa was the most critical continent in terms of America's struggle with the USSR, a finding that mandated that the United States devise ways to have continued access to its minerals and other resources critical to maintaining

U.S. military superiority. Nixon soon became known as the administration's expert on Africa.

Then Senator John F. "Jack" Kennedy, a member of the Senate's
Foreign Relations Committee (FRC), became the Democrats' expert. When the State Department created the post of deputy assistant
secretary of state for African affairs to oversee a new, standalone African Bureau, Kennedy received permission from FRC chair J. William
Fulbright to establish and chair a subcommittee on Africa. Earlier,
while in the House of Representatives, Kennedy had been on a foreign affairs subcommittee on Africa, and as a senator he had already
stunned the Eisenhower administration by insisting that the United
States must help all peoples under colonial subjugation in their fights
for independence, and by characterizing the United States' official
stance in Algeria as wrong for backing the colonial power over those
whom Kennedy labeled moderate revolutionaries. After he assumed
his new chairmanship, Kennedy raised his level of rhetoric against
the administration's policies:

> The most powerful single force in the world today is
> neither communism nor capitalism, neither the H-bomb
> nor the guided missile, it is man's eternal desire to be free
> and independent. The great enemy of that tremendous
> force of freedom is called, for want of a more precise term,
> imperialism—and today that means Soviet imperialism and,
> whether we like it or not, and though they are not to be
> equated, Western imperialism.

The Western imperialists he had in mind were the French, whom
he castigated for exiling and executing some Algerian revolutionary
leaders.

Events in Africa were mandating that some change in the U.S.
relationship to the African peoples must be made—but Eisenhower's
"personal conviction," he wrote around this time, was "that almost

any one of the newborn states of the world would far rather embrace Communism or any other form of dictatorship than to acknowledge the political domination of another government even though that brought to each citizen a far higher standard of living." When his National Security Council took up NSC 5719/1, which would guide a new policy for sub-Saharan Africa, it declared that America's purpose was to see "Africa South of the Sahara develop in an orderly manner towards self-government and independence in cooperation with the European powers."

Those two objectives were antithetical—even the authors of the policy document acknowledged that. But they believed that the United States had no choice but to pursue what they called a "middle ground," painting that as a rational course. It was hardly rational; as a later note to the policy revealed, it was based on a skewed and biased view of Africans: "To a considerable extent, the African is still immature and unsophisticated with respect to his attitudes towards the issues that divide the world today. The African's mind is not made up and he is being subjected to a number of contradictory forces."

The problem for the AASF was that this NSC policy-guidance document, at once timid and deeply flawed, would not only shape how the United States acted toward various countries and areas of Africa but would also deeply affect how the U.S. State Department would specifically relate to the foundation's efforts to aid colonial Kenyans. The government's stated need to adhere to the "middle ground" made the AASF effort seem all the more radical, because its operations, as a later news report said, were akin to sticking a thumb in the eye of the British colonial system.

But something radical in relating to emerging nations was badly needed, as philosopher Eric Hoffer wrote at the time, because "our generosity, diplomacy, and propaganda have not won for us a marked measure of wholehearted adherence" from those nations. Hoffer noted that the underlying reason for the failure was that the United States treated new nations, and those aspiring to independence, as though they were "weak"—an approach that failed because the weak frequently feel that generosity is just another form of oppression. "My hunch is that in mastering the art or the technique of helping the weak to help themselves, we shall solve some of the critical problems which confront us . . . in our foreign affairs."

Mboya's dream concerned precisely that point: He wanted Americans to help his young countrymen and countrywomen to help themselves, to afford Kenyans the opportunity to bootstrap themselves into the future. In Mboya's vision of the airlift, students would have to obtain scholarships and collect money for living expenses on their own before U.S. benefactors would be permitted to assist them.

A t stake in the march on Washington in the spring of 1957 and in the congressional session was a mild Civil Rights Act, the first in nearly a century to have a chance of being passed despite the objections of segregationists because it was being championed by Senator Lyndon Johnson, the majority leader and a Southerner himself. Martin Luther King, Jr., and his lieutenant Ralph Abernathy met with Nixon in the Capitol building and made plans for the vice president to come to a Southern city to address a future meeting of a presidential council that Nixon chaired. King told Nixon that he, Abernathy, and other African-American leaders had all voted for the Republican ticket in 1956, and that if enough progress on civil rights was made they would turn out the African-American vote for the next election, presumably for the Republicans, a message that Nixon quickly conveyed to Eisenhower and the cabinet. After the meeting, King told a friend that Nixon "was a mixture of enthusiasm with pragmatism, whose general stance was that he would help the cause of civil rights if he could do so without getting hurt politically."

Nixon worked assiduously for the passage of the 1957 Civil Rights Act, putting the arm on Republican senators. Eisenhower told one senator that the bill was as mild as he could politically make it. The House passed it but a filibuster in the Senate created an impasse. An amendment was introduced that would require a jury trial if the federal government indicted anyone for violation of another person's civil rights. Southerners assumed that in any such jury trial in the South, obtaining a conviction would be impossible; labor unions also liked this amendment, as it would allow them to circumvent the power of a single, local, antiunion judge to break strikes, which had frequently happened. The NAACP asked Eisenhower to veto the bill if it contained the jury-trial provision, arguing that no bill was better than a bad bill; so did Ralph Bunche and Jackie Robinson. "HAVE WAITED THIS LONG FOR BILL WITH MEANING CAN WAIT A LITTLE LONGER," Robinson's telegram to Eisenhower read. But Martin Luther King, Jr.—also an enthusiast and a pragmatist—was for the bill, even in adulterated form, because it would encourage and enable more African-American voter registration.

Although some liberals voted against its passage, John Kennedy went along with the compromise at the request of Johnson. At this time, Kennedy's many biographers agree, Kennedy was not in the forefront of those pushing for civil rights.

The bill passed, and King wrote to Nixon, "Let me say . . . how deeply grateful all people of goodwill are to you for your assiduous labor and dauntless courage in seeking to make the Civil Rights Bill a reality. This has impressed people all across the country, both Negro and white. This is certainly an expression of your devotion to the highest mandates of the moral law. It is also an expression of your political wisdom."

A week later, and pursuant to a plan established to gradually desegregate the schools in Little Rock, Arkansas, nine young African-American teenagers attempted to walk into Little Rock's Central High School. They were blocked by armed elements of the Arkansas National Guard, on the instructions of Governor Orval Faubus. This produced a national crisis and focused international attention on what President Eisenhower might have to do to support *Brown* and the Civil Rights Act of 1957.

During his first term Eisenhower had shied away from leadership in the arena of civil rights. Moreover, as sympathetic biographer Stephen Ambrose asserts, "By refusing to take the initiative or otherwise provide leadership, he had put himself in a position in which he could only react to events, not control them." The previous June, Eisenhower had said that he would never send federal troops to carry out a judge's orders; but now this was precisely the prospect that faced him. A federal judge issued an injunction to Faubus to stop blocking the school. Eisenhower, on vacation in Newport, Rhode Island, met with Faubus and thought they had agreed to a compromise, but Faubus then reneged, merely replacing the Arkansas National Guard with the Little Rock police and continuing to prevent the nine students from attending Central High. Angered by Faubus, and urged on by the moral and legal necessities of the situation, Eisenhower ordered that U.S. Army units proceed to Little Rock, confront the protesters with bayonets fixed, and make it possible for the African-American teenagers to finally begin their classes.

Eisenhower's decisive action on behalf of civil rights and integration was widely reported and celebrated throughout the United States and the rest of the world, and served to restore some of the prestige that the United States had been losing in the eyes of Africans. America's deeds were once again as good as her words.

As Bill Scheinman grew more interested in Kenya as a country, he also increased his attention to the individual students; rather than simply writing checks for their education and airfare, he spent time with them, commiserating with a young man heading off to Little Rock and Philander Smith College who worried about his safety there. Scheinman assured him that he would be okay, but suggested that he study hard so that in a year he could transfer north to a college that offered the engineering degree he wanted.

Two years later, when the airlift began, Philander Smith in Little Rock offered partial scholarships to many of the Kenyans. The college became the destination for seven young Kenyans in 1959, and the same number journeyed there in 1960. Among them were Haron Andima, Sam Mutsiya Ngola, Peter Makau, Joseph Maitha, and George Samuel Okello-Obong.

Haron Andima, a mathematics student at Kisii secondary school, almost did not make it onto the airlift. One of nine children of a family whose father had died young, Haron had a brother who had been imprisoned without trial for two years for "agitating against the British." The only literate member of his family, Haron wanted to write a letter to the authorities protesting his brother's imprisonment and discussed it with a local Catholic priest, who encouraged him to write it. He sent the letter, but then became afraid of reprisals. He spoke to the head of his school, a British expatriate, about the letter and his fears, and the headmaster said, "I'll take care of it." He was as good as his word, and so Andima felt able to apply for and accept the scholarship at Philander Smith. Eventually he would transfer to Hunter College in New York City, and go on to earn a doctorate from New York University and establish a career as an academic.

In the year before the first airlift, Samuel Mutsiya Ngola was living in Nairobi and was taking training courses to be a hospital inspector. He wanted to better himself by going to the United States for education, but when he and other trainees showed up in their schoolboy shorts to try to enter the American consulate and ask for college applications, they were blocked by the police. They had to run away lest they be arrested as troublemakers. Ngola figured out that it was his clothes that had betrayed his intention, and so changed out of his shorts and into long pants. Thus attired, he was able to walk into the consulate unimpeded, and to find information there about colleges in the United States that might offer scholarships to someone with his school record and training. Eventually, Ngola would continue his education in the United States through to completing a doctorate in economics—as would his fellow Philander

Smith schoolmates from Kenya, Peter Makau, Joseph Maitha, and George Samuel Okello-Obong. As Barack Obama, Sr., did, they would bring their doctorates and expertise in economics back to Kenya and aid in the country's development.

All of that lay in the future in mid-1958. Jomo Kenyatta was still in detention, and some Elected Members of the Legislative Council were talking openly about appointing someone else as head of their independence movement. Scheinman wrote to Kiano that "regardless of any statements made by Mr. Odinga, it seems to me that it ill becomes any Elected Member to deny Kenyatta." He suggested that Kiano, Mboya, and the other African members put out a joint statement that would "terminate the controversy" by calling for Kenyatta's release and asserting that Kenyatta "is fully capable of determining what future role he may wish to play in consultation with present African leaders." Scheinman's and Mboya's thoughts were alike on this point and on many others. The joint statement of the elected African members on Kenyatta's future role, written by Mboya, was a turning point in the long march toward independence.

Mboya's ability to reach across tribal and party lines and to stress the need for unity among the African Elected Members helped him to become their leader. He was continuing to grow in stature throughout Kenya and abroad. His celebrity, his ability to inspire confidence, his intelligent analyses, and his base in the East African unions assured that.

But the London and Nairobi governments had rejected Mboya's proposals for added African representation, wider plebiscites, and an end to the Emergency. And so, biographer Goldsworthy writes, on the eve of Mboya's departure for the pan-African conference at Accra that Nkrumah had convened, "Tom Mboya must have felt that he had reached a most worrying political impasse." But when Mboya stepped off the plane to attend this first All-African Peoples Conference—200 delegates representing 200 million people—he learned that Nkrumah had unexpectedly and at the last minute appointed him its chairman. This, Mboya later wrote, was "the proudest day of my life." In a speech, Mboya addressed directly the colonial powers that several generations earlier had taken part in what was known to history as the "scramble for Africa." "Your time is past," Mboya told the colonial powers. "Africa must be free—scram from Africa."

That was in the headlines. Behind the scenes, Mboya and Kiano met with George Houser and Bill Scheinman, who were also attending the conference, for ACOA. Houser noted for his ACOA board that the conference's theme was anticolonialism, and that conferees were exhorted to do whatever they could to end colonialism. One specific way of working toward that goal was the focus of the meetings with the Kenyans.

Scheinman told Mboya that the airfares to transport individual students were growing too burdensome for him to handle alone, and suggested that to bring down the cost per student, they must charter a plane. Mboya was enthusiastic. He and Kiano assured the Americans that they would have no difficulty in filling the charter's eighty-one seats.

They did so because they knew that when independence came someday, while they and their handful of well-trained peers would be the new country's cabinet ministers, there would be an urgent need to staff the upper levels of the new government's bureaucracy. As Kiano later recalled, "We knew that if independence comes and we become ministers and so on, but we don't have the personnel, then this kind of independence would be very weak." Nkrumah, to take Ghana through a similar start-up period, had had to retain the country's white bureaucrats, government functionaries, and inspectors because there were not enough properly trained Africans to handle the jobs.

Mboya had discovered to his chagrin that "many Kenyans could not take up the scholarships they had been offered at American institutions because they could not raise the travel money." The only logical and economic way to bring over a large group, he, Kiano, Scheinman, and Houser agreed, was with a charter. To raise thirty to fifty thousand dollars for that charter would also require an organization capable of completing the paperwork tasks associated with vetting, transporting, and caring for a large group of young people.

The larger goal of that airlift and of the new organization—working toward the end of colonialism—was reflected by a letter to Scheinman from one of his Kenyan correspondents, who wrote that his efforts on behalf of young East Africans to date "cannot pass unnoticed" by the small but growing band of them that was accumulating in U.S. colleges. "It is very impressive and significant for it obviously manifests how keenly you are associated with those [men who are] helping materially . . . the thousands of Africans now oppressed by European imperialists, to fight for their freedom." Houser was also impressed by Scheinman, sending him a note after the Accra conference: "In spite of whatever your 'problems' may be, you are a very generous fellow, and this is not too frequent an accomplishment for mankind."

In ACOA board meetings Scheinman discussed the charter idea. ACOA was not officially interested in assisting students, but fellow board member Montero was, and Scheinman tapped him to become vice president of the new African American Students Foundation and to work on rounding up funds. Montero, in turn, asked Kheel to help. Kheel joined the AASF board as secretary-treasurer and provided Montero with an office inside his law firm and with the shared services of Kheel's secretary.

Scheinman, Montero, and Kheel could only devote part of their time to the AASF endeavor, and so sought a student adviser who would also function as an executive director supervising the New York office. Montero then recruited Cora Weiss, wife of ACOA board member Peter Weiss. The Weisses had recently returned from an extended trip to Africa, and were quite sensitized to the issues involved. They, the Kheels, and the Monteros were neighbors in the Riverdale section of the Bronx, and knew one another. They decided that none of the AASF principals—Mboya, Kiano, Houser, Scheinman, Montero, Kheel, or Cora Weiss—would take a salary, and they all would try to keep office expenses to a minimum, even in Kenya, where the office would be situated in Mboya's labor union building, so that as much as possible of the expected donations would be put into chartering the plane.

"It is my wish," Scheinman wrote to Kiano, "that you and Tom [Mboya] have full authority as to the use of any monies received by the Foundation and that the two of you jointly determine which students shall come here each semester." This was an important principle for both American and African leaders of the AASF: that Africans, rather than Americans or British colonials, would choose the students for the chartered flight, which they were already referring to as an airlift. Kiano had a doctorate in letters and was the director of the Cultural Society for the New Africa; he and Mboya decided to bring in a third man to help choose among the candidates. He was Kariuki Njiiri, son of an important Kikuyu chief, a recent graduate of Lincoln University whose wife, Ruth, like Kiano's wife, was American-born. While the Njiiris had been in the United States, they had grown close to Scheinman; he had attended their wedding in Brooklyn, and when he visited Kenya he had paid a courtesy call on the chief. The Njiiris and Scheinmans both had small sons the same age. Kariuki Njiiri's job in Kenya was as an adult literacy officer for the government, and it took him all over the country.

Mboya would tour the United States in the spring of 1959 to help drum up support for the airlift. He already had open invitations to speak to such as groups as Martin Luther King, Jr.'s Southern Christian Leadership Conference, and at Howard and many other universities. Kiano would also return to the United States during that period.

Mboya and Kiano had long since convinced Scheinman that there should be a business component to his involvement in Kenya's future, which enmeshed Scheinman in underwriting various endeavors. Kenyan governmental regulations restricted "the repatriation to the country of origin of profits, dividends, royalties, etc., nor of the original capital investment," as a colonial official put it in a letter to Scheinman, but the American was not seeking to turn a profit, at least not for himself. The idea of the ventures was to further the push toward independence by use of key equipment, such as a printing press to counter the government's refusal to publish pro-independence literature. His ventures were also intended to generate capital within Kenya that could be used for other necessary projects, and to provide income to Mboya, Kiano, and others while they went about their nonpaid activities, in much the same way that Martin Luther King, Jr.'s activities were supported by Belafonte and others because King's modest salary would not cover his expenses as a leading civil rights activist. At Accra, Kiano added to this wish list a petrol (gasoline) station, so they could more readily get around the country to spread the word. Later, Kiano would suggest a business of exporting parrots and monkeys.

A month later, Scheinman wrote to Kiano to explain that a proper business structure—a jointly owned holding company—had to be in place before he could transfer funds. Kiano became testy: "Obviously, Bill, something has gone wrong somewhere. And it is going to be very difficult to carry on our devoted task for Kenya's freedom together when there is obvious lack of mutual confidence and trust." Kiano hoped that Scheinman was not being "influenced by the many rumors and tales" about him, spread by the likes of *Life* and *Time* and the colonial Kenyan Information Service. "PLEASE SEND CHECK FOR PETROL STATION BY MONDAY NAIROBI ADDRESS FORMAL OPENING THIS WEEK DONT FAIL US," Kiano soon cabled. Scheinman sent the money but was troubled, writing back that if, as Kiano wanted, the initial investment was turned into a revolving fund to underwrite various ventures, then the profitability would decline and with it the holding company's usefulness to the freedom cause. In London, Mugo Gatheru—a partner in the press enterprise—got wind of these other schemes and warned Scheinman not to become too deeply involved in business with Kiano, whom Gatheru no longer trusted. Scheinman also had to turn down Kiano's requests to fund the air passage of three students right away, cabling that "INDIVIDUAL TICKETS PURCHASED NOW MAY MEAN SACRIFICE SEPTEMBER PROJECT CHARTER," and suggesting that the three delay their departure until they could be booked on the chartered plane. Kiano saw the light and wrote back, almost apologetically, that he had perhaps overpromised to the three applicants but would insist that they wait, and would see to it that the Nairobi end of the AASF became better organized for the big push for the fall.

Mail and telexes flew back and forth between AASF offices in Nairobi and New York, most signed with the exhortation "*Uhuru*," the Swahili word for approaching freedom. There was similarly no doubt as to the intent of the impending airlift: to give the lie to British protestations that the East Africans were not educated enough to enable their countries to deserve independence or to be capable of sustaining it once achieved.

The idea of an African American Students Foundation was straightforward: It would be privately funded; Africans would select the students; students would obtain scholarships directly from the wide variety of educational institutions they would attend; and the process would continue mostly independent of supervision by both the U.S. and colonial Kenyan governments. Also, the students to be served by the AASF were to come only from areas of Africa—from Kenya, Uganda, and Tanganyika, in the first batch—that were attempting to rid themselves of British colonial control.

The simplicity of the AASF approach masked how sharply it contrasted with the existing structures for bringing international students to the United States. The State Department had a program for that purpose, administered by an outside contracting entity, the

Institute of International Education (IIE). Because the IIE was government-funded, in conformance with U.S. policy it dealt only with established overseas governments, which meant that only candidates approved by an African government were deemed eligible for the program. The IIE program had been designed mainly to educate the elite from European countries at carefully selected U.S. colleges, and when it expanded to include students from African, Asian, and South American countries, its criteria and methods did not change much. So while independence movements were emerging all over the globe, there was no corresponding action on the educational front from the State Department, its grantee, or from the large private foundations—Ford, Rockefeller, and Carnegie—to help students from colonial territories seeking independence. The fledgling AASF applied to all those foundations and was turned down.

The IIE scholarships were awarded by the U.S. government, not by the individual colleges and universities, though the colleges were permitted to pick and choose among the candidates, taking only those who met their standards and rejecting all others. In most instances, State Department employees acting on behalf of various colleges and universities made the final choices, a selection process that routinely excluded nonmainstream applicants. The IIE and State used this method to prevent situations such as one uncovered by a British colonial official when he went to check up on students from the British Commonwealth countries in the United States; he found a group of Hong Kong Chinese students who had accepted offers from various California junior and community colleges in order to get into the United States, expecting once in residence to be able to transfer to the better-accredited institutions that had previously, through the U.S. government programs, refused to accept them.

The first big AASF-ACOA event was to be an April 15, 1959, fundraiser at Carnegie Hall for Africa Freedom Day. Kheel was the chair of the program, produced by Cora Weiss with Houser and

ACOA staff, and the entertainment included Belafonte, Langston Hughes reading his own poems, and several well-known musical groups. Mboya was to be the star speaker. As he was preparing to leave Kenya for the United States, his home and office were raided, and the editor of his party's newspaper and the party secretary were arrested for subversion. Houser wrote Mboya that in the event Tom was detained, they would turn the Carnegie Hall event into an international protest forum. That proved unnecessary, as Mboya was given the proper exit visa to travel to the United States.

Cora Weiss was detailed to pick him up at Idlewild International Airport in New York, and to have a pastrami sandwich and a sour pickle waiting. She drove Mboya directly to an office building in Manhattan and waited in the car until he returned. "I later learned that he was visiting Jay Lovestone," Weiss recalled in a recent interview.

On the evening of April 15, 1959, the capacity crowd at Carnegie Hall saw on display the flag of the Algerian independence movement, at a moment when the United States had still not recognized that movement. The display caused some Israeli dignitaries to exit the hall. The forthcoming airlift was described and donations were pledged, some as small as a dollar, a few in the thousand-dollar category. Before the close of 1959, eight thousand small donations would be received, totaling thirty-five thousand dollars.

On another evening in New York, banker David Rockefeller was the host for a dinner for Mboya, and Mboya also visited Washington, meeting with union leaders and politicians including Nixon and Hubert Humphrey. Later, on the West Coast, Mboya met Senator Jack Kennedy. "I think we found a lot of interest in each other immediately," Mboya later wrote, adding that Kennedy had really impressed him, perhaps because the two men found that they "were in a lot of agreement about the whole area of American foreign policy as it affected the African scene." For instance, Kennedy had recently told an audience in Palo Alto, in sentences that could as easily have been penned by Mboya:

> Most of all, [Africans] want education—for education is in
> their eyes the backbone to gaining and maintaining the poli-
> tical institutions they want. . . . Education is, in truth, the
> only key to genuine African independence and progress. . . .
> [I]f these new states and emerging peoples turn bitter in their
> taste of independence, then the reason will be that the West-
> ern powers, by indifference or lack of imagination, have
> failed to see that it is their own future that is also at stake.

Kennedy made a variant of this statement at a dinner in New
York for the American Society of African Culture, also addressed by
Congressman Diggs and Kiano, saying that "[a] strong Africa can
only result from a strong people. And no people can become strong
in a climate of servitude and social indignity." Kiano appealed for
American families to house and feed students coming to the United
States to attend school, and warned that many Africans "feel hurt,
angry, sometimes impatient to read some experiences accorded Negroes here. . . . Until the American people . . . wipe out color bars in
America, free African nations and freedom-loving African nationalists will always have a heavy heart and strained friendship for democratic U.S.A." According to a later article that drew on Kiano's
reminiscences, at this dinner he and Kennedy discussed educational
problems in Kenya, and "Kennedy appeared to be receptive."

Scheinman accompanied Mboya on some stops of a countrywide
speaking tour that had Mboya at a podium as many as six times a
day, every day, for six weeks, more than a hundred speeches in all.
Flyers sent out to prospective venues quoted *Life* magazine's recent
description of Mboya as "[a] superb political speaker with an actor's
sense of drama . . . Intellectually quick, courageous, dedicated."
Echoing these observations were local and college newspaper reports that followed his various appearances. "The second American
tour was a time of sustained acclamation: a triumphal progress," as
biographer Goldsworthy puts it.

Martin Luther King, Jr., had been eager to have Mboya speak to the Southern Christian Leadership Conference—Bayard Rustin had conveyed that wish several months earlier. As the day for the African Freedom dinner approached, King hastened to change the date on which he was honoring one of his heroes, the pacifist A. J. Muste, because Mboya's tight schedule only allowed him to be in Atlanta on May 13.

In the headlines at the time of the African Freedom dinner in Atlanta was the lynching of Mack Parker, an African-American who had been arrested in Mississippi for raping a pregnant white woman. Before his trial commenced, he had been abducted from jail by eight to ten hooded men, beaten, killed, and dumped into a nearby river, where his chained body was found floating just a few days before Mboya and Scheinman arrived in Atlanta.

Mboya and King, who had wanted to meet for some time, got along well and understood one another. They would shortly begin a correspondence that would continue for the rest of their lives. The Kings were going to sponsor a half-dozen airlift students. Speaking that night, Mboya expounded on themes that he had frequently expressed during this visit to the United States, for instance, on the television programs *Meet the Press* and *Today*. In addition to warning about the danger of Communism gaining ground in Africa because the United States refused to support the African peoples' anticolonial efforts, he highlighted the "simple" things that Africans sought in their independence movements. An Atlanta listener found most memorable Mboya's point that "[m]aybe America and Africa are not speaking the same language. For example Americans speak of refrigerators to preserve food; Africans' problem is to get food. While Africans are seeking to get a man under shelter, America is projecting a man into outer space."

Although many African-Americans, and even a few of their leaders, still believed that the fight to end segregation in the United States was of a very different sort than that faced by African nationalists,

King disagreed, stating unequivocally at the dinner, "Our struggle is not an isolated struggle. We are all caught in an inescapable network of mutuality."

In a thank-you letter a month later, Mboya was effusive: "I have always been impressed and inspired by your devoted and dedicated leadership in the struggle for equality and dignity of man. . . . It is particularly significant that you succeed in putting forward your ideas and championing our coloured people's cause without emotion, hate, or fear." In the next paragraph he asked King to sponsor or find a thousand-dollar sponsorship for a Kenyan who was to go to Tuskegee in the fall.

King wrote back, similarly full of praise for Mboya, willing to find underwriting for the Tuskegee student, and "absolutely convinced that there is no basic difference between colonialism and segregation. They are both based on a contempt for life and a tragic doctrine of white supremacy. So our struggles are not only similar, they are in a real sense one."

Edith Gitau was twenty-three when she headed to Southwestern College in Winfield, Kansas. A seasoned and well-trained teacher, she had taught at the Mary Leakey School for Girls in Kenya and at a secondary school in Uganda. In order to obtain a seat on the airlift she had to promise in writing to Ruth Njiiri, the American-born wife of Kariuki Njiiri, who was helping to sift the applicants, that "upon my return to Kenya, I would help fight ignorance and poverty— the 2 enemies destroying my community—through education, and thus make a difference," she recently recalled in an e-mail. At the orientation in New York City, an earlier arrival, Zacchaeus Chesoni, a future attorney general of Kenya, spoke to her and told her she sounded more like a social worker than a teacher, and advised her to switch to that profession. So did the administrators at Southwestern, after they tested her.

Edith's white roommates were surprised "that I was not clothed according to their expectations—no wild hair, bare feet, [not] grass-skirted!" She experienced discrimination for several months. "Taking meals in the dining room was a very unpleasant experience because no one wanted to share a table with a black girl," she recalled. When she attended church services off campus, the first few times she had to sit alone in a pew "because of my color." These and similar incidents continued to occur "until people discovered I was not a Negro."

She thought the distinction between whether she was an American or an African black was stupid, but recognized that it allowed her to participate more fully in campus life. Even so, when she went to off-campus restaurants with a group of friends, the restaurants refused to serve them so long as she was part of the group. There was even an incident at a nursery school where she was a practice teacher: The all-white children thought she must be "dirty—soiled" because of her color, until she showed them the palms of her hands, which they decided were "clean."

Once past these initial barriers she was able to fully participate in campus life. She joined clubs and sororities, became a runner-up in a beauty-queen contest, and was taken on breaks to roommates' homes and ranches, where she was allowed to work side-by-side with them, cementing relationships with classmates that she maintains to the present day.

In late 1963 she went to Athens, Ohio, for a foreign-student ecumenical conference, and there met James Gitao, another religious-minded airlift student from Kenya who was studying at the University of Stockton in California; he had wanted to transfer for some time but had decided to stick it out there until graduation. In 1964 they married and both moved to UCLA for graduate work. In 1966 Edith was hired by the Ford Foundation in Nairobi, and James went into business. Her initial duties at Ford also brought her into contact with Kenya's business community. James developed and ran a coffee farm as Edith rose in the Ford Foundation hierarchy to become the regional administrator for East Africa. Both devout, they continued their church activities. Husband and wife collaborated on an affili-ated property management company, Akiba.

During her years at Ford, Edith kept reminding herself of her pledge to Ruth Njiiri to work to rid Kenya of its twin evils, poverty and ignorance. After nineteen years at Ford, in 1985, she resigned to run Akiba; in 1992, with the help of her father—a mechanic, mason, and carpenter—they put up a block of flats in the Kangemi area of Nairobi, known for its slums. "On completion in October 1992," she confides, "I could hardly rent them at a reasonable price because they were too posh for a slum area. It was at this point that I decided to turn the block into a school as part of my campaign to fight igno-rance and poverty."

She opened the religious-based Akiba School—the first private elementary school in the Kangemi district—in January 1993. To Edith's delight, its first pupil on its first day was a girl named Faith, who was then joined by a half-dozen others, taught for the semester by four faculty members. Each year thereafter the school expanded in terms of both number of pupils and number of grades taught. Edith added a second block of flats to accommodate them. In 2000, the high school opened; today there are nearly four hundred stu-dents in Akiba's primary and secondary grades. "Running this school where the majority [of students and their families] can hardly pay school fees is a challenge, but I thank God that we make a difference in their lives," Edith notes. A third of the children are sponsored by donors, many of them from church groups in the United States. Edith handles the administrative duties at Akiba, leaving the educa-tion to trained teachers who are occasionally supplemented by vol-unteers from the U.S. church groups.

4

THE HARAMBEE KIDS

The entire continent of Africa was in the midst of upheavals in 1959. *The Economist* commented,

> Africa is at one and the same time undergoing an agricultural revolution, an industrial, technological and urban revolution, a social revolution and a political revolution; it is passing from a feudal and indeed, in places, still pre-historic age into the atomic age in a matter of decades. It is recapitulating the history of the last five centuries of European society in fifty years.

The pressures of these revolutions were as keenly experienced in Kenya as anywhere else on the continent—but Kenyans felt blocked from making progress toward independence. When Tom Mboya returned from his American tour in the spring of 1959, after receiving an honorary doctorate from Howard, he was detained two hours at the Nairobi airport so that his belongings could be searched for subversive literature; this, he thought, was an excellent reminder of how the government treated its African citizens, the prominent as well as the anonymous.

The Emergency had not yet been lifted, Kenyatta was still in confinement, and the independence movement faced other problems. Two new political parties had been formed, one a reactionary white-settlers party and the second a self-proclaimed moderate white party; these put pressure on the fourteen African and Asian (Indian and Pakistani) Elected Members of the Legislative Council to form a third, "multiracial" party in order to have the best chance of obtaining concessions from the government at a route-to-independence conference scheduled for London in early 1960. More than two dozen other African countries were already on track to become independent in 1960, but Kenya's timetable was still vague.

Of the elected African members, most were from the smaller tribes, the exceptions being Mboya, Kiano, and Odinga (who were from the Luo and Kikuyu tribes). The latter two men, previously the radicals, had indicated their willingness to go along with the multiracial party notion while Mboya had been in the United States. But when Mboya came home and reentered the political fray, he loudly voiced suspicion of the multiracial-party approach. He did not advocate a blacks-only African Nationals party—that was illegal under Kenyan colonial law; moreover, he was on record as encouraging Europeans already in Kenya to remain and work with the black majority. But he insisted publicly that the multiracial-party notion was just another way for Europeans and Asians to maintain power and prevent the much larger black majority from exercising it in correct proportion to its numbers. The authorities clamped down on Mboya, restricting his venues for speeches and even forbidding him to use loudspeakers to carry any speech beyond the confines of the auditorium. Mboya repeatedly defied the restrictions, and the controversy kept him in the headlines and augmented his power.

When a daylong meeting of the fourteen nonwhite Legislative Council members drafted an agreement to establish a multiracial party that would be pledged to achieving representative self-government by 1968, nearly a decade away, Mboya refused to sign. A heated argument ensued. Mboya wanted to use a refusal to sign to undermine the edict forbidding an African Nationals party; the others did not. The chairman issued an ultimatum to Mboya: "You can sign or go to hell."

"Thanks very much. I will go to hell," Mboya replied in a line that soon became famous in Kenya, and walked out. Kiano, Odinga, and another member followed him, now also refusing to cooperate. The high-profile opposition of these Kikuyu and Luo representatives made it clear that from then on, gradualism was unacceptable. "Tom Mboya shows a steely contempt for moderation and half measures," *Time* observed. "His platform: complete equality for Kenya's blacks and whites by 1960, common schools for all races, and a ban on further white immigration to Kenya."

While the political jockeying continued, Mboya, Kiano, and Njiiri evaluated applications for places on the airlift and interviewed the applicants. In the summer of 1959, only about 150 Kenyans were studying for bachelor's or master's degrees outside of Africa: 74 in Great Britain, 75 in India and Pakistan, and a handful in the United States. Kenya's colonial education system did not qualify very many to go abroad each year—a few hundred at most, out of a population of six million Africans. Critics such as Mboya charged that the scarcity of candidates for higher education was a deliberate outcome of an educational system that at each step up the educational ladder provided fewer and fewer educational facilities. Above the primary school level, bottlenecks prevented most students from going to intermediate school, and almost all from making the jump from intermediate to secondary schools, the equivalent of American high schools. Mboya recounted the story of an education officer in the Nyeri district who "had the sad job of allocating 25 secondary school places among pupils from more than 40 intermediate schools." The Cambridge certificate examinations provided another stopping point, as some secondary schools did not prepare their students adequately to pass these examinations; students who did not take them or who failed were ineligible for college-level study abroad.

Since the Emergency had been declared in 1952, the educational situation had worsened. An already-extant shortage of qualified teachers was exacerbated by the forced closing of the teachers college that had been established by Koinange and run by Kenyatta; the government had forbidden other schools from hiring the fired teachers, leaving them unable to find employment as educators and thinning the number of qualified instructors throughout Kenya. The British had not liked the aggressive fundraising campaign among the African population that had led to the establishment of this teachers college and of other independent schools, and further decried the teachers college for allegedly providing the Mau Mau movement with political indoctrination and intellectual cover.

Mboya, Kiano, and other East African leaders understood that the educational problems in Kenya, Uganda, Tanganyika, and the Rhodesias lay deeper than the Emergency. They charged that the "tapering pyramid" of African colonial education—whether run by Great Britain, France, or any of the other colonial powers—was designed to keep down rather than to lift up, to deter the growth of precisely the sort of educated critical mass of people that would demand a greater say in their own governance and would also possess the training and the qualifications to earn enough money to pull significant numbers of them out of poverty.

Adding to the difficulty for students, the opportunities that had been made available to them in the United States, prior to this time, were meager pickings, indeed—five scholarships for Kenya in 1957, nine in 1958. Robert F. Stephens was then the cultural affairs officer for the American consulate in Nairobi. In his forthcoming book, *Out of Kenya: An Educational Odyssey*, he writes that even that increase was hard-won through "constant entreaties and a flood of dispatches." Stephens had been posted to Nairobi from Washington in 1957 to be in charge of the office of the U.S. Information Service (USIS). One of his first tasks had been to accompany Scheinman and Mboya on their 1957 tour of Kenya. His association with the two men had made him enthusiastic in support of their efforts.

The USIS office became a focal point for students seeking to go to America for higher education. That office was not in the consulate but on the second floor of an old commercial building overlooking Nairobi's outdoor market for produce and handcrafts. "Often," Stephens recalled, "the traffic noise and hawkers' cries made conversation in my office a challenging proposition." He became convinced that the United States was missing a great opportunity to influence an entire generation of Kenyans prior to the colony's inevitable achieving of independence. Accordingly, Stephens put together a small library of U.S. college catalogs in the USIS office.

He found it "frustrating" that Washington required a Kenyan who wanted to study in the United States on a U.S. government scholarship to have two years of schooling beyond high school, when the collegiate entrance requirement for U.S.-educated applicants was simply a high school diploma. He chafed at the notion that all British colonial students aiming to go to U.S. colleges on U.S. government scholarships should be chosen in London; that, he judged, was "discriminatory" because "it totally ignored Kenyan realities and left out of the process the presumably better informed American consular representatives on the scene." In communicating with Foggy Bottom, Stephens rang the anti-Communist bell, arguing that East Africa desperately needed to send students to the United States to ready their countries for independence and subsequent close ties to the West. He convinced the State Department to roll back the 1959 U.S. government scholarship requirements for Kenyans to just having a Cambridge certificate, dropping the added requirement for two years of postsecondary schooling.

State's loosening was also attributable to an overall, though gradual, shift that was taking place in the wake of the death of John Foster Dulles in the spring of 1959, a shift away from Dulles's doctrinaire anti-Communism that had mandated continuing close ties with colonial regimes in Africa. State was also being pushed in this new direction by the election in 1958 of an even more Democratic Congress, which had increased the power of foreign-relations overseers Senators Fulbright and Kennedy, and other serious critics of the Dulles procolonial policies.

Compared to American applicants for college slots, the Kenyans were at a disadvantage because of the nature of their culture and their previous schooling. They lived in a mostly nonliterate milieu, and spoke English as a third language, learned after their own tribal language and Swahili, the lingua franca of all of East Africa. Perhaps more important, many students who had been in government-run schools rather than in those operated by religious groups had been taught mostly without books and by rote, in a system descended largely unchanged from that developed by Joseph Lancaster of London in the 1820s, which had been used in missionary and colonial school systems throughout the less developed world, including Great Britain's African colonies and the Native American reservations of the United States. Lancaster's system, a recent critic wrote, "promised wholesale acculturation and social control at discount prices" and was generally used in places where the number of properly trained teachers was low, as it was in East Africa.

Another roadblock was race. Although some American colleges were prepared to categorize the Kenyans simply as foreign students, there were dozens of institutions, primarily in the South, who would not accept them because they were black. It was for this reason (and for the lower tuition fees) that so many of the Kenyans accepted invitations from historically black colleges rather than from comparable white colleges in the United States.

But the Kenyan applicants also possessed some distinct advantages over the usual incoming American freshmen. They were older, nineteen to twenty-nine rather than seventeen or eighteen, since they had had to wait years longer for the opportunity to study abroad. Many, like Pamela Odede, had attended technical college for a year or two before being selected for the airlift program. Virtually all had worked—toiled hard throughout their young lives outside the classroom, in addition to attending school—at a time when most American college freshmen had not. Most of them had also personally taken charge of securing their own admissions to college, generally without the assistance of guidance counselors or family members, since relatively few applicants came from literate families. Many applicants, as with Barack Obama, Sr., were quite persistent, writing to twenty or thirty schools before securing definite admittance and partial or full scholarships. Such letters were not only difficult for them to write but also costly. Each initial inquiry missive cost fifty pence; sending a completed application would entail more postage and, often, a ten-dollar application fee—more than the average Kenyan earned in a week, which made the resulting acceptance letter enormously valuable in their eyes and augured well for their determination to succeed in college. So overwhelmingly poor were they that many felt the need to attend the U.S. college that offered them the most money, rather than attending the most prestigious college that accepted them. Obama Sr. once told a reporter in Honolulu that he had also been accepted at Morgan State in Baltimore and at San Francisco State, but chose to come to Hawaii because of its more exotic climate, which he had read about and seen photographs of in *The Saturday Evening Post.*

In terms of motivation, these students were infused by the understanding that, unlike most American-born students, they were studying for a cause beyond themselves.

Many were not only the first in their families to attend college but also the first in their villages and clans. They knew they were the hope of their communities, knew that when they returned to East Africa they were expected to devote their lives in important ways to their fellow countrymen rather than solely to self-aggrandizement. As one student later said, "I am not here [in the U.S.] on my own." Mungai Mbayah, later a student spokesman for the 1959 airliftees, expressed the thoughts of the whole group: "We all have a responsibility ahead. We will all be called upon to give public service when we go back to Kenya. Nothing short [of that] will be acceptable to our people and to those who enabled us to come here to study."

Gordon Hagberg, who had been a public affairs officer in the U.S. Nairobi consulate, later explained in an article that the same social forces that pushed Africans toward independence also impelled them to become better educated:

> Education is seen as a means to an end . . . as the means to getting wealth and power which the Western man had by virtue of his education. . . . There is a widespread stirring among Africans which reflects an inner urge to discover themselves and to realize their full potential in this world of science and industry. It is not unlike the awakening experienced earlier in the Western world, except that the pace has been accelerated.

Hagberg was sympathetic to such aims but initially wary of the AASF approach to meeting them, especially as he worked at the time he wrote the article for an entity, the International Institute of Education, whose fiefdom was challenged by the idea of an airlift. Stephens was better primed by his understanding of the East Africans' need, and by Mboya's approach, to rebel against the formal State Department posture that hewed only to the support-the-colonial-government line, and he went out of his way to aid the Mboya program.

It may seem surprising to you to get this appeal for HIGHER EDU-CATION from a person unpopular, semi-educated, poor and above all, unknown to you."

"I humbly beg to place before you a request and I hope it would be given sympathetic considerations as I was informed is your natural function."

"I intends to work there to cover some of the expenses as my father's yearly income is not so big. Every small help the foundation will be able to give will be greatly appreciated and the reward of it would be beneficial to promote better understanding and friendship between our two countries."

"It is not my intention to trespass unduly on your time by sending you a long letter. However, an appeal like this, which necessarily requires the unburdening of one's heart, may often tend to be somewhat detailed."

"Father's maximum yearly salary about 773 dollars, mother's earnings, nil. On my father therefore depend a large family of ten including our aged granny. Our dad (God bless him) has not spared pains and has even denied himself and the family bare necessities of life in an heroic endeavour to give us children as good an education as possible within the limits of his tiny resources."

"Personally, I have gained full Tuition, Room, and Boarding

scholarship at Oklahoma City University. . . . I am completely desperate and unable to raise any money to meet my travel expenses to the States. I don't know whether you will kindly offer me some advice in order to overcome that difficulty of mine."

"My people are severely oppressed in every walk of human development. This has been possible because of the disservice of the colonial government. It is not to the benefit of the Africans who are the majority."

"I'm at present taking my studies at St. Bernard's College in Uganda. I'm a Kenya man and my age is 20 years. I beg for a vacancy in your place as well as a aid."

"For interest sake, I would like to inform you that I had been offered a chance at Oakwood College last year but I failed to fill and send back the forms I was sent to fill because of financial difficulties."

"My brother has provisionally been accepted in one of the Colleges in the U.S.A. . . . I request your organization as to whether something can be done for any assistance to cover this journey. My parents are ordinary poor peasant who cannot even manage to look after their life properly and thus no way can be explored for the futures of their children. I am now trying to build up if possible and hope that you will do your best to help me."

"My plight is somewhat regrettable. I am due to enter Boston College of Business Administration in September next. I had hoped to earn the $2,000 first year fees from a book I started writing, 'Black Rhodesia Under the White Men's Rule.' . . . I am an African 23 years of age and as I write this letter, am more than a 1,000 mile from home. I am a Southern Rhodesian but since the February arrests, it is most unsafe for me to go home."

"I passed Junior Leaving Certificate and I am completing Form IV this year at the Kenya Indian High School in Mombasa. I am sitting for senior Cambridge certificate this year and I hope I shall pass it. I have been accepted to join the University of New Mexico Albuquerque within the end of this year [but] the director of admission told me that the University is not in position to offer me financial aid."

"There is no degree-awarding educational institution in Kenya, my country. Makerere College is the only college for the four East African Territories. As such, Kenya sends less than a hundred students every year to the College."

"I'm a Kikuyu in tribe and I am so young that I am very interested for so any superiority as I have been detained for a long of 5 years since Emergency declared in Kenya (1952) but now I am free."

"I am born of very poor parents with my home in Kenya. I had 12 years of education but financial disablement proved the main barrier behind my failure [to go on]. . . . I have been with the Education Department as a teacher for roughly seven years."

"I understand that the American way of life is more satisfying and happy than any other system in the world. . . . I trust that, by bowing before your said Honourable Council, it would be kind enough to relief me from all my worries and in which your generosity help would be highly appreciated by both hands."

These and hundreds of similar letters poured into the AASF from many channels, addressed to Scheinman in New York, or Mboya, Kiano, Njiiri, and the American consulate in Nairobi, or to ACOA, or to various donors such as Jackie Robinson, when it became known in the press that he was involved. In many instances, the processes of vetting and accepting a candidate were complex. A typically convoluted one involved the efforts to assist the best student in a girls' school in Nyasaland who wanted to attend one of America's most prestigious child development institutes, Merrill-Palmer in Detroit. A prize pupil at a school founded by the Phelps Stokes Fund in Nyasaland, she appealed to Phelps Stokes, which forwarded her request (and a recommendation) to ACOA, who passed it on to the AASF in New York. Scheinman and Montero wrote several letters to the Detroit school, obtaining verification and clarification, but left the ultimate decision on the young woman's transportation to Mboya and the Nairobi AASF office. Once she was vetted, arrangements had to be made separately for all three legs of her journey—by bus from her home area to Nairobi, by plane to New York, and by bus from New York to Detroit—before all the parties were satisfied that she would be able to matriculate at Merrill-Palmer. Unfortunately, the process took so long that she missed the 1959 plane and had to wait until 1960.

In order to grant a student visa, Washington required that a prospective student have a passport, a guaranteed return ticket home, proof of admission to an American college, evidence of a scholarship or other way(s) to earn the money to remain at the college, and three hundred dollars in cash. Of these requirements, the major stumbling block was cash in hand: Three hundred dollars was several times the eighty-four-dollar annual per-capita income of African Kenyans. Most individual students could not amass it alone, no matter how many after-school jobs they held. It could only be raised by soliciting relatives, friends, neighbors, and local merchants. Many prospective students were given a *harambee* party—*harambee* means "to have everyone pull together"—to which guests would bring money or goods that could be auctioned for cash. The celebration might be a bonfire-lit evening or a tea party. It could not be a political gathering because those were outlawed, but many tea parties were organized by political and union leaders who prodded their followers and members to attend. Many airlift-generation graduates recalled spending dozens of afternoons sipping tea in private dwellings, receiving gifts as small as a few pence as they struggled to accumulate the needed three hundred dollars. In commercial districts they knocked on shop doors, obtaining significant contributions from Kenya's Asian proprietors of shops and service ventures whose enterprises depended on African customers. Mboya and other Legislative Council members leaned on the Asian community to chip in, and it did, handsomely.

The largest part of the burden of raising funds, though, fell on the students' families, whose sacrifices were often acute, involving the sale of parcels of land that had been hacked out of the savannah over the years or of prize goats, cattle, and the like. Many gifts and funds came from people who were themselves not literate but who understood the value of an educated person to the community and were quite willing to assist a relative, neighbor, or clansman. If the students felt keenly their responsibility to their communities, it was in part because the communities had happily assisted their children to go into the larger world and become educated, on the joint expectation that the children would then return home to enrich others' lives. A curious paradox was at work: Neighbors and clansmen contributed to send the community's scions to be educated and eventually come back to lead—though the donors lived in a tribal culture in which leadership was hereditary, they were unconcerned that a radical change in the community might be produced if future leadership eventually passed to the better educated, rather than to the tribal leaders' sons who did not have as much education.

There were 140 serious applicants for places on the September 1959 charter, which could seat 81. The applicants came from about a dozen tribes and included students from Uganda and Nyasaland. The trio of Mboya, Kiano, and Njiiri interviewed most of them, individually and sometimes as a panel. Most applicants were able to satisfy the requirements of both the U.S. government and the Kenyan colonial government, and were thus eligible for passports and visas; some, like Barack Obama, Sr., who was headed for Hawaii, did not board the charter plane but were assisted in other ways once at American colleges.

East Africans were also being courted to attend school in Moscow and in Soviet bloc countries—and with better scholarship packages. In addition to full tuition scholarships, all expenses were to be paid at the "University of Friendship of Peoples" in Moscow, including airfare for one trip home for each year of study. Some students did go to the Communist capitals, but more of Kenya's eligible students believed that if such respected people as Mboya, Kiano, and Njiiri thought that the United States was a better place to be trained—one that was more in the mode of the democratic governance they hoped to have in independent Kenya—then they should go to the English-speaking United States.

The Luo applicants tended to seek Mboya's protection, the Kikuyu, Kiano's, although both men tried hard to avoid giving preference to their own tribes; Mboya, whose Council district and union fiefdom was primarily Kikuyu, was especially conscious of the need to be atribal. One felicitous nontribal selection was a well-known Nairobi student athlete, a Goan, Francis Santiago, who had received an athletic scholarship to Howard Payne, a Baptist college in Texas.

The selections were mostly made on merit, but in Kenya it was always important for an applicant to any position—student, employee, or union leader—to be recommended by a person of influence, and the successful applicants for airlift places generally had references from people known to the selection committee. The preponderance of applicants were Kikuyu and Luo, though the eventual mix included students from eight different tribes. Many Kikuyu were at a disadvantage in applying because the colonial government, in its 1952 sweeps, had destroyed the records of the Kikuyu school system that had been established by Koinange. (This was not unique to Kikuyu; Obama Sr., a Luo, also had difficulty in procuring his school records.)

Sometimes Mboya, Kiano, and Njiiri would deadlock on an application; Bob Stephens joined the discussions and, he recalled, acted as a referee. "My insistence was that academic qualifications and not tribal identities be the criterion for selecting candidates," he wrote in a recent letter. The political strain that was driving a wedge between Mboya and Kiano was put aside during their deliberations over students for the airlift. Stephens later wrote that Mboya, whom he admired for many reasons, "could be crafty, secretive, imperious, always in control of the situation," while Kiano, a man whom the chancellor of the University of California system once characterized to Stephens as the brightest foreign student who had ever attended the university, was quiet and scholarly.

There was push-back from the Kenyan government, which disliked the entire idea of allowing African students to go to schools of their own choosing in the United States rather than having them accept, in a docile way, the government's right to choose the best and brightest of them to be schooled in Great Britain. But once the students had procured admissions and scholarships to American institutions, and the charter was arranged, the colonial government was somewhat stymied in its objections. Not so the acknowledged leader of secondary education in Kenya, Carey Francis, headmaster of Alliance, which each year sent a few of its graduates to Oxford, Cambridge, and St. Andrews. Francis had a low opinion of American universities. He wrote, "The frenzied thirst for and confidence in overseas education was a major difficulty for Kenya. To many the nature of the course [of study] was immaterial so long as it was a course and one course led not to work, but to another course. . . . [I feared that] in a few years, many would return disillusioned and embittered, unfitted for any useful work, with fourth-rate degrees from fifth-rate universities."

There also were grumbles from applicants who did not make the cut, and from students who thought they should have been chosen but did not apply because they lacked patronage and were certain that without it they would be rejected. Mboya answered these young critics in an interview in Nairobi's *Sunday Post*: "Those who have criticized our endeavors are usually those who have done the least to help themselves." He advised such critics to contribute to the program to assist the students, and not "to sit around and hope for free gifts and bemoan the fact that not all people get them."

Those chosen for the first airlift included Dorcas Boit, by then twenty-two, the teacher who had not dreamed of going to college out of Kenya because so few places for African women were available in Great Britain, but would now be able to attend Spelman College in Atlanta; the Maasai Geoffrey ole Maloiy, who had been chagrined to learn that Harvard would not take him yet because he lacked a basic scientific education, and had found an alternate place to provide him just that, a veterinary college in the middle of Iowa; the teacher Cyrus Karuga, by then twenty-nine, who had finally been released from prison after five years, and would attend a college in Nebraska, though he would have to leave his beloved wife behind to do so; Isabelle Muthagi, who had now turned thirty and would leave behind her husband and three children to teach Swahili at Howard University while she took classes there; Sam Mutsiya Ngola, the young man in shorts who had cadged entry to the American consulate and managed to earn a scholarship to Philander Smith; and Evanson Gichuchi. The previous year, despite Gichuchi's having been awarded a scholarship that Njiiri had arranged at Lincoln University, at the last minute he was bumped off the small list of people to be transported by Scheinman. This year, better understanding the relative clout of the individuals on the selection panel, Gichuchi had sought help from Kiano as well as from Njiiri, and finally won his ticket to America.

Six dozen more students were deemed qualified and credentialed enough to take seats on the charter. Among them was Pamela Odede. Daughter of a senior Luo chief, she had been at Makerere for two years before applying to and obtaining a scholarship from Western College for Women in Ohio. The same description that American newsmen would soon apply to Dorcas Boit also fit Pamela: "intelligent, slim, articulate." For years, Mboya had been a tribal and political friend of Pamela's father, and recently Pamela and Tom had become romantically involved. On the eve of her departure for the United States, they announced their engagement.

While Scheinman, Montero, Kheel, and the Weisses were convinced that by enabling East Africans to study in the United States they were furthering not only the aims of the East Africans but also the best interests of the United States, to many other Americans the connection between the interests of the United States and the forthcoming airlift was not as obvious. To raise money and consciousness for the airlift and any further assistance to the students, that connection had to be made palpable. So Scheinman and Montero drafted a fundraising letter that they wanted to have signed by one of the country's most recognizable African-American celebrities. They debated whether this should be baseball star Jackie Robinson, singer Harry Belafonte, or actor Sidney Poitier. Eventually, Montero recommended that all three sign it. Scheinman agreed. The celebrities proved to be amenable, and looked at drafts of the letter until there was one that all three approved and signed. The thrice-signed letter went out to thousands of people, asking them to help underwrite the airlift.

The jointly signed appeal was unusual because Robinson, Belafonte, and Poitier were not frequently in agreement philosophically or politically, even in regard to the pace of civil rights progress. Robinson, who liked to say he was independent but regularly supported Republican causes, had retired from baseball and was an executive with Chock full o'Nuts, a coffee company whose shops were ubiquitous in American big cities. With a coauthor he had written a bestselling book and currently wrote a weekly newspaper column carried in the *New York Post* and newspapers in other cities. Belafonte, having recently released the first album ever to sell a million copies, was wildly popular. The most liberal of the three men, the singer had a long history of support for good causes—civil rights, alleviating poverty, and free speech. While Belafonte had championed Paul Robeson, the singer, actor, and social activist who had been hounded for his open embrace of the Soviet Union, Robinson had testified against Robeson to a congressional panel. Poitier, starring in *A Raisin in the Sun* on Broadway, was a centrist when compared to Belafonte and Robinson, though a reliable supporter of liberal causes.

Their one-page letter, sent to many thousands on the mailing lists of several liberal organizations, called the recipients' attention to "an urgent matter which we are confident will appeal to your sense of fair play." Recounting Mboya's recent trip to the United States and his drive to educate Kenyan students, the letter asserted that "under the repressive colonial system . . . higher education is not available to Africans" in Kenya. Fortunately, the letter continued, more than forty institutions of higher learning, from Harvard to the University of Hawaii, had responded to Mboya's appeal and had offered scholarships. Reporting that the students had already raised considerable money in Africa to cover most of their expenses, the trio appealed for contributions to cover the $39,000 cost of the charter airplane. "We have personally pledged part of this, but we cannot do it alone."

Robinson had agreed to contribute four thousand dollars, annually, for a variety of scholarships; some would go to Kenyans already studying in the United States, the others to those who would be matriculating that year. In a *Post* column a week later, Robinson reported that an Elks chapter in Detroit had signed on to help sponsor a Kenyan medical student at Michigan State, and that a passerby on the street had stopped him to say he had already mailed a check to the AASF. "Now, while Africa is struggling to free herself from her chains," Robinson wrote, "is the time to make friends and influence people—for if we fail, there are others who are eager to gain a foothold there with distorted propaganda about America."

There would eventually be eight thousand responses to AASF appeals in 1959; in terms of fundraising efficacy, the first letter was a home run.

A predictable outcry from the British government objected to the AASF assertion that there were no opportunities for higher education for Kenyans. In a letter to *The New York Times*, the colonial attaché in Washington, Douglas Williams, claimed that 451 "Kenya Africans" were taking college-level courses, 79 at the Royal Technical College in Nairobi, 325 at Makerere, 45 in the United Kingdom, and 2 in Canada, all supported by "bursaries" from the Kenyan government. "Any suggestion, therefore, that the Government of Kenya is indifferent to the needs of Kenya Africans for higher education is unwarranted."

Scheinman cabled Mboya with the text of the attaché's letter to the editor and urged him to write a quick response. But feeling that the letter had to be answered immediately, Scheinman sent his own to the *Times*, which was printed. It pointed out that the newly founded Royal Technical College was a training institute that did not offer degrees, and that it was the only institution physically in Kenya and "not precisely a shining example of generally available 'higher education' in Kenya." Makerere was also a technical training school; moreover, Scheinman charged, the "bursaries" given to students were far from complete, and the Kenyan students who wanted to attend schools outside of the country were almost entirely unable to choose which college they could attend in Africa or in the United Kingdom. Finally, the total of 451 college-level government scholarships provided for a population of six million Kenyans was proof itself of the failure of the colonial government to properly attend to African educational needs.

The fundraising letter from the three celebrities also produced a short article on the front page of the *Times* in August, and prompted a phone call to Scheinman from the State Department. "That must be an error," Scheinman later recalled the State Department representative saying to him about the *Times* article, because, this man said, the department was not bringing to the United States anything like the eighty-one students from Kenya that were to be on the charter. Scheinman patiently explained that these students had obtained their own scholarships and that the AASF was simply paying their transportation costs to the United States.

A few recipients of the fundraising letter, and a couple of readers of the *Times*, did not think that bringing large numbers of East Africans to the United States was a good idea. They said that it was premature, or that the U.S. higher education system could not absorb so many. A Ugandan student at a U.S. college complained to the *Times* of his inability to land a summer job or adequate housing in New York City because of racial discrimination. "Billions of dollars can be poured into Africa [by the U.S. government], but if you [white Americans] are hostile to us while we are students in this country, well, billions might aid progress, but you will not have won our hearts to call you friends and trust you."

In the last few days before the plane was to leave Nairobi, Mboya, Kiano, and two Indian employees of a travel agency, as well as Bob Stephens and a visa officer from the American consulate, vetted documents and dealt with the students. "The colonial government and Education Department dragged their feet and placed obstacles in the way of students obtaining passports, though they abstained from blatant attempts to block their departure," Stephens later wrote.

Eighty-four people were on the list to be airlifted, but the plane could only take eighty-one; arrangements were made to have the extra three fly on a commercial plane. Seventy-nine students from Kenya and one each from Uganda and Tanganyika were to go aboard the charter—sixty-eight young men and thirteen young women, the largest contingent of East Africans ever to travel out of the African continent for study at a single time. That there were thirteen women was also remarkable, considering that Kenyan society was highly patriarchal and that there were far fewer secondary schools for women than for men.

The plane was scheduled to leave the still-small Nairobi airport in the middle of the night. Nonetheless, a crowd of five thousand gathered for the send-off and listened patiently to farewell addresses by Mboya, Kiano, and others. "The colonial authorities were nervous and the police were very much in evidence at the airport," Stephens recalled.

When the propeller plane finally lifted off on its first-leg flight to London, the crowd cheered and cried.

After an overnight stop in London, the chartered plane landed at New York's Idlewild International Airport on September 9, 1959. In the crowd to greet the arrivals were a dozen or more Kenyans who were already studying in the United States, such as Wanjohl Waciuma of Harvard. The AASF delegation was led by Jackie Robinson, who welcomed the students, spoke to several of them, and introduced them to the press.

Mungai Mbayah and Dorcas Boit read statements on behalf of the students, and they and others answered questions. Reporters were delighted with Geoffrey ole Maloiy's tales of his Maasai hunting trophies, appalled at Cyrus Karuga's report of having spent five years in jail for associating with Kenyatta, and amused by student stories of herding goats or cattle on the savannah before they were old enough to go to school, as well as charmed by the students' articulateness and serious miens. Eight were to study premed courses; the same number indicated an interest in the law. The press could not get over its astonishment that seven of the students were heading to Little Rock—a city whose segregation struggles had been heard of around the world. "I want the experience," said one of them; "it might be useful when I go back home." Jackie Robinson told his column readers how impressed he was with the students to whom he had spoken, adding, "I couldn't help but feel that here undoubtedly was a whole group of potential Tom Mboyas, Kwame Nkrumahs and Nnamdi Azikiwes."

Cora Weiss worked with many of the students in New York, handling the details of their college careers. She recalled that most of the airlifted students did not come from the elite: "The few that the British considered the 'best and the brightest' were going to Oxford and Cambridge. Those who came to the U.S. were bright enough, though more earnest and hardworking. But they were the most highly motivated students that I've ever met. Nothing was going to stop them from getting an education."

The *Chicago Daily News* observed that the airlift project was "mud-in-the-eye to the white supremacy specialists in Africa who prefer their Africans docile and uneducated. It is also a powerful rebuttal to Communist propagandists selling the fiction that Americans are somehow linked with African white supremacists." And *Time*, which featured a photo of three of the students, commented that the event of the students' arrival in the United States "was not one to make British colonial officials cheer."

A reporter for the *Amsterdam News*, a New York City African-American paper, was annoyed that the airliftees steadfastly refused to discuss the internal affairs of Kenya during their press conference or in individual chats. "There are more students in Nairobi waiting to come to America to study," Mungai Mbayah explained. "We must be careful [or] they will suffer by not being allowed to come. And we must return and live there, and we could be picked off." After another twelve hours had elapsed, when the reporter spoke to some of them again, "they did loosen up" and provided the reporter with some choice quotes about their "English slave lords," the Emergency restrictions on travel from one district in Kenya to another, and the unjust imprisonment of Kenyatta.

The students were taken by chartered bus to the Hotel Martinique, opposite Macy's department store, a cornucopia that delighted the students even though they had no spare money to spend on its wares. They stayed two nights and were exhorted by the AASF to eat breakfasts and lunches at the cafeteria called the Automat, rather than be lured into restaurants that would cost them too large a fraction of their precious resources. Dinners were provided as part of the three-day orientation. The African-American community and ACOA had lined up an array of speakers and counselors that included playwright Lorraine Hansberry and other prominent people. Part of the orientation was held at the Church of the Master in Harlem, and participants included representatives from the NAACP, the Phelps Stokes Fund, and New York's Central Labor Council.

Among the handouts at the orientation sessions was a fifty-six-page pamphlet published in 1957 by the Phelps Stokes Fund, *African Students in the United States.* In a section entitled "Education of the Negro," the pamphlet noted that until *Brown* in 1954 there was a lot of segregation in the United States, and that this was "destined to change," but that while "[c]onditions are improving in the South . . . Negroes are still far from having equal opportunities in the educational system." It suggested that obtaining a part-time job, North or South, would not be easy, because "[w]hile the African student may not be at a particular disadvantage in seeking employment on the campus he is at a very distinct disadvantage in the outside community where the average employer may have no sentimental interest in the African student nor sympathetic understanding of his problems." Summer work, the pamphlet said, would be "even more difficult" to obtain.

The toughest language of the pamphlet was in "Personal Problems"; African students—presumed by the pamphlet to be male—needed to understand that American behaviors were different than their own, this section said, and to abide by American standards. These included "the worth of the individual man; the concept of the monogamous family as the unit of society . . . the belief in the dignity of manual labor . . . emphasis upon the simple moral values of right versus wrong and honesty embodied in the Christian religion . . .

and equality of the sexes." Beyond these were the canons of "etiquette" and "good manners," punctuality, the keeping of promises, "not to monopolize the verbal intercourse," and to treat others as he wished to be treated. "He should forget who he was at home (Prince or Chieftain's son) for such a reputation will not long sustain him in the democratic society of America and not at all in his struggle for academic success." And he must not misconstrue a young woman's agreement to go out on a date as evidence of "sentimental interest" in him.

Thus fortified and warned, and after visits to the United Nations, the Statue of Liberty, the top of the Empire State Building, and City Hall, the eighty-one students were put on trains and buses for their collegiate destinations. Before they left, their papers were rechecked once again to make certain they would be properly received and matriculated at their respective colleges. Upon his return to his office Scheinman found a thank-you letter from Tom Mboya for all that the AASF team in New York had done for the students. "The greatest thing in man's achievement," Mboya wrote, "is the knowledge that he is needed and that he can give."

Fred Egambi Dalizu was one of several Kenyans who had eagerly enrolled at Lincoln University, in Pennsylvania, with the help of Njiiri, a recent graduate. But once there, Dalizu became dissatisfied. He was interested in political science, for which the place to be was Washington, D.C., and so he managed a transfer to Howard, another historically black college. There he found courses more to his liking, and took up with a social group that combined the interests of Africans, African-Americans, and West Indians. In that setting he met Jean, a young African-American woman with two children from a previous marriage. Nicknamed "Clicky," in her childhood Jean had somersaulted and backflipped well enough to be part of halftime shows for the Harlem Globetrotters, and as an adult loved to dance. Shortly, Fred and Jean were engaged.

Upon his graduation the couple moved to Southern California, where he pursued his master's and doctorate at Claremont, and Jean, who had worked for the federal government in Washington, found a job at the university as a secretary to help provide for their growing family, which eventually included their two children as well as Jean's two from her first marriage. His 1969 doctoral thesis was on Kenyatta's "agitational and integrative politics." "When I got my doctorate, my Ph.D.," he later recalled, "we recognized [Jean] by awarding her a 'PHT,' pushed husband through." For his civic work, he was also awarded the key to the city of Claremont.

Within a few years he was recruited to join the faculty at the University of Nairobi, and the family transferred to Nairobi. However, Dalizu later recalled, his wife was unable to find a suitable job there, and returned to the United States with the two teenage children for another seven years, during which the couple commuted and wrote lots of letters. Fred continued teaching and research in Nairobi, publishing on Kenyan and American political subjects. In 1983 it was finally possible for Jean to move permanently to Kenya, and the Dalizus built a second home in Migori, 175 miles west of Nairobi. When the children went off to college in the United States—a large percentage of airliftees continued to send their children to U.S. schools, even when no scholarships were available—Jean sent them photos of the animals on their farm.

In the 1980s Jean Dalizu landed a job at the American Embassy in Nairobi that everyone agreed was a perfect match for her outgoing and welcoming personality. Technically it was under the U.S. Department of Defense in the attaché's office, but mainly it involved liaison with Kenyans and hospitality for visitors; she kept a supply of M&M's to give out to homesick Americans. Her duties included payrolls, traveling arrangements for VIPs, and the evacuation of Americans from trouble spots in Africa.

In 1994, after twenty years on the faculty, Fred Dalizu retired from the University of Nairobi; the couple bought a four-acre property

near Nairobi and made plans to build a home, but the plans kept being delayed because Jean was enjoying her work. Though sixty-one
years old and a grandmother, she would not consider retiring. Early
on the morning of August 7, 1998, she caught the 6:50 A.M. shuttle
and was in her embassy office when it was car-bombed by Osama bin
Laden's men. She died in that attack, as did the consul general and
eleven other Americans, along with more than two hundred Kenyans. Another four thousand were injured. Also on that morning,
the embassy in Dar es Salaam was hit by car bombs, with some loss
of life. These were the deadliest attacks on American overseas facilities since the end of World War II. Only one of the American victims
of the Kenya attack was buried in Kenya: Jean Dalizu.

In 2001, Fred Dalizu traveled to the United States to give testi-
mony about the death of his wife in the trial-in-absentia of bin Laden
for the 1998 bombing, after which he returned to Kenya, where he
rejoined the University of Nairobi faculty.

5

THE COLLEGE EXPERIENCE

A few East Africans matriculated at such highly regarded academic schools as Georgetown University, Michigan State University, the University of Southern California, Bowdoin College, La Salle University, and Skidmore College; more at religious-oriented schools such as Iowa Wesleyan College, Moravian College in Pennsylvania, and St. Francis Xavier University in Nova Scotia; and the largest fraction at historically black schools such as Howard, Spelman, Morehouse, Tuskegee, Lincoln, Philander Smith, Chicago's Roosevelt University (where the student body was mostly from the inner city), as well as at small colleges such as Cascade College in Oregon and Diablo Valley, a community college in Northern California. The "Harvard to Hawaii" boast of the AASF publicity materials included some students who had arrived earlier on tickets provided by Scheinman, and some who, like Obama Sr., were on Jackie Robinson scholarships and other assistance provided through the AASF.

On their inland journeys from New York City to their respective schools, some of the East Africans, especially those who traveled by bus, experienced their first taste of American racial discrimination—being refused service when trying to buy a soda, directed to use the "colored" washroom or drinking fountain, or simply snubbed by white passengers. Though startled, they were not discouraged. A later survey revealed that only a quarter of them were bothered by such discriminatory incidents; by contrast, a contemporaneous survey of African students in Great Britain reported three-quarters of its respondents as having been discriminated against during their stays in that country.

Upon arrival in American colleges, they resided in dormitories. If there were two East Africans of the same sex they were roomed together, but more frequently the East Africans were paired with foreign students from other parts of Africa or Asia; they were occasionally assigned to a room with an African-American roommate. A few of the women attending liberal arts colleges were paired with white roommates; one of the more interesting pairings, at Western College for Women, was Pamela Odede with Donna Shalala, later secretary of health and human services under President Bill Clinton. Dr. Shalala recalled in a recent interview that Tom Mboya, Pamela's fiancé, visited the campus often, "meeting the African students on campus and just hanging out with us. He always spoke of the promise of Africa."

Almost all of the East African students had difficulties with their academic classes, partly because English was not their first language and they did not write it as well as they spoke it, but mainly because they were unused to forms of instruction that required a deeper response than a memorized answer. Many did not readily grasp the notion that in a discussion class—literature, history, economics, law—there was no one correct response, and that their participation in the discussions would affect the grades they would receive. During their first year at American colleges, very few of the East Africans were A students; many just scraped by academically until they were able to master the process, after which their grade point averages steadily increased.

Far more difficult for the students than the academics, Geoffrey ole Maloiy would remember, were the social problems—racism, culture shock, and acute homesickness; some airliftees, he recently recalled, "had a problem managing time being far away from home, and setting priorities right was a real issue." Maintaining focus on the long-term goal—in Maloiy's case, medicine—was essential, and that meant paying much more attention to classes than to the social environment, and working toward transferring to schools that were more in line with the students' ultimate goals. Pella College was unable to satisfy Maloiy, and after a semester he looked into transferring; by the following academic year he had gone farther north, to Vancouver and the University of British Columbia, to earn his BS. Harvard was still his goal, and he would get there eventually. Amram Onyundo Okal, who could not obtain veterinary training at his current school, the Tuskegee Institute, was thinking of transferring to a Canadian school; his eagerness to go north was heightened when he tried to buy a sandwich at a white lunch counter and was briefly arrested.

Chicago in 1959, Philip Ochieng recalled, was "a redoubt of racism," but he and John Kang'ethe got along well enough there, "painting the town red." He found it "extremely strange" that "for some reason, black African students were treated much better than black Americans," since the Africans were "much blacker than most black Americans." Only years later would Ochieng figure out that when the African students opened their mouths and did not spout American slang, the whites recognized them as foreigners who would soon return home and therefore "posed no threat," which permitted the white Americans to be friendly to the Africans.

Longing for home, in this alien culture, could be quite acute. Regina Katungulu, the only African woman at Skidmore, was described by her adviser as having "desperate homesickness, which she does not easily admit," though she was well liked on campus. Her homesickness would be relieved the next year when another Kenyan woman joined her at Skidmore. Francis Mwihia was terribly lonely at Moravian College in Bethlehem, Pennsylvania, despite living in the home of one of the professors, until he could arrange for his wife, Kathleen, to leave her post in New York and join him there.

Shortage of money was a problem for nearly all the students. Obama Sr. joked to a reporter that his living expenses in Hawaii were three times what they had been in Kenya. "My money was supposed to have lasted a year and a half but it looks like I'll be working to supplement my income next semester," he said. Many of the other Kenyans received the same sort of economic shock during their first months in the United States.

The reason that the social aspects gave the East Africans more trouble than the academic courses was that life at an American college was at once so different from what they had known, and so intriguing. The warnings in the Phelps Stokes booklet, they found, were on target: They had difficulty gauging the meaning and the degree of seriousness in the relatively loose and open relationships with members of the opposite sex, in classes and in social situations, that were the norm in American colleges. Most East Africans had been taught not to talk to an age peer of the opposite sex unless chaperoned and during a formal courtship. Similarly, because in their homeland the students had been treated as members of an educated elite, they looked down on those whom they perceived as not sharing the same elevated status, such as cafeteria workers, groundskeepers, and teaching assistants. This fault was exacerbated when the students applied for jobs to supplement their meager stipends, and found that the only positions available to them were as janitors or dishwashers. One Kenyan at Philander Smith refused a job cleaning toilets even though he desperately needed to make money to remain in school. Others there, including Sam Ngola, were told they had to perform such work as a concomitant of their scholarships; they did, but soon made plans to transfer.

The East Africans had expected segregation in the South and had not anticipated it in the North; but in general wherever they found it they endured it, judging it not as bad as colonial Kenya's antiblack attitudes and strictures. The students most affected by American segregation were those raised in rural areas of Kenya who had previously seldom encountered whites.

A universal feeling among the East African students, both those at historically black colleges and those at mostly white colleges that included a few nonwhite classmates, was that African-Americans treated them with indifference rather than as brothers and sisters. Here was the greatest split between the attitudes of civil rights leaders such as King, who understood the deep ties between African-Americans and Africans, and young African-American students who had plenty of their own hurdles to overcome and seemingly little empathy to spare for Africans. In part that was due to the attitude of the East Africans, some of whom looked down on African-Americans as relatively ignorant, unlettered, and uncouth. One African wrote of his grievances anonymously to a Nairobi newspaper, in the form of a letter warning next year's airlift applicants that the United States was "not a land of milk and honey." Kenyans should watch out for cars that sped along streets faster than anyone ought to be driving, con artists, and high food prices, and above all they should be wary of fellow students.

Most of the white students will treat you with great contempt
while a few others may show ironical and insidious interest. . . .
There are, however, a few minority groups like the Jews, some
of whom may show genuine interest. . . . In the event of discrimination, do not expect sympathy from the American
Negro, especially in the North. To him you will be a link [to]
a regrettable past.

Distancing the East Africans from their white American college
peers was the fact that the Africans, in order to come to the U.S. colleges, had surmounted grave difficulties in their home countries,
which had deeply affected them. One had seen his father killed by
the Mau Mau and his brother killed by the Kenyan security forces.
Several had relatives imprisoned for years during the Emergency.
Many had never been in a big city before going to Nairobi for the
airlift. Their experiences with discrimination were also dissimilar to
that of most African-American students. For instance, when traveling in the United States, some of the Africans discovered that if they
wore Western dress they were hassled, but if they wore African dress
they were not. Airlift student Mahmood Mamdani from Uganda,
who came to study at the University of Pittsburgh, recalled in a recent e-mail that "[o]ur hosts always told us: 'Wear your national dress
when you go out to restaurants or public places.' As we realized that
the national dress differentiated us from Americans of color, we
came to realize discrimination was less about color than about the
history of slavery and subordination."

In social gatherings, the African students were expected to know
how to dance and to show off their moves when asked, even if they
did not wish to. They also had to endure silly and ignorant questions
from the groups that invited them to speak about Kenya. Obama Sr.
found that his audiences' main misconceptions about Kenya were
that it was a teeming tropical jungle and that the country was not
ready for self-government. "Nobody is competent enough to judge

whether a country is fit to rule itself or not," he told a reporter, as he had told such audiences.

> If the people cannot rule themselves, let them misrule themselves. They should be provided with the opportunity. We are not trying to drive the white man out of Africa; we want to work with them but not for them. If I come to America, I work and am employed, but I don't tell you how to run your government. We need outside help in the form of capital and technical aid. Any new nation needs this. This is all my people are asking for.

After settling in, many airlifted students wrote thank-you letters to the AASF, Scheinman, Mboya, and the trio of Belafonte, Robinson, and Poitier. A typically effusive one was sent to the three celebrities from Joseph B. Magucha, a freshman at Greenville College in Illinois, a Methodist college just north of St. Louis, Missouri. Robinson reprinted the letter in his column. Magucha thanked Robinson and associates for bringing all the students, "and me in particular," to further their studies in the United States, "which without your sympathy and consideration" would not have happened, and he wondered:

> It has always been a puzzle to me why you and your colleagues took such a brave task of bringing some of us to study over here as if you were our own fathers. . . . I believe, as any one of the students, that you are not only treating us as brothers and friends but also as sons of the new future of Kenya. . . . Those of us who came here for studies have a big duty to do; a duty even bigger than the one you rendered us. For how else shall we repay the debt we owe to our people in general, and to you in particular, if we cannot . . . teach our brothers the right of human dignity, which is indeed indivisible?

Magucha asserted that his goal, and that of the other students, was independence for their country, and not just any independence but a society "where social justice prevails," which he believed could only be achieved through education of all of Kenya's people, the ultimate task awaiting the graduates upon their return home.

Robinson told his readers that the impact of the AASF program was growing, that applications for the next airlift had been pouring in from other territories still under colonial rule, because "this has been the first partnership . . . to begin to break down the barriers to the African's right to educate himself." He beseeched the public for $121,500 to transport three planeloads of Africans the following fall, and by doing so to "affect the course of history."

A more formal thank-you to Mboya, Kiano, Njiiri, Scheinman, and everyone from the assistants at the American consulate in Nairobi to George Houser was signed by the three spokesmen for the students: Dorcas Boit of Spelman, Mungai Mbayah of the New School, and Harrison Bwire Muyia of Wayne State University. It went out in the form of a letter to the editor of the *East African Standard*, whose stories and columns had frequently contained criticism of the airlift:

> History alone shall record the success of this project, which serves as a model not only to our country, but to all the people of the African continent. . . . We who have been so lucky to get this chance look forward with a determination to pursue and fulfill our intellectual obligations; and happy will be the day when our country and our people can enjoy the achievement of this whole exercise.

Around the United States, groups of individuals took it upon themselves to support dozens of airlifted students, financially in some cases, but mostly in terms of moral and quasi-familial support—taking the students into private homes, providing them with better meals and bedrooms, and assisting them in getting along in the United States. One cluster of helpers was in the Riverdale section of the Bronx, where the Weisses, Kheels, and Monteros lived. Their extra bedrooms and sometimes their floors were frequently filled with East African students on semester breaks and weekends who came from outlying colleges to the Big Apple for excitement and to meet others with whom they could converse in tribal languages. In later years, some would consider having slept on the floor of the Weiss home a badge of honor. Cora Weiss, only a few years older than the students, became a den mother to many, fielding worried phone calls and letters, doling out emergency AASF grants of twenty-five and fifty dollars, and arranging visits to doctors when necessary, including an abortion for one distraught young woman. Arthur Krim, a lawyer and motion picture studio executive, and his wife, Mathilde, a well-known microbiologist, took in many of the students who studied in New York or who came to New York on vacation. Haron Andima, a frequent guest at the Krims', recalls that some of the East Africans he met there became friends although they had not known one another previously.

Other centers were in Pittsburgh, where the newspaper editor P. L. Prattis and the Steel Workers union were the mainstays; in Atlanta, centered around Martin Luther King, Jr., whose support also extended to students going to Alabama State College in Montgomery; in Detroit, spearheaded by a local Elks lodge; and in Chicago, where Professor Frank Untermeyer of Roosevelt found American couples willing to provide room and board for three students at Roosevelt and another at the University of Chicago, and five Chicagoans willing to contribute five hundred dollars apiece for these students' ancillary expenses. Philip Ochieng and John Kang'ethe, who had been classmates at Alliance in Kenya, shared a room at the home of an African-American pharmacist, Charles Thompson, while attending Roosevelt. In Chicago, as in New York, Pittsburgh, and Berkeley, the sponsoring organizations or informal groupings were initiated by or included whites.

The Berkeley support group became the most formal and organized of these. It was convened by Gikonyo Kiano's friend and the former supervisor of his Berkeley doctoral committee, Dr. Robert Scalapino of the University of California at Berkeley, who was a widely published scholar with expertise in Asian affairs. With his wife, Dee, Scalapino had visited Kiano in Kenya in 1958, and soon agreed to sponsor seven students from the 1959 airlift. Most of these did not qualify right away for the California State University system, and were enrolled at Diablo Valley, a commuter school that had no facilities for housing students. Dee Scalapino urged her friends and neighbors to take in these students and to find jobs for them that would help them pay for their room, board, and extra expenses. Each weekday Mrs. Scalapino drove the students to and from the Diablo campus, twenty-five miles northeast of Berkeley. Shortly, to assist and counsel the Kenyans, she established a more formal structure, a nonprofit Committee for African Students. It consisted of seventeen whites and seventeen African-Americans—medical doctors, professors, clergy, a lawyer, the head of the Oakland NAACP chapter, and others. These thirty-four people then undertook fundraising to help present and future East African students; as the California State system did not offer scholarships to foreign students, the group lobbied the governor, Pat Brown, and obtained contributions from him and from individual members of the Board of Regents. In the years to come, the Committee for African Students enabled forty more Kenyans to attend colleges in the San Francisco Bay Area. Many of those students matriculated first at a Bay Area community college, Diablo Valley or a similar school, and then after a year of proving themselves in an American institution were easily able to transfer into a four-year college within the California State University system, or to equivalent colleges in other states.

Groups in other cities also took the opportunity of close interaction with the students and the colleges to plan for the future. When P. L. Prattis and Tom Murray of the Steel Workers visited the University of Pittsburgh chancellor, they extracted a promise for the university to provide more scholarships for East Africans in the coming years. The reason, Prattis stated in a letter to Scheinman, was, "They feel that the U of Pgh should be importantly related to emergent Africa, and, as Tom [Murray] stressed, should help to prevent Uganda, Kenya and Tanganyika from becoming the broad highways over which the Soviets might reach to Central and South Africa."

Mboya had not accompanied the students to New York because, among other reasons, he wanted to attend an important conference at Moshi, on the slopes of Mount Kilimanjaro in Tanganyika, convened by Dr. Julius Nyerere, the leader who would become prime minister when that territory achieved its independence in 1960. It was a conference of PAFMECA, the Pan-African Freedom Movement of East and Central Africa. Also in attendance were delegates from Uganda, Zanzibar, and the Belgian Congo; Nyerere told them that the conference's demand for "self-government now" was "not extremism but . . . the most moderate demand for us to make," since they were pledged to multiracial societies and were opposed to both "white racism and black chauvinism." The conferees from the various territories had much in common with one another. Men from the Nyasaland area and from Uganda railed against the imprisonment of their leaders and declarations of emergencies, as the Kenyans did. Nyerere and Mboya had both made attempts in the past year to unite disparate factions in their homelands so that they could together press for independence. A PAFMECA resolution warned the people of the Belgian Congo, who were to vote in a forthcoming election, to "beware of any attempts, however subtle, by Belgian officials to divide the people in order to [continue to] rule."

Mboya came away from the conference with a pledge from Nyerere to work with the AASF board in East Africa, and to help collar other education-minded officials from neighboring territories for that purpose. The 1959 airlift had been criticized for giving seventy-nine of the eighty-one places to Kenyans and not taking enough students from the other colonial territories; the recruitment of Nyerere and the other East African officials was an attempt to rectify that, as their presence on the AASF board would spur applications from students in their areas.

An October election in Great Britain returned an even larger majority of Conservatives—a blow to Kenyans' hopes for independence, which had been identified with the Labour Party—but also the resignation of colonial secretary Alan Lennox-Boyd. He was replaced by the much younger Iain Macleod, who agreed with Prime Minister Harold Macmillan that it was no longer worthwhile for Great Britain to retain a tight hold on its African colonies. In an early speech to Parliament, Macleod said that one of his first tasks would be to bring the Emergency in Kenya to an end. Simultaneously, an edict was passed in Kenya that allowed black as well as white Kenyans to own land, and the government applied for a loan from the World Bank to help indigenous tenant farmers purchase their farms. After this, Evelyn Baring, the colonial governor who had instituted the Emergency, retired. On November 10, 1959, Macleod in London and the new governor in Nairobi announced that the Emergency was about to end. Ten days later, the sparring African parties led by Odinga and Mboya agreed to join forces for the conference in London that would determine the precise route to Kenya's independence and its timing. One of the group's first decisions was to hire, on the recommendation of Scheinman and Montero, American attorney Thurgood Marshall—the chief counsel for the NAACP who had argued convincingly to the Supreme Court in *Brown*—to advise them on drafting a constitution for an independent Kenya.

Meanwhile, across the Atlantic in America, the changing political climate in Africa became an issue for the forthcoming presidential election campaign. Many Democrats as well as Republican Vice

President Nixon were lining up to try to be Eisenhower's successor. One of them, Senator Hubert H. Humphrey, warned in an address at the time of the 1959 airlift, "Africa's current economic weakness and racial conflicts provide ample opportunities for Communist penetration." He damned with faint praise the Eisenhower administration's recently added attention to Africa—"We have been moving in the right direction"—but said this was "too little and too late." When the United States had to vote in the United Nations on matters pitting colonies against the colonial powers, he lamented, "we seem to forget our traditional principles of freedom and human dignity." To combat this, Humphrey called for increased educational exchange with Africa.

Similar sentiments and proposed remedies were also increasingly to be found in the public utterances of Kennedy and Nixon. But while these political leaders all embraced the need to educate young Africans in the United States, the American educational and philanthropic establishment as well as the State Department were not interested in doing so by aiding the AASF or by adopting the airlift model. As Albert G. Sims, a leader of the IIE, would later write, "The airlift caused a latent but growing concern about the quality of the foreign student movement to surface conspicuously. What standards and criteria were the colleges and universities using in admitting these students from abroad? What was being done to ascertain the adequacy of the finances of the foreign student applicant? And what damage was being done in this process to the reputation of U.S. higher education around the world?"

As Sims's questions suggest, the AASF model for bringing not "choice" individuals but planeloads of East Africans to the United States was perceived by the established institutions as a threat. George Houser recalled that the IIE objected to the AASF program primarily because the IIE viewed the airlift and its student beneficiaries as causing problems for all other international students—and for the IIE's primacy in the field. The IIE, as the State Department's designated agency, and the African-American Institute (AAI), a group consisting of leading academics and representatives of the larger U.S. foundations, did not like their fiefdoms and procedures being implicitly questioned by the AASF and its "crash" program. Nor did the Ivy League, as represented by Harvard's dean of admissions, David Henry, who in the fall of 1959 announced a program to bring the best and the brightest of Africa's students to America's top colleges on full four-year scholarships, beginning the following fall.

A Harvard graduate and former prep-school English and history teacher, David Henry had been dean of admissions at Harvard for eight years before hatching his big idea. According to Houser, Henry tried to lure Mboya out of the AASF program and into his own, promising more and steadier support—the AASF program was clearly hand-to-mouth, and was currently seventeen thousand dollars in debt for the 1959 airlift, as Henry knew from AASF pleas for funds. Mboya flirted with the Dean Henry idea but soon discovered that it had quite a few strings attached, including giving up control of the student selection process. He rejected the Harvard dean's blandishments.

Shortly, Mboya succinctly listed the criticisms of the AASF approach in an article in *Harper's*:

> The pioneering, shoestring, crash-through quality of our approach, our free-enterprise solicitation of scholarships by going to the donor colleges directly—these have been interpreted as unwillingness to coordinate our efforts with those of other foundations. Our eagerness to have as large a number of grants as possible has been viewed as a lowering of standards and political patronage in the allocation of grants has been charged.

Scheinman, Montero, Kheel, Weiss, and their associates reaffirmed their commitment to Mboya and to the AASF's current method of choosing students, amassing scholarships, and raising funds privately; but they also acknowledged the need to regularize the program more so that it would not always be hand-to-mouth. One of their plaints was to Tom Mboya, to better organize the Nairobi office. Mboya shot back a request: Send him an appropriate secretary, perhaps an American as efficient as those in the office of Martin Luther King, Jr. Scheinman immediately wrote to King, saying that he would pay for such an African-American woman to go to Kenya, and pleading for a recommendation of a secretary who had "first-rate shorthand . . . a girl with courage because at any time the Kenya government would evict her from that country," and above all "emotional maturity, particularly insofar as personal relations with her boss were concerned. As you know, Tom has a strong appeal to the ladies and if this ever got the best of her, her work would suffer." King wrote back six weeks later, saying, "I do not know anyone with the necessary qualifications who is presently available."

Bill Scheinman liked to fly, but his trip down to Washington was not for pleasure. He was visiting Joseph Satterthwaite, whom he had met socially. A career diplomat who had served as head of the legation at Damascus, Satterthwaite had become assistant secretary of state for African affairs. Scheinman needed Satterthwaite to obtain money from State for the 1960 AASF airlift program, then being planned to bring over at least triple the amount of students assisted in 1959, students from a half-dozen East African territories that were either still under colonial rule or, as with Tanganyika, just emerging from it. The Scheinman trip was a bust, as were several others that he had made to see Satterthwaite. "Whenever I asked him for help," Scheinman later recalled, "it was 'No, no, no, we can't do that.' Completely negative." Mboya also saw Satterthwaite in Washington and was given the same dismissive response.

Preliminary applications for the 1960 airlift were coming in, and this batch of students were even better prepared and better credentialed than the first year's. For instance, Samuel Okello On-yango, a mathematician, was a graduate of a teacher training college and a former headmaster who would enter Morgan State College as a junior. Another stellar applicant was Stephen Misati Machooka, twenty-three, a farmer and promising long-distance runner who was eager to enter Cornell as a freshman because it had a very good agri-cultural school. Charles Angwenyi, son of a Kikuyu chieftain, had been accepted at Colby, a small college in Maine, where he would study economics. Grace Wagenna, thirty-one, a welfare worker, teacher, and the headmistress of a home economics center, would at-tend Howard. Muthoni Muthiga, a married woman who wanted to be a lawyer, would go to Philander Smith. James Marangu would go to Olivet Nazarene College in Illinois with the objective of eventu-ally earning a doctorate in genetics. Miriam Khamadi, the would-be poet who had won all of the prizes at her secondary school, wanted to attend the Quaker college in Iowa, William Penn, and Maina wa Kinyatti, the firebrand would-be historian, wanted to become part of Michigan State University's first group in its African studies program.

A visit from Tom Mboya to the Catholic archbishop of Kenya had resulted in a dozen opportunities for graduates of Kenya's Cath-olic schools to study in religious-oriented colleges in the United States, including two young women at Mount St. Scholastica and a young man at St. Benedict's, its brother school in Atchison, Kansas. One of the young women, known then as Mary Jo Wangari, was in-terested in cell biology.

But few of these bright young people would reach their destina-tions without a major infusion of help to the AASF, as airlifting and assisting 250 students in 1960 would cost far more than Schein-man, Jackie Robinson, former ambassador W. Averell Harriman, and the thousands of smaller donors could handle. Support was needed either from the U.S. government or from a large foundation.

Though the State Department had repeatedly said no, the AASF believed that this decision was political and could be reversed. The New York and Nairobi AASF offices remained committed to a three- to four-planeload 1960 airlift and were planning to assist even more students in the future, so everyone pressed on, because on the East African side the need and the talent were palpable, and on the American side—despite the scoffing of Dean Henry—the resources were available; many colleges were more than willing to offer scholarships to those East African students.

Evidence of that willingness came from a daring and highly successful AASF mailing. From the standard guide to American colleges and universities Scheinman had selected 425 accredited schools in the United States and Canada that were not whites-only. He and Montero drafted a letter to these 425, soliciting scholarships, that would go out over the signature of Dr. Ralph Bunche, recipient of the 1950 Nobel Peace Prize. Bunche liked the idea but said he could not sign the letter because of his position as undersecretary-general of the United Nations, and suggested that his wife, Ruth, an AASF board member, should do so instead. In a stroke of public relations genius, Montero conceived the idea of having the letters to the presidents of these 425 institutions, requesting scholarships for East Africans, bear stamps showing that they had been mailed from the UN post office. He and Cora Weiss lugged all of the letters to the UN post office in shopping bags, and mailed them. "In many cases," Cora Weiss recalled, "these were the first letters the college presidents had ever received that came directly from the U.N." The postmark, UN stamp, and signature provoked immediate and courteous attention.

Some colleges declined to offer scholarships, for various reasons. Among them was the University of Minnesota, which had joined Dean Henry in his program "to improve the methods of selecting students from Africa." But for every such rejection there were many acceptances: Nearly half of the colleges responded favorably, two hundred promising immediate tuition scholarships for the 1960–61 academic year, others, because that year's scholarships were already distributed, promising them for future years. Even the schools that declined for technical reasons—state schools, for instance, were forbidden by law from promising scholarships to groups, and could do so only to individual applicants—praised the AASF for the "important work you are doing." Some collegiate offers were accompanied by personal guarantees from the presidents and chancellors. Wake Forest's president pledged one thousand dollars for every student who qualified for admission. North Carolina's governor pledged summer jobs for every African student on his state's campuses. In a letter that summed up the sentiments of many college officials who pledged scholarships, Kenyon's president wrote, "The justification for this grant . . . is not so much a charitable consideration as it is based upon the hope, and faith, that the youth from Africa will make a tangible contribution to the undergraduate life at Kenyon College, and this to better understanding."

Harold Case, president of Boston University, perhaps stimulated by the Ruth Bunche letter and his two months' tour of Africa, proposed that each of the two thousand colleges and universities in the United States invite two African students to study for the 1961–62 school year. The Soviets, he pointed out, were increasing their publicity about the University of Friendship of Peoples that would open the following fall with three thousand to four thousand students from Africa, Asia, and Latin America. "Under my proposal," Case said, "we would steal from Russia any propaganda value its new university would have."

The comparison with the Soviets was underscored by a report to Scheinman from John Murra, a Vassar anthropologist and ACOA board member, who at a recent All-African Peoples Conference had chatted about the airlift with delegates from Rwanda, Zanzibar, and Basutoland. He reported them as being "staggered" and "startled by the amount of preliminary and individual work that must be done to

secure the scholarship" in the United States, because of the "relative
ease with which scholarships to Eastern Europe and the USSR were
secured. . . . Admission to such universities is negotiated by a group."

The colleges' response to the Ruth Bunche letter, Scheinman
later recalled, was "absolutely fantastic." The number was so large
that the organization could not answer them all. After making copies, the AASF in New York sent the response letters in several boxes
to Mboya in Nairobi, where he and his associates pursued each positive one, writing directly to the college involved, nailing down the
specifics of each offer and what the college would require from the
candidates, and matching prospective candidates with the offering
institutions.

As for the initial batch of airliftees, by their second semesters at
their colleges, many were eager to transfer. Their eyes were
mostly cast north and east, toward more prestigious schools and
schools that offered course concentrations that were more in line
with their aspirations—engineering, medicine, business administration, and other similarly practical fields. "The colleges they started
in were often not the colleges they ended up graduating from," recalled Cora Weiss, who oversaw and facilitated many of the transfers. The students presumed that after having done reasonably well
in an American college for a year, they would be more likely to earn
merit scholarships at higher-end universities—and, in general, they
were correct. Oliver Mbata was able to transfer from Foothill College in Los Altos to the University of Wisconsin. Several Kenyans at
Diablo Valley found their way into the California State University
system. Cyrus Karuga transferred from Nebraska to Rutgers. In
later years, when listing their academic credentials some students
would routinely omit from their résumés their community college
beginnings, preferring to feature the more prestigious schools from
which they eventually graduated.

Some students in the Deep South transferred to flee the area's overt discrimination. Three Philander Smith students were among seven from historically black colleges in the South who were able to transfer to Fairleigh Dickinson in New Jersey because Mboya and Cora Weiss personally visited its president, and because a professor at the newly accredited university was starting an African studies program. One was Muthoni Muthiga. After the transfer, she felt liberated, able to travel around on weekends to the homes of class-mates, mostly white young women, to attend summer classes at Yale, even to work in a department store to earn extra money. She acceler-ated her studies so that she would complete undergraduate work in three years and then enter law school.

Other East African students wanted to transfer but could not do so yet, as their grades had not yet reached a level that would make them attractive to better schools. And some ran into roadblocks. Martin Luther King, Jr., had promised Justin M. Kitonga that he would be able to transfer from a smaller school to Alabama State, but when the governor of Alabama forced the president of Alabama State to fire faculty members for supporting student protests, King had to apologize to Kitonga because the university president had not been able "to st[i]ck with his promise" to facilitate the transfer, and so King could not "advise [him] to come at this point." Kitonga un-derstood, and transferred to a small religious college in Wisconsin. Interestingly, those attending religious-based colleges did not seek to transfer as eagerly as did those at secular colleges.

Philip Ochieng recalls two surprises of his and John Kang'ethe's first winter in Chicago. "It was the first time that we ever saw a white person laboring—shoveling snow—with his own hands," he recalled in a recent newspaper column, since at home all manual labor was done by Africans. The second surprise: "[T]hat white girls (our co-eds) readily chummed up to us suggestively. Soon we would partake of the forbidden fruit. Romantic appointments took place thickly between Caucasian and African." In addition to Ochieng, a half dozen of the male students commenced liaisons with white American women; at least four of these pairings produced children, some within the borders of a marriage, some out of wedlock, with the progeny thereafter being raised by their mothers in the United States while the Kenyan fathers moved on. "I had no contact with my biological father until I found him on the Internet," wrote the daughter of one such marriage.

Today the most well known of such pairings is that of Barack Obama, Sr., and Ann Dunham in Honolulu. Obama Sr., then attending the college of business administration at the University of Hawaii, was living at the YMCA when the pair met in a Russian class. He was an honors student, popular and quite recognizable on campus, and a founder of the university's chapter of the Foreign Students Association. Obama Sr. left Hawaii after graduation and moved to Harvard University for graduate work, leaving his wife and infant son, Barack Jr., behind. Shortly after that, Dunham filed for divorce.

In several of these pairings the men had previously been married in Kenya and had left wives and families to come to the United States. Tom Mboya received letters from Obama Sr.'s Kenyan wife and forwarded them to him. But in as many other instances, Kenyan wives of airliftees later obtained scholarships through the AASF to join their husbands in the United States. Nicholas Mugo, at a junior college in South Carolina, did well enough there that when he transferred to Lincoln he was able to bring over his wife, Beth, who finished high school in the United States and then obtained a business degree from a Delaware college. When Simon Thuo Kairo transferred from Northeast Missouri State Teachers College to Long Island University he brought over his wife, Nellie, and their two children; later the family transferred again, to Huron College, a small Presbyterian school in South Dakota, where Simon and Nellie were the first Africans ever seen in the town of Huron.

As with Simon Kairo, in the spring of 1960 about forty of the 1959 airlift students planned to go to New York City to seek summer jobs, since they had discovered very few positions available in the small towns and universities where they had been residing during the school year. For such students to have paying jobs, rather than unpaid internships, was essential, because if their monetary resources were inadequate, they risked being declared indigent by the Immigration and Naturalization Service and could be deported.

The AASF determined that it had to assist the students in finding jobs, even though this task went well beyond the organization's original charter. The board members called in favors, particularly from the labor movement. Ted Kheel prevailed on Harry Van Arsdale, head of the New York City Central Labor Council, to find a dozen or more jobs for students; Frank Montero leaned on his numerous contacts; and other board members telephoned or wrote to friends to provide temporary employment for one or more students. Scheinman kept a half dozen busy in his factory in Little Ferry, New Jersey. Thanks to Jackie Robinson, some were hired by Chock full o'Nuts, others by that chain's rival, Nedick's. Cora Weiss bore the brunt of these searches, importuning her neighbors in Riverdale to provide room and board for the summer influx of students, and sending out AASF letters to potential employers and even to *The New York Times* and *The Riverdale Press* seeking "earning for learning" jobs.

"The Foundation had expected that a fair number of jobs would be available" from department stores Macy's and Saks Fifth Avenue, which traditionally hired summer help, Cora wrote in a memo, but she learned that nearly all such jobs had previously been promised to sons and daughters of the stores' regular patrons. For jobs in summer resorts, the AASF had to help the students reach New York City, where interviews were being held before the end of the school year, and then get them back to school to finish up the semester.

There was a backlash of sorts against this search for summer jobs, or perhaps it was a prank: Someone used the AASF name to place an ad in *The Village Voice*, an alternative weekly, in fake Swahili, translated as asking "Can You Help. 15 African College Students from

Kenya Urgently Require Summer Employment Starting at Once." It took repeated correspondence to convince the *Voice* that the ad was illegitimate.

The quest for summer jobs was reasonably successful. No students were deported, and many succeeded in amassing experience that was useful to them in applying for on-campus or near-campus positions during the next school year.

An even larger task lay before the AASF: to raise three times the amount of money that it had managed to find in 1959, for a September 1960 airlift that Mboya and Kiano were already estimating would take at least three charter planeloads of students from a half-dozen East African territories. Considering the difficulty in raising the money to cover its 1959 deficit, the new fundraising goal was daunting for the AASF, but necessary: 250 education-hungry East African students from territories on the verge of independence were depending on them to realize their dreams of a college education.

For the young Protestant woman known at St. Cecilia's School in Nyeri as Miriam or Mary Jo Muta Wangari, coming to New York City in 1960 "was like landing on the moon," she later wrote. Agape at the speeding cars, the elevators, the escalators—she lost a shoe in one of the latter—she was abashed at a rest stop on her bus trip to Atkinson, Kansas, when she was prohibited from buying a cola because she was black. Wangari was one of a half-dozen Kenyans whose scholarships were the by-product of interchanges between the Catholic bishop of Nairobi, Mboya, and Catholic-run colleges in the United States. Another such student was her close friend at St. Cecilia's, Agatha Wangeci, who also went to Mount St. Scholastica; a third, from a similar school for boys, would attend the Mount's counterpart school for men, St. Benedict's. For Wangari, Mount St. Scholastica was academic heaven; she dived into biology classes, worked on minors in chemistry and German, and studied English and American literature, which she had previously known nothing about but came to love. "I marveled at the freedom that the students had—young men and women kissing in public, and watching films with romantic scenes," she noted. In her school in Kenya she had only been permitted to watch Westerns with the romantic scenes edited out. To attend parties where men and women danced with each other, rather than in single-sex groups, was "incredibly liberating." She also began to question her faith, as her school years overlapped with the Vatican II changes in the liturgy and rules for participation by the laity. The changes were relatively minor but, she recalls, "they made me think. Had God changed his mind? Was that possible? All this was strange and disconcerting, and forced me to reflect on my faith."

She was greatly "impressed" by Americans' "generosity to us Africans at a time when there was so much conflict between the races in the U.S.," she later wrote. In an interview for this book, she recalled that "my teachers became almost like parents to me," that her fellow white students "couldn't have been more generous to me," and that when her roommate took her home, the roommate's mother "treated me as one of her children—imagine, at that time, embracing a little black girl. I was very lucky. Now I am proud to say that I, too, have roots in Kansas, just like President Obama."

Her introduction to the world of African-Americans came slowly, as she attended church services in an African-American part of segregated Atkinson. During her summer job in a biological tissue lab in Kansas City her boss took her to a Nation of Islam service; she reacted negatively to its assertion that Jesus had been a black student at the University of Alexandria. This, she later wrote, "was not only untrue but sacrilegious." After a summer in Pittsburgh, where she worked at a bio lab, she made plans to attend graduate school there. Her years in Atkinson, she wrote, "nurtured in me a willingness to listen and learn, to think critically and analytically, and to ask questions"—thought processes that had been damped down during her education in Kenya, but which she recognized as being central to what she would be able to achieve in life. "There is a persistence, a seriousness, and a vision to America," she concluded.

Attending the University of Pittsburgh for graduate school in 1964, she wrote a thesis on assisting women in rural areas. Recruited by the Kenyan government in late 1965, she returned to Kenya expecting to be part of the faculty of the University of Nairobi. But upon her return she was confronted with tribalism. The job in the zoology department at the University of Nairobi had been given to a person from the professor's own tribe, to which she did not belong. She also encountered gender bias, being a woman in a field (cell biology) dominated by men. "Tribalism and other forms of corruption," she later wrote, were becoming "the most divisive factors in our society." She stayed with Agatha Wangeci and other friends until a brother-in-law could arrange a post in a new veterinary school at the University of Nairobi, in an anatomy department. Eminently qualified to be a microanatomist, she was hired and found that her new laboratory was just across the quad from the zoology department that had spurned her.

As with many U.S. college graduates who returned to Kenya in this period, she soon dropped the Mary Jo and Miriam names—these English-heritage appellations now felt like "slave names"—and became known as Wangari Muta, for "Wangari, daughter of Muta," her father's name. She moved into a flat near the university, became a supervisor for the women's dormitory, and soon met Mwangi Maathai, who had also studied in the United States and was an executive for Colgate-Palmolive as well as a budding politician. They became engaged, and a short while later Wangari left for a twenty-month stint in Munich to pursue her doctorate. Mwangi "worried that I might stay in Germany longer than was good for his plans," and sent her letters imploring her to return so they could start a family. They married in 1969, and he ran for a seat in Parliament. During the campaign Wangari was accused of "being a white woman in a black skin," and was very conscious that her university-level position and work on behalf of rural women might be bad for her husband politically.

The assassination of Mboya in 1969, the arrest of Odinga, and the banning of his opposition party "effectively brought an end to the multiparty system in Kenya," and it also helped to defeat Wangari's husband at the polls. He returned to work for Colgate and prepared for a second run in 1974, while Wangari gave birth to two children and completed her doctorate—the first woman in East and Central Africa to receive that degree. By 1974 she was a full lecturer at the university, a popular teacher, and an activist involved in environmental affairs. Returning home to the Nyeri area to visit her family, she wrote, "I saw rivers silted with topsoil, most of which was coming from the forest where plantations of commercial trees had replaced indigenous forest [and] noticed that much of the land that had been covered by trees, bushes, and grasses when I was growing up had been replaced by tea and coffee." She worked with the National Council of Women of Kenya to provide better access to clean water and firewood for rural women.

From those interests, she gradually evolved the "green belt" program that combined environmentalism with help for women. At first she simply studied the issues: The women lacked "water, energy, and nutrition," all of which depended on the environment. After understanding the issues, she recalled, "We had a choice. We could either sit in an ivory tower wondering how so many people could be so poor and not be working to change their situation, or we could try to help them escape the vicious cycle." She opted to find and implement solutions, and did so, she believed, "as a result of my education as well as my time in America: to think about what can be done rather than worrying about what cannot."

The solution she found was to plant trees to provide wood for cooking, protect watersheds, and provide fodder for livestock and fruit for human consumption. It was a simple yet elegant and quite practical solution to rural deforestation, despoliation, and poverty.

From the time that she founded the green belt movement in 1977, longtime friends such as Agatha Wangeci worked in it as her colleagues. Eventually, this program resulted in the planting of forty million trees in rural Kenya to restore the environment devastated by overfarming from commercial plantations. The green belt program expanded beyond the borders of Kenya, and Wangari became one of the planet's leading environmental activists.

For her efforts Wangari Maathai would be jailed and beaten, lose her university position and her life's savings, and be divorced by her husband on the grounds that her public posture as a thorn in the government's side was incompatible with his position as a government minister. She fought the Daniel arap Moi government on many fronts, and friends felt that only her international renown kept her from being killed or exiled. Despite the difficulties, she remained, as she put it in the title of her autobiography, "unbowed." Eventually, the Kenyan government swung a bit toward supporting her efforts. She won election to the Kenyan Parliament in 1999, and in 2004 was awarded the Nobel Peace Prize, the first time that prize had ever been earned by an environmentalist or an African woman.

6

CRISIS TIME: KENNEDY VERSUS NIXON *on the* AIRLIFTS

In one of his 1959 speeches regarding Africa, Senator John F. Kennedy staked out an advanced position for the forthcoming election by calling for "a new American policy toward Africa" and chastising Nixon for talking about "winning the battle for men's minds" when what was needed was action, since "the people of Africa are more interested in development than they are in doctrine." He proposed the establishment of an African Educational Development Fund. By February 1960, Kennedy had sharpened his Africa rhetoric and refined his plan for educational and economic aid. He expressed his theme in a Palo Alto speech: "[N]o area of the world deserves more of our knowledge and attention while getting so little as the great, throbbing continent of Africa."

Two months later, also in Palo Alto, Vice President Nixon—similarly pursuing his party's nomination for the presidency—warned that the United States would have to come to grips with emerging independent Africa and that old methods "won't necessarily work to insure progress in areas of high illiteracy and no industrialization."

Bill Scheinman of the AASF, who had previously ordered copies of Kennedy's Africa speeches from the senator's office, immediately sought to obtain copies of Nixon's, believing that it provided added rationale for the airlifts. He needed such ammunition because on December 10, 1959, the State Department had definitively said no to supporting them, although the AASF continued to hope that this decision could be reversed or, if not, that State would steer outside assistance to the project. Absent any form of blessing by State, the AASF was finding it very difficult to secure funding from large private foundations or even to obtain commitments from smaller ones.

The AASF's New York headquarters was now in the Seagram Building, a glass-front skyscraper in Manhattan designed by Ludwig Mies van der Rohe, in an office within the suite leased to Milton Gordon, a friend of Kheel's. Gordon had been a television and film producer whose big winner was *Lassie*. In 1959 he had sold his production company for millions of dollars and bought a Wall Street brokerage. The new AASF office was small but had room for Montero, Cora Weiss, and Mary Hamanaka, a Japanese-American whose internment in a California camp during her childhood made her quite sensitive to the pressures felt by the East African students.

While Weiss and Hamanaka dealt with the students, Montero and Scheinman looked for funding. Montero implored John H. Johnson, publisher of *Jet* and *Ebony*, to permit the AASF to use their subscription lists for a public appeal. Johnson, who had accompanied

Nixon to Accra in 1957, declined. Mboya used a meeting in Nairobi with the Reverend Billy Graham, a closer Nixon friend, to plead for support, and Montero followed up, writing Graham, "You indicated you were going to attempt to obtain scholarship aid for African students in this country." Not much came of that approach.

Only a few months were left before planes had to be chartered and places on them allotted. American universities had offered a half-million dollars in scholarships, and potential airliftees had amassed several hundred thousand dollars to defray their expenses in the United States. Mboya, Kiano, and Njiiri, along with Julius Nyerere of Tanganyika, Abu Mayanja of Uganda, Hastings Banda of Nyasaland, Joshua Nkomo of Southern Rhodesia, and Kenneth Kaunda of Northern Rhodesia, were encouraging and selecting applicants. (Nyerere and the other East Africans had all visited the United States and its educational institutions within the previous year.) But all of this effort might go for naught if enough money to charter the planes was not found, and found soon.

Much as the AASF wanted to operate outside of American politics, and had done so in 1959, this year that would be impossible. The 1960 presidential election promised to usher in significant changes because Eisenhower and his age cohort, the country's leaders since World War II, would be succeeded in office by younger men, of the generation who had actually fought on the front lines in that war's battles. Nixon and Kennedy had both served in the navy during World War II; fifteen years after Japan's surrender, they were the leading candidates for their parties' nominations.

Jackie Robinson was going to have to choose between them for someone to support, and, he later wrote, "Frankly, I didn't think it was much of a choice." He had campaigned for Hubert Humphrey in the primaries because he admired the Minnesota senator's long-term commitment to civil rights, but after Kennedy defeated Humphrey, and Nixon had fended off all challengers on the Republican side, Robinson recognized that he ought not remain neutral.

For decades, African-Americans had been sympathetic to Republican candidates, for two reasons: African-Americans still viewed the Republican Party as the party of Abe Lincoln, who had freed the slaves, but perhaps more important, they viewed the South, where many African-Americans lived (and in which still more had relatives), as controlled by segregationist Democrats. So while in 1952 Democratic candidate Adlai Stevenson had polled 79 percent of the African-American vote, in 1956, running once more against the incumbent Eisenhower, Stevenson had managed only 61 percent of that vote. Just as important, among the states won by Stevenson in 1952 and lost by him in 1956 were Louisiana and Kentucky, states that had substantial African-American populations. These trends had encouraged Republicans to think that African-Americans would continue to vote for their party in increasing numbers. Early 1960 polling gave them additional reason to believe so, because the potential African-American vote was reported as evenly split between the parties—not only in the South, where many more African-Americans would be voting for the first time, but also in the North.

The 1960 election was going to be the first in which the African-American vote would be large enough to affect the outcomes in many states. African-Americans were able now to vote in more states than in 1952 or 1956, and their percentage of the population in Northern cities had increased. Both parties courted them, the Democrats very carefully, to avoid losing the votes of the more numerous Southern whites that were critical to any potential Democratic victory.

Politically Robinson was officially independent, not a registered member of either party, although he had been philosophically in line with the Republicans throughout his public career, influenced by the conservatism of his most influential boss, Brooklyn Dodger general manager Branch Rickey, and by that of his current corporate employers at Chock full o'Nuts. In the spring of 1960 Robinson traveled to Washington, where he had arranged to meet with both candidates separately, on the same day.

Robinson already knew Nixon, had been corresponding with him for some time, and believed that Nixon had amassed "a fairly good track record on civil rights." But he also noted "a great deal of suspicion in the black community about Nixon, primarily because so many black people were disenchanted with the Eisenhower Administration." Prior to this meeting, on May 18, on behalf of the AASF Robinson had sent the vice president a proposal for an airlift. Africa was then much in the news; just a few weeks earlier, sixty-nine protesters had been killed by South African troops in the Sharpeville Massacre, and in reaction Robinson had chaired a conference that called for a boycott of South African goods. "As we both know," Robinson wrote to Nixon, "the question of race relations is no longer an American problem solely, but in harsh reality, a vital world problem as well . . . because of the moral leadership expected of the United States government and its people." After detailing the history of the AASF, he asked, "[C]an some transport be found for these [East African] students among the agencies of the United States Government? The African leaders have suggested an airlift of the U.S. Air Force planes to dramatize this airlift before the world." Robinson followed up with a telegram to Nixon's executive assistant, Robert Cushman, on June 9, saying that the AASF had "HAD NO RESPONSE" from the appropriate person at State. "TIME IS SHORT CAN YOU SPEED DECISION. WILL COME TO WASHINGTON TO DISCUSS IF NECESSARY." Cushman replied, "YOU WILL BE HEARING FROM [State] SHORTLY." To emphasize the urgency, Scheinman sent copies of Robinson's May 18 letter to Senators Jacob Javits and Hugh Scott, as did Montero to pollster Louis Harris and other influential people, and Kheel to Attorney General Rogers; Kheel had previously been instrumental in obtaining a private luncheon with Rogers for Robinson, at which Robinson had pleaded the AASF's need for transport.

Nixon responded to Robinson on June 13 that he had asked State to give the transport request "serious consideration," but pointed out some difficulties with the request: The air force was required to charge passengers in such operations, and "funding and fiscal problems" had been exacerbated "by Congressional cuts in the President's proposals." Despite Nixon's urging, no decision from State had been forthcoming when Robinson met Nixon and Senator Scott in the vice president's office.

Civil rights was in the headlines. African-American college students had begun sit-ins at Southern lunch counters, and Martin Luther King, Jr., had embraced their cause, thereby raising it in the consciousness of the mainstream press. King was also in the headlines because he was being prosecuted in Alabama for tax evasion and being sued as a codefendant in the libel case that would be known, when it reached the Supreme Court, as *New York Times Co. v. Sullivan*.

Robinson's meeting with Nixon went smoothly until the vice president interrupted it by taking a phone call, during which he told the caller, "No, well, I can't do that. I'm tired of pulling his chestnuts out of the fire." Robinson concluded that Nixon had uttered these words to leave the impression in Robinson's mind that Nixon was putting distance between himself and Eisenhower, because Nixon sensed that this was what Robinson wanted to hear. "It had the feel of a cheap trick," Robinson later wrote.

Kennedy disappointed Robinson even more. When they met at the home of Chester Bowles, a former Connecticut governor and ambassador who was a foreign policy adviser to the candidate, Kennedy was "a courteous man, obviously striving to please," but "couldn't or wouldn't look me straight in the eye." More important, Robinson sized up Kennedy as a man who "knew little or nothing about black problems and sensibilities. He himself admitted a lack of any depth of understanding of black people." Although Robinson recognized that Kennedy seemed very willing to learn, wanted him as a tutor, and hinted at offering money to Robinson to perform that tutorial task, Robinson refused to get "on board the bandwagon." He told Kennedy in a letter to look people in the eye, and was subsequently "amused" when Montero apprised him that during his own encounter with Kennedy, the senator "didn't take his eyes off him for a minute."

Harry Belafonte garnered similar impressions of Kennedy in the spring of 1960. One evening, the candidate invited himself to Belafonte's New York apartment and asked two questions—why Jackie Robinson would ever think of supporting a Republican candidate like Nixon, and could Belafonte find some African-American "stars" to offset Robinson's likely endorsement of Nixon. It was Kennedy's pattern, Belafonte recalled in a recent interview, to identify a constituency of electoral concern—working-class mothers, suburban young parents, African-Americans—and then find a prominent person respected by that constituency to endorse him, and hope that endorsement would sway the constituency's voters. In their three-hour discussion that evening, Belafonte, as Robinson had, found Kennedy to be woefully ignorant about African-American affairs and issues but willing to learn. Unlike Robinson, Belafonte agreed to help Kennedy learn, suggesting, among other avenues, that he get to know Martin Luther King, Jr. Kennedy avoided saying directly that King was a minor celebrity compared to Belafonte or Robinson, but the implication was clear to the singer. Belafonte countered by contending that celebrities were no longer important to the black vote—issues were. "Forget me. Forget Jackie Robinson and everybody else we've been talking about. If you can join the cause of King, and be counseled by him, then you'll have an alliance that will make the difference." Kennedy agreed to try, and Belafonte later phoned King and urged him to get to know Kennedy. King and Kennedy then met for a private breakfast in New York, after which King told Harris Wofford, a white civil rights lawyer who had worked with him for years and was becoming close to the Kennedy campaign, that the candidate lacked a "depthed understanding" of the civil rights issues.

Kennedy publicly released a letter to Robinson expressing full support for civil rights; Robinson told the press that after his interchanges with Kennedy he was "not nearly as critical as I have been," but would not endorse him. Rather, "despite my reservations," Robinson decided to back Nixon and to campaign with him. The ex-ballplayer soon appeared on platforms with Nixon in white communities, and in black communities set up his own rallies, drawing such large crowds that the Democrats sent Harlem congressman Adam Clayton Powell to conduct rallies before or after his.

The Kenya constitutional conference in London in January 1960, known as the Lancaster House conference, had emphasized the urgency of turning the governing of Kenya over to its indigenous peoples. The new colonial secretary, Iain Macleod, was convinced of that necessity but also worried that if independence came too swiftly, or not under the right circumstances, it would result in bloodshed. Mboya gave in somewhat to accommodate Macleod; this did Mboya little good at home. His name was not immediately put forward as a future cabinet minister, though Kiano's was. Mboya's problem could be traced in part to the jealousy he was evoking because of his popularity in the West. Scheinman reported by letter to St. Clair Drake, the Roosevelt University sociology professor then teaching in Accra, that he had been told by friends that Nkrumah had been "selling the line to some of the expatriate Kenyans that Tom is, in fact, leading an anti-Kenyatta movement."

For years, Mboya had backed the notion that Kenyatta must be the new country's first prime minister upon his release, and now went a step further: He called for the African Elected Members of the Legislative Council to resign if Kenyatta was not freed. His rivals did not like that stance, and initially tried to exclude him from being a mainstay of a new political party being established, the Kenya African National Union (KANU), formed from thirty smaller political organizations. But during the course of a contentious one-day organizing conference Mboya emerged as KANU's general secretary. He did so, biographer Goldsworthy writes, because "of all the African politicians, he was still the best deliverer of goods, still the most effective of patrons." His ability to extract scholarships from the United States was an incontrovertible demonstration of that attribute.

London had suspended the previous Kenya constitution and installed a "caretaker" colonial government—but had not agreed to a definitive timetable for handing over power to an African-led government. Citing the unrest in the Belgian Congo, which was about to become independent, London refused to let go in Kenya and even made plans to move more troops into the colony.

At around the same time—May 1960—the education minister of the Kenya colonial government charged in the Legislative Council that the 1959 airlift students were so underfunded that some were starving, and mounted other attacks against the AASF program. A Kenya Education Fund had been established by Mboya and his associates to solicit contributions from within East Africa for the students to be airlifted; the Nairobi police department shortly denied this fund's application for "a permit to collect funds throughout Kenya for the purpose of assisting students."

The adviser to British colonial students in America, Kenneth D. Luke, then charged in a letter to *The New York Times* that some of the 1959 airliftees were indigent—some even starving—and that many were doing poorly in their classes because they had been improperly prepared. His letter to the *Times* was one result of his recent, very rapid journey around the United States to survey British territorial students, a survey that, when released, concealed as much as it exposed.

After a career in the British Foreign Service that began before World War II, Luke had taught English at the Choate School, a top-tier prep school in New England, for several years before being hired in 1960 by the British Embassy in Washington to replace Bernard Mellor, a former registrar of the University of Hong Kong, as the adviser to British-territory students in the United States. Mellor's exit had been hastened by his authorship of a book published in the spring of 1960, *The American Degree*, in which, according to Luke, Mellor "recommended that [British] colonial students seeking to pursue advanced degrees in their home countries should enroll in universities with excellence in the field chosen, rather than in liberal arts colleges." Albert Sims of the IIE and Gordon Hagberg, now with the African-American Institute—organizations that had quite a bit of experience with Africans in American four-year liberal arts colleges—objected loudly to Mellor's slap at U.S. collegiate education, and Luke was chosen to replace him.

Upon being hired, Luke immediately began a tour of the entire United States and Canada that took him three months, and during which he visited some of the 3,900 British students from twenty-six countries and territories attending American and Canadian institutions of higher learning. While on his grand tour, he had his secretary send a letter to all 81 of the airliftees—and to no others among the 3,900—in which Luke asked for their assessment of their own financial situation, a transcript of their grades, and a letter of recommendation from their campus's foreign-student adviser. The letter, dated April 27, 1960, closed with this sentence: "If you do cooperate to your fullest capacity, I believe that something can be done to alleviate your position."

Some of the students forwarded the letter to the AASF. Scheinman quickly sent a copy to Mboya, noting that it was likely "an attempt to embarrass us," since Luke had been "rather critical of our efforts in the past."

The student and faculty-adviser responses to Luke's letter were many and varied, and he collected them in a document, initially labeled "confidential," that he sent to his superiors in June 1960. His conclusion as to the impoverished state of the Kenyans was based mostly on their letter responses, rather than on his visits to campuses, and was clearly colored by his original letter's last line: Since he said he might provide help if they cooperated, there was an incentive for students to say that they needed such assistance. Nonetheless, Luke concluded, "What must be prevented if at all possible is a continuation of the flow to North America and in particular to the United States, of underfinanced students, who are sometimes poorly qualified." He was also incensed about students attending such schools as Diablo Valley community college only so that they could later transfer into California State institutions that would not have previously admitted them because of their academic records in Kenya.

Luke did visit some of the students, and in his evaluation wrote paragraphs about a few, such as Dorcas Boit at Spelman, one of the spokespersons from the 1959 airlift. "I think Dorcas is not very happy at Spelman, although she is charming and has created a good reputation there. She wishes either to teach or work in Community Development, and is not sure whether she can manage to qualify for either. . . . Needs $300 to end of year to supplement her scholarship." Luke's assessment did not jive well with Dorcas's Spelman adviser's report: "Miss Boit's academic record is satisfactory. . . . Contributes much to the college community." Luke similarly wondered if Fred Egambi Dalizu, recently transferred from Lincoln to Howard, would make it in his new school, considering that he had flunked one course at Lincoln and was "short of funds." Since Dalizu would graduate and continue on to a PhD, and Dorcas Boit would become a campus activist and go on to a fine career in Kenya, Luke's assessment of these two students was neither sensitive nor prescient. Of Geoffrey ole Maloiy, Luke wrote that he was having difficulty adjusting to his environment in Pella, Iowa, and "his instructors are of the opinion that he does not grasp scientific principles easily," a conclusion belied by Maloiy's soon-demonstrated ability to win a laboratory teaching fellowship at Harvard. Even when Luke was complimentary to students such as Angelina Wokabi at Clarke College in Dubuque, acknowledging that she had almost made the dean's list in her first year, he chose to highlight her "failure to mix socially, probably due to limited funds and concentration on course work."

The AASF staff—who did not receive a copy of Luke's detailed list until months later—made a round of phone calls to ascertain if the students were really in such bad shape financially, and were told by them that for the most part they were managing.

Luke's trip and his impressions were also the basis for an attack in a letter from the colonial attaché in Washington, Douglas Williams, to Mrs. Ralph Bunche. Williams, who had written the previous fall's inflammatory letter to *The New York Times*, complained to Mrs. Bunche that her scholarship-solicitation letter to 425 American colleges and universities—which Williams admitted that he had not actually read—maligned the British and their provision of higher education for East Africans. Montero provided Mrs. Bunche with a detailed memo to answer Williams's charges. For instance, to refute the notion that the AASF was really providing "spoils" for "certain African politicians whom they favor," Montero named the leaders other than Mboya—Nyerere, Kaunda, and the several other Africans on the AASF board—whose countrymen and countrywomen were to be part of the 1960 airlift. Montero closed with a reminder to Ruth Bunche that "we are not anxious for controversy," seeing as how they were currently engaged in "delicate discussions with Vice-President Nixon" about using air force planes for the September airlift.

As country after country in Africa scheduled its independence ceremonies—seventeen of them in 1960—American newspapers also reported the large efforts being made by the USSR and even by West Germany to cultivate and assist the new and emerging nations. On July 5, 1960, a *New York Times* editorial railed against the "timorous Administration and Congress" that had not risen to the challenge posed by these emerging nations that were so economically, politically, and educationally needy. "There is no time to lose, yet there is not much evidence that the depth of the problem has really been grasped in Washington."

Only after Russia and Red China trumpeted that they would give scholarships to would-be college students from the Congo and Guinea, a thousand from each new country, did the Eisenhower administration announce that the United States would also give such scholarships, to three hundred Congolese and three hundred Guineans.

On July 7, Satterthwaite finally replied to Robinson. While noting Nixon's interest, he wrote that "[u]nfortunately, it does not appear possible to comply with either of the two proposals mentioned in your letter to the Vice-President," one for the air force to supply the transport, and the other to use funds from a presidentially designated Special Program for Tropical Africa to underwrite private charter planes. Satterthwaite said that he had discussed these matters with the Department of Defense and other agencies, but had received no encouragement.

Among the AASF's first responses was a long telegram from Robinson to Nixon on July 11 expressing "GRAVE DISAPPOINTMENT AND DISSATISFACTION" with the State Department's turndown. The telegram cited the ongoing problems in the former Belgian Congo as evidence of what could happen if future leaders no longer believed in democracy and in U.S. sympathy for their cause. Robinson pleaded with Nixon to get State to make the airlift possible,

> AS TANGIBLE EVIDENCE OF ADMINISTRATION DEDICATION TO CIVIL RIGHTS SINCE AMERICAN NEGROES REGARD SUCH A PROGRAM AS PARAMOUNT ISSUE [AND] AN INDEX OF FUTURE DOMESTIC AND INTERNATIONAL POLICIES STOP WE MUST NOT WAIT UNTIL IT IS TOO LATE IN THESE SEVEN AFRICAN COUNTRIES AS WE DID IN GUINEA AND NOW IN THE CONGO.... YOUR RESPONSE AS PRESIDENTIAL CANDIDATE WILL REVEAL MANNER IN WHICH OVER-ALL PROBLEM WILL BE MET

Scheinman and Montero flew to Washington for a July 14 meeting with State to attempt to have the decision reversed. One State participant was C. Kenneth Snyder, program officer for Africa in the education and cultural affairs bureau. In the three-hour meeting, additional reasons were given for the rejection, among them, State later wrote in a memo, dissatisfaction with the student selection process and "disquieting reports regarding certain aspects of the management and support of the students while they were here." State wanted the AASF to operate only through the IIE, its officially designated outside agency for the "selection, placement, and every day care of the students." If the AASF would not do so, then transport for the students was out of the question. Montero and Scheinman would not agree, and were told that the decision for State not to participate had been made at the "top," presumably by Secretary of State Christian Herter.

Robinson continued to pursue Nixon, hoping to have the State Department fiat reversed. But because it remained in place, Satterthwaite's turndown provided the rationale for the large U.S. private foundations to also decline to aid the airlift. The only foundation of any size willing to step in was Phelps Stokes and, Scheinman recalled, "they had no money." The two foundations had been cooperating for more than a year, with the AASF remitting checks to Phelps Stokes to be sent on to colleges as tuition payments for several of the students.

In desperation the AASF decided to bring Tom Mboya to the United States for a personal appeal. He was initially reluctant to come, writing to Scheinman, "I feel it would not be wise politically for me to make such a trip," and enclosing an article from a Nairobi newspaper, a poll showing that he "outstripped" even Jomo Kenyatta in terms of popularity in Kenya. Most politicians might find such a poll flattering, but Mboya sensed that Kenyatta's closest associates would not like the poll findings and might agitate against Mboya in his absence, as had happened to him earlier when he had gone out of the country for a week or more. An election was coming up. Nevertheless, when Scheinman and Montero told him that this was a do-or-die moment, he agreed to come.

The conference on education in East and Central Africa, under the auspices of the Phelps Stokes Fund and of a small foundation led by Peter Weiss, was a venue to which the AASF invited many of its critics, including the IIE, State, and the major foundations. The thought was to get these people together in one place so that Mboya and the AASF could make their most persuasive pitch on behalf of the airlift. The hope was that at least one foundation would agree to contribute, which would enable the AASF to more effectively pressure State and/or the other foundations.

Meanwhile, Montero, Scheinman, Kheel, and others made approaches to John F. Kennedy, who that week was accepting the Democratic nomination at the party's convention. The AASF had previously approached other senators on the Foreign Relations Committee but all had shied away, lauding the AASF but not wanting to become involved. Kennedy was the AASF's best hope. He was scheduled to stay at the family compound in Hyannisport, Massachusetts, for a few days after the convention and before setting out on the campaign trail. Scheinman and Montero worked on obtaining an invitation for Mboya to discuss "African affairs." There were interchanges with Kennedy's press secretary, Pierre Salinger; his aide on civil rights matters, Harris Wofford; and his brother-in-law R. Sargent Shriver, Jr., whose bailiwick included the Joseph P. Kennedy, Jr., Foundation, named for the senator's elder brother, killed in combat in World War II. In all of the preliminary communications, no specific mention was made of the airlift.

The Phelps Stokes conference on higher education in East and Central Africa featured such panelists as Snyder and officers of the IIE, the AAI, the Carnegie and Rockefeller foundations, the American Society of African Culture, and other organizations. Maida Springer and George Houser were there, as was an aide to Senator Kennedy. Kenneth D. Luke, the British government's adviser to African students in the United States—the man who had charged that the 1959 airlift students were starving—asked to attend and was immediately put on a panel. Participating in that panel's discussion, in front of an audience well grounded in the subject, Luke backtracked on his prior assertion that some airliftees were starving, saying this had now been "refuted," but he continued to insist that some were "underfinanced . . . so hard-pressed that [the student] has to go begging to the affluent society and bear the loss of dignity involved."

Other participants, particularly those from establishment institutions like the IIE, were also tough on the AASF. While an internal IIE report acknowledged that "[i]t is too early to judge the probable results of the current AASF program," Barbara Walton, the report's author, nonetheless charged at the conference that "[a] program which selects those students who can raise the most money, and places them at institutions which offer the best scholarships, cannot be expected to make a systematic contribution to the solution of Africa's educational or social problems."

Scheinman addressed his remarks at the conference to State's Snyder. Raising the issue of the administration's recent and sudden offer of scholarships to the Congo and Guinea, made only after the Russians and Chinese had made larger offers to those new countries, Scheinman asked, "I want to understand the logic behind that decision—what sense does it make to do that [for the Congolese and Guineans] and not help 300 Kenyan students who have made their own scholarship arrangements?"

"Well," Snyder responded, "I wasn't part of that decision. That was a political decision that I wasn't part of." According to a later press account, Snyder was very precise about why the State Department could not fund the AASF airlift:

On that point we can give you a clear answer. When we are
dealing with independent countries like Guinea and The
Congo, we have a certain ability to plan our own program.
When dealing with any colonial area, it means we must be
conscious of our relationship with the colonial powers still administering the area. . . .

Despite the contentiousness, the conference participants all acknowledged the AASF's basic premise: the urgent need for Africans
from emerging nations to be educated immediately, and in larger
batches than the U.S. government had previously been willing to
support.

Maintenance of the status quo, however, was the establishment's
priority, and ten days later, when a draft "statement of general principles" from the conference was circulated, Peter Weiss had to fight
to have that statement reflect more of the AASF guidelines than of
the mainstream's don't-rock-the-boat conclusions. In its initial form,
the resolution said flatly that only the U.S. government was capable
of handling an increased flow of students from Africa, and implied
that only those eligible for admission to the top thirty U.S. colleges
would continue to be acceptable in such a program. Weiss railed
against "talking about an education program for the elite," arguing,
"The crying need today . . . is for the mass training of the second and
third echelons of leadership and administration, and it is precisely
here that American higher education, with its partly realized dream
of putting college degrees within reach of every student possessing
the required intellectual equipment, has its positive contribution to
make."

The AASF did more than talk about broader education for Africans. The organization consistently assisted students of promise who
had not been in the echelon of those that the Kenyan government
agreed to send to Oxford, Cambridge, or St. Andrews. In later years,
the achievements of those AASF-aided East Africans—who began

their collegiate careers at nonelite campuses such as Philander Smith, or at religious-oriented ones such as Moravian, or at junior colleges such as Diablo Valley, and then went on to more prestigious schools for their masters and doctorates—would prove Weiss's point.

During the Phelps Stokes conference, Mboya did not stay with Maida Springer, as he had on previous visits to New York, but at the Barclay Hotel so he could meet there with another hotel guest, Prime Minister Patrice Lumumba of the newly independent Republic of the Congo, who had come to New York to ask for U.S. and UN assistance in dealing with the Katanga province, a resource-rich area that was threatening to break away. Refugees from the fighting, mainly white Belgians, had been streaming into Nairobi and warning Europeans that the bloodbath might envelop Kenya, too, if Kenya continued on the path toward majority black rule. Lumumba was openly courting assistance from Moscow.

Eisenhower's military aide and close friend, General Andrew Goodpaster, would shortly write to Secretary of State Herter, "The Congo crisis points up one of the world's most urgent needs: The absence of trained and educated people to take over leadership and administration of the new African nations." But the notion that such assistance ought to be offered to territories that were not yet independent never entered his thinking.

On July 26, 1960, Montero, Mboya, Scheinman, and Mboya's brother Alphonse Okuku Ndiege flew by private plane to Hyannisport to meet with Senator Kennedy at the family compound. Three hundred newspeople were camped out at the gates. Harris Wofford, the close adviser to Martin Luther King, Jr., and the coauthor (with King, Bayard Rustin, and Chester Bowles) of the civil rights plank in the 1960 Democratic Party platform, was perhaps the most impressed onlooker in the room when Mboya and Kennedy met to talk. "Seeing the easy rapport of these two young men each heading for the top leadership of his nation, I had a sense that day of the far-reaching changes to come in the relationship between America and Africa," Wofford later wrote.

Mboya and Kennedy talked for an hour about African affairs, and Mboya never mentioned the airlift. After a break to see his doctor, Kennedy returned and asked if they had come for a specific reason. Scheinman explained the situation in detail: scholarships collected, money raised in East Africa, the State Department and all the major U.S. foundations turning down the AASF request, and a hundred thousand dollars needed. He mentioned that the AASF program had been criticized from all quarters. "What were the criticisms?" Kennedy wanted to know. "That we sent unqualified students to unqualified colleges," Scheinman said, and explained why neither charge was valid.

Mboya asked if Kennedy, as chairman of the Africa subcommittee, could intercede with State; according to a later memo, Kennedy said that "if Mr. Nixon had tried and failed, he could do little there." They discussed private funding. Kennedy wanted to help in some way, and promised five thousand dollars from his family's foundation, even though it was not in the educational field. He made the promise twice more, and phoned his brother-in-law R. Sargent Shriver, Jr., executive director of the family foundation, to ask him to get in touch with the other foundations, in the hope that if Rockefeller, Ford, and the others knew that the Kennedys were contributing, perhaps they would as well. A later report said that Kennedy also consulted his brother Robert, his campaign manager and the president of the small Foundation for All-Africa, which assisted African students in the United States.

"We felt something ought to be done," Kennedy later said on the Senate floor. "To waste 250 scholarships to this country, to waste $200,000 these people had raised, to disappoint 250 students who hoped to come to this country, it certainly seemed to me, would be most unfortunate, and so we went ahead."

On July 26 Senator Kennedy decreed that the initial grant to the

AASF and Shriver's beating of the bushes for more money were to be done quietly, that the whole matter should be "kept out of politics," because if his opponents knew that Kennedy was using his family money in such a way, they might misconstrue his gesture as crass or inappropriate, a political move for the purpose of obtaining more African-American votes.

A publicity photo was taken of Mboya and Kennedy, and a release prepared that said they had conferred about various situations in Africa, including that of the Congo. No mention was made whatsoever of the airlift or of Kennedy's largesse.

On the ride back to New York, Mboya said to Scheinman, "Well, at least we have $15,000." Scheinman was puzzled. "He said $5,000 three times," Mboya explained.

Shortly Mboya returned to Kenya, and within days fractured his skull in an automobile accident that sent him to the hospital for a brief stay.

Shriver's calls to the other major foundations, made on July 27 and 28, confirmed what Scheinman had told Kennedy. Some foundations said they might be willing to participate later, but not now. On July 29, when Senator Kennedy learned from Shriver that the other foundations would not help in the current airlift, he recommended that the family foundation contribute the entire amount, in order to secure the charter, and suggested adding ten thousand to the ninety-thousand-dollar charter cost to cover the expenses for a fact-finding group to go to Kenya and participate in the selection process.

That was the word passed to Montero and Scheinman by Shriver and Wofford at lunch at the Mayflower Hotel in Washington on August 10: The Kennedy Foundation would underwrite the air charters, for $100,000, and would also provide up to an additional $100,000 for support of the students while they were in the United States to allay criticism that the students didn't have enough money to sustain them while studying. There was to be an advisory board for this project, and Shriver had invited the IIE and the AAI to participate, along with such dignitaries as Representative Diggs. A panel that included IIE and AAI representatives would go to Nairobi to check out the AASF operation, make certain that the students were qualified, and so on. The proposed panel members would meet the following week in Washington. Shriver reiterated to Scheinman and Montero the warning not to publicize the grant in any way. Elated, the two sent a telegram to Mboya: "WE HAVE HIT THE JACKPOT." They also informed the members of the AASF board of their good fortune.

On Friday, August 12, Shriver called Montero to say that meeting would be on Monday, August 15, at 2:30 P.M. in the Kennedy Foundation's Washington office, currently situated within the Democratic National Committee headquarters.

By August 12 the Nixon campaign had learned of the potential Kennedy Foundation underwriting of the airlift. Jackie Robinson, who had pushed Nixon hard to lean on the State Department, was one likely source, but later Kennedy would tell the Senate that he and his associates believed the leak had come from one of the foundations canvassed by Shriver. In any event, James Shepley, a Nixon campaign aide, became involved. Shepley was a former Washington bureau chief of *Time* magazine, known as "Brass Knuckles Shepley" for his hard-biting style, formed in part when he had been an assistant to General George C. Marshall at the end of World War II. Robinson phoned Montero at home and asked him to call Shepley, which he did. Shepley announced to Montero that he knew about the Kennedy Foundation's $100,000 offer; Montero later told colleagues that in this conversation with Shepley he neither confirmed nor denied the Kennedy Foundation's offer but did acknowledge that a private foundation was willing to underwrite the airlift. Shepley asked that Montero hold off accepting the offer until Nixon had a chance to reverse the State Department's refusal. They agreed to speak the following day. In that Sunday call, Shepley said he was going to take up the matter with Undersecretary Douglas Dillon; he did not as yet have an answer but expected to have an affirmative one before Montero's Monday afternoon meeting with Shriver.

This, Montero's version of the sequence of events, was later contradicted by Robinson in a column contending that on Sunday, August 14, he and Montero discussed the likely State contribution "in front of witnesses," and that "no contribution beyond Sen. Kennedy's personal $5,000 had yet been received [by the AASF]." That Montero's version is more likely than Robinson's is suggested by the participants of the meeting at Shriver's office: Hagberg of the AAI; Sims of the IIE; Dr. Fred Patterson, president of Phelps Stokes; and a representative of the Foundation for All-Africa. They would not have been there had a large commitment not already been made.

On Monday morning, Shepley kept in touch with Montero by phone, saying he would take up the matter with Dillon as soon as the undersecretary finished testifying on Capitol Hill. A few minutes before the Shriver meeting, Shepley reached Montero with word that he was authorized to make a definitive offer for State to fund the airlift up to $100,000, and asked him to contact an assistant secretary of state, who would verify that.

While Montero and Scheinman were in their Kennedy Foundation meeting, Shepley told Robinson that State would be financing the airlift, and Robinson and his writing colleague began to draft a column to run in the Wednesday *Post*, which began,

> Good news is all too rare these days, but on Monday I received a call from Washington which added up to just that. Jim Shepley, an aide to Vice President Nixon, called to tell me the State Department has decided to pick up the tab for the three planeloads of African students which the African-American Students Foundation is bringing over this year to study at American universities.

Montero told the assembled group in Shriver's office about Shepley's phone call; Shriver said that the AASF was, of course, free to accept the government's offer rather than the Kennedy Foundation's. Montero and Scheinman wanted to accept both offers so they could stockpile money toward future airlifts, but, Scheinman later recalled, a phone call to Mboya revealed his preference for the "private" offer. Montero also worried that State's commitment was still not firm and might eventually have unacceptable strings attached.

As Montero and Scheinman argued in a lengthy backgrounder for the Kennedy campaign, their goal was to change minds at State: "It is hoped that this incident will focus the attention of the State Department on the needs of the non-self-governing areas in Africa and that the reaction of the State Department in this situation means that it will also be alive in the future to the urgent needs of Africa in higher education."

In the meeting in Shriver's office, Montero and Scheinman reported that a major U.S. airline, which had previously agreed to furnish aircraft for the airlift, had suddenly declared it had no aircraft available on the specific September dates required. Montero and Scheinman guessed that State might have exerted pressure on the airline to withdraw and force the AASF to accept the government's offer.

At this meeting it was decided that a group of advisers, including Montero, Hagberg, and Sims, would travel to Kenya to check out the student selection process and other aspects of the airlift in advance of the planes leaving Nairobi, and perhaps accompany the students as they flew into the United States.

Montero and Scheinman left the meeting still under the prohibition against publicizing the underwriting, which Shriver had reiterated. But Montero felt obligated to phone State and then Shepley to inform them that the AASF had accepted the Kennedy Foundation's offer. According to a later document, Shepley was upset at their "turning down the United States Government," and implied to

Montero that the Nixon camp might retaliate by suggesting to the press that the Kennedy donation was politically motivated.

Senator Hugh Scott of Pennsylvania, although a freshman senator, had been in the House of Representatives for many years and was a Nixon associate, one of the vice president's surrogates on a "truth squad" who responded to supposed untruths voiced by the Kennedy campaign. On the Senate floor on Tuesday, Scott announced that the State Department had offered $100,000 to bring the 250 East African students to the United States.

That day, Robinson called Montero and read him his column for Wednesday, with its "good news is all too rare these days" theme, and its crediting of Nixon for having spurred the State Department to come up with the $100,000. Montero pleaded with him not to publish the column because the AASF was going to accept the Kennedy Foundation money, but Robinson insisted on going ahead. It was published on Wednesday, August 17, and early that evening Senator Scott took the Senate floor again to announce, "I have been informed that the long arm of the family of the junior senator from Massachusetts has reached out and attempted to pluck this project away from the U.S. government. At this moment, they appear to have been successful because they are offering more than the U.S. government has offered." Scott said he could understand this action only in the context of the "pressures brought about by the Kennedy people and their anxiety to take over the function of government in advance of an election." Scott went on to suggest that the donation from the Kennedy family foundation would be "an apparent misuse of tax-exempt foundation money for blatant political purposes."

This was the first public notice of the Kennedy Foundation's commitment to the AASF airlift. Although Kennedy had probably not meant to keep it under wraps forever—it was too good a publicity boon to forsake—he had not wanted it to become public without controlling its release. However, if he rather than Scott had made it public, it might not have been as important an issue in the campaign.

Scott's announcement, which the senator thought would help Nixon's campaign by implying that Kennedy money was being used to buy black votes, had unforeseen consequences.

Kennedy and his advisers understood that he must respond quickly to the accusations of meddling and impropriety. At the campaign's request, Montero sent the senator a telegram stating flatly that the "OFFER" from the State Department "WAS ONLY MADE AFTER THE [AASF] WHICH HAD REPEATEDLY REQUESTED HELP DURING THE PAST 12 MONTHS AND WAS FINALLY TURNED DOWN LATE LAST MONTH WAS SUCCESSFUL IN OBTAINING A GRANT OF $100,000 FROM A PRIVATE FOUNDATON." Montero labeled as "REGRETTABLE" Scott's "ATTEMPT TO REAP POLITICAL ADVANTAGE FROM THIS NONPOLITICAL EDUCATIONAL PROGRAM," and expressed the hope that State's $100,000 could be used for "OTHER AFRICAN STUDENTS ON A CONTINUING BASIS."

On the Senate floor on August 17, Kennedy read into the record the Montero telegram, as well as portions of the earlier Satterthwaite letter to Robinson and other documents provided by Montero and Scheinman, and recounted his meeting with Mboya at Hyannisport and the evolution of the family foundation commitment. He called the Scott attack "the most unfair distorted, and malignant, attack to which I have been subjected in my 14 years in politics. . . . I will say to the Senator [Scott] that I think it is unfortunate that he has chosen this means of attacking me and the foundation, suggesting that we wish to spend the money improperly." He urged Scott to have Shepley do as Montero suggested, see to it that the State Department's $100,000 was used to bring additional African students to the United States, an activity that he, Kennedy, as chairman of the Subcommittee on Africa, "would be delighted" to approve.

The overwhelming response of the other senators, Republicans as well as Democrats, was to back Kennedy in this dispute. Republicans Javits and John Sherman Cooper rebuked Scott. Even Nixon repudiated Scott's remarks; Nixon's campaign spokesman responded to a newsman's query by saying that "it was 'a fair answer' that the Vice-President did not share Scott's views."

"Who is this Mr. Shepley and what position in the government does he occupy? How did this Mr. Shepley go to the State Department and get this money?" Senator Fulbright fulminated on the Senate floor. "Has the State Department entered politics? Has it become the handmaiden of Mr. Shepley?" The chairman of the Foreign Relations Committee followed up his remarks by a long letter to Secretary of State Herter demanding a full explanation of the affair and specific answers to thirteen questions, among them, "When did the Department [of State] reverse its earlier decision? Who participated in the decision?" In an accompanying speech in the Senate, Fulbright also threatened punitive action if there had been outside pressure on the State Department to provide funds for the airlift—"an unacceptable interference with the orderly conduct of our foreign policy . . . for partisan political purposes."

Herter assigned Assistant Secretary William Macomber, Jr., to respond to the Fulbright letter, and Macomber dived into the task.

The controversy continued to flare. On Friday, August 19, Robinson's column for the *New York Post* began with an uncharacteristic statement: "I don't mind admitting it: I was wrong." The admission, however, was not that he had ignored Montero's warning against writing the "good news is rare" column but rather that he had bad information at the time of composing that column—in effect, though this was not overtly stated, that Montero had withheld information. "The integrity of a good many people has been laid open to question during the current row," Robinson wrote, adding, "If anyone is to blame, it is this reporter." He apologized to his readers and to Shepley for the mistake. After this incident, Montero and Robinson rapidly grew apart, and Robinson also cut back on his time commitment to the AASF, though he remained very much a champion of the airlift and a provider of scholarships. He also began to question his embrace of Nixon and how the vice president's campaign had been using him.

The Scott-Kennedy imbroglio was grist for many media mills, discussed and dissected in newsprint, magazines, and television and radio commentaries. The conclusion of most media evaluators was that Scott had not done the Nixon campaign much good by his mean-spirited and error-filled attack on Kennedy—and that the program in question, the airlift, was a good thing for America as well as the East Africans. The African-American press reaction was even more pointed. Some black newspapers saw racism in Scott's remarks, and nearly all concluded, as P. L. Prattis wrote in *The Pittsburgh Courier*, "One of Nixon's henchmen showed State the deep point that the Kennedy gift would be worth a lot of Negro votes, which it would be best for Nixon to have in a tight contest, so all of a sudden State recalled that it had been for the project from the beginning!"

On Monday, August 22, Macomber sent the State Department's response to Fulbright, who released it to the press. In his long letter, Macomber asserted that his recent conversations with Dillon and Herter revealed that neither had had any knowledge of the previous AASF requests for assistance. Macomber then went on to advise Fulbright that Dillon's special assistant had "received assurances from the financial section of the Bureau of International Educational and Cultural Affairs . . . that there were funds legally available for such an airlift." Finally, Macomber asserted that the department had reversed itself on funding the airlift because the AASF had agreed to work through the good offices of the IIE.

All three assertions raised more questions than they answered. Macomber's statement that Herter and Dillon had not known about the AASF requests—which may have been true—belied what State officials had previously told Scheinman and Montero, that the decision to deny the request had come from the top. The second assertion, that State funds were available, refuted the officials' earlier, categorical denial that any such funds were permissible. As Scheinman insisted in a telegram to Fulbright—which Fulbright also gave to the press—the prior turndowns by State had always been on the basis of "A LACK OF FUNDS." Scheinman also rejected Macomber's third assertion, that the AASF had agreed to work through the IIE and that this change in the AASF stance was what had finally permitted State to allocate funds for the airlift; that assertion, Scheinman said in the telegram, was "NOT IN CONFORMANCE WITH FACTS."

The immediate uproar over the Kennedy Foundation's commitment to the airlift died down, but the matter continued in the news, as the delegation of advisers to the Kennedy family foundation prepared to embark for Nairobi on a fact-finding tour. There would be similar publicity about the airlifts when the advisory panel returned, and more when the students arrived in September. In short, the airlift matter would continue to reverberate throughout the fall and thereby to have an impact on the eventual outcome of the presidential campaign.

F amilies in Kisii, in the southwest of Kenya, tend to run large, and to farm intensely; Kisii is one of the most densely populated and intensively cultivated areas of the country. The secondary school there, in the late 1950s, was small, only around two hundred students, and admission to it was highly competitive. Three of its graduates who, earning spots on the 1960 airlift, went on to education in the United States and to interesting careers are Steve Machooka, Charles Angwenyi, and Haron Andima.

Stephen Misati Machooka, eldest of ten children of a Kenyan farmer, had been a good student at the local primary school, seven miles from his home, and had developed his running ability by running to and from the school every day. In secondary school he was coached in the long distances by a Kenyan who had taken seventh place in the five-thousand-meter race at the 1956 Olympics, and his running abilities improved even more. Nicholas Otieno, an earlier airlifted student, then a graduate student at Cornell, returned home on a visit, heard about Machooka, and recruited him, helping him obtain a scholarship to Cornell's famed agriculture school for the fall of 1960. Once at Cornell, Machooka proceeded to shatter school, intercollegiate, and international meet records in the mile and to become a Cornell star athlete. A particularly sweet Machooka victory, memorialized in a photo in *The New York Times*, was when he beat the Oxford star in a combined Penn-Cornell vs. Oxford-Cambridge meet. This was years prior to the era when Kenyans began winning long-distance races in international competitions; Machooka, a later analysis for a sports magazine concluded, was the man who ignited that particular sports revolution. A runner who competed against Machooka in intercollegiate races explained to the reporter, "The thought back then was that black people couldn't run distance. But not only was [Machooka] good, this guy was great."

"Steve was unprepared for our cold climate," a Cornell classmate recalled. He required boots and outdoor clothing, for which the AASF sent him small sums. But he did not realize that while running in the cold he would need gloves, and thus had to run one particularly cold and sleety marathon with socks over his hands. He won anyway. His celebrity in the United States moved the AASF to ask him to write a letter detailing his progress, which was then mailed out as a fundraising appeal.

An avid "ag" student, Machooka also developed a taste for Handel, Mozart, and chess. During semester and summer breaks he stayed in New York, sometimes at the home of the Kheels, who were Cornell alumni, or nearby in Riverdale at the home of Sylvia "Frankie" Levey, a recently divorced biologist and the vice president of the American Cancer Society. Levey was the mother of two teenaged boys; one, Bob Levey, later a columnist for *The Washington Post*, remembered Machooka as "the most unassuming, most talented" person. On a windy, fifty-degree day Machooka headed out of the Levey home in a running outfit, and when Bob asked where he was off to, he said he was "just going for a run" in nearby Van Cortlandt Park. Bob soon found out that Machooka had won the Heptagonal, a race among seven top colleges, in that hilly park. He was the first black man ever to win part of an all-Ivy competition, leading his team in the relays.

In Machooka's sophomore year his grades went down, and his professors advised him to spend more time on his classes; he cut back on his track commitments, and when he was ready to return, a few months later, he contracted the mumps and was sidelined for many more months. Eventually he did run again competitively, and made the dean's list as well as the cover of *Track & Field News* magazine.

The Kisii area was populated mostly by the tribe of that name, but was near Luo and Kikuyu lands, and Charles Angwenyi's father was the senior Kikuyu chief nearest to the school. As had Machooka, when Angwenyi went to New York on breaks from attending Colby College in Maine, he stayed with the Kheels and the Leveys. He owed his scholarship to Mboya's having convinced Colby's president to furnish one. Angwenyi studied international economics and finance; Kheel's children, a few years younger than Angwenyi, remember him as studious and as good company. Like Machooka, Angwenyi became a member of the Kheel brood, then numbering six children. He found a quote that he liked and sent it to the Kheels because he thought it fit them: "Life must be revealed not as a dubious and pointless struggle but rather as a meaningful and magnificent privilege, a torch that must burn as brightly as possible before it is handed on to the next generation." Steve Machooka developed enough family feeling for the Kheels to trade birthday poems with Bob Kheel, also at Cornell.

> Some day in Biblical ages a word passed;
> You will thereby get yourself a son and . . .
> So here you are and your name will be Bob.

During Angwenyi's senior year at Colby, he convinced a bright cousin from Kenya to attend that school as well. After graduation, Angwenyi pursued further studies in finance and economics at the University of Massachusetts.

Bob Levey recalled that these two Kenyans had a great influence on his life by "teaching me that there was a larger world out there" and by being so "energized" and enthusiastic about the United States. The impact on his mother, he remembered, was even greater: Once her two sons were safely into college, Frankie Levey obtained a Fulbright scholarship to teach in Ethiopia for a year and then in Kenya, where she remained on the faculty at the University of Nairobi for an additional ten years before returning to the United States.

Haron Andima was of the Kisii tribe, one of nine children whose father died when Andima was quite young. He had begun his U.S. education at Philander Smith, then transferred to Hunter College in New York, often staying in the city with Arthur and Mathilde Krim. At Hunter, he recalls, he was the only black in his class, though others followed in later years. After earning his bachelor's degree he went on to graduate work at New York University, paying for his studies by working for the City of New York as a statistician, and supplementing that with similar work for a hospital. He became involved with an African-American woman, and they planned to marry. First, however, he wanted to return to Kenya, doctorate in hand. They both went, but Andima lacked a high-level patron and therefore was not sponsored for jobs that he thought he deserved. He visited his family—none of his brothers and sisters had graduated from college, though some had been through high school. After a year, he and his girlfriend returned to New York, married, and found jobs in academia.

In 1964 Steve Machooka graduated from Cornell and returned with his American bride to Kitale, in rural Kenya, to raise crops and livestock. He no longer ran competitively, but his prowess was evident in pickup soccer games. During her pregnancy Betty Machooka returned to the United States to have her child, and eventually moved back permanently so that their daughter could attend school in the United States while Steve and their son, Bob, remained in Kenya.

Machooka taught agricultural economics at two small Kenyan universities and served as a field controller for the Ministry of Finance, working with local groups to improve crop production using the latest cultivation methods. His son, a Nairobi lawyer, recently recalled that throughout his father's career, Machooka had two professional objectives: "One, to be of service to mankind and to serve in those areas where his professional competence could be exploited, and two, to support and promote the development of Africa. So committed was he to these ideals that he long ago gave up the luxury of city life to work among the people in the rural areas."

After taking an advanced degree in production management economics in Great Britain, on his return to Africa Machooka expanded his reach by working for the Pan African Institute for Development in Zambia to achieve water independence in rural Zimbabwe, Tanzania, Swaziland, Malawi, Lesotho, and Botswana. In the 1980s he joined the Lake Basin Development Authority in Kenya. The vast Lake Victoria area, home to twelve million Kenyans, has extensive fisheries and mining facilities in addition to farming; it was a good match for Machooka's agricultural and development skills, and he eventually became the Authority's executive director. He also continued to be interested in long-distance running, assisting several Kenyan runners, including a nephew who trained in the United States and became an All-American.

Charles Angwenyi worked in the banking industry in the United States before being recruited to join the Standard Bank in Nairobi. Frankie Levey stayed with Charles and his wife, Susan, in Nairobi for a while before moving into a place of her own. The Angwenyis named their first child Ann in honor of Kheel's wife, and a few years later Charles wrote Ann Kheel that her namesake "spoke English, Swahili, and Kisii, not necessarily in that order." He also became the

Africa editor for an international magazine for which Ted Kheel served as publisher. In 1974 Angwenyi stood for election to the Kenyan parliament but lost. After his defeat he devoted himself to international banking, and was sent to Great Britain for additional training. This led to his appointment as chairman of the Bank of Kenya, the Kenyan national bank, an important factor in the country's development process. In this prestigious position he traveled the world; when in the United States for various conferences, he visited his American friends and sponsors. His daughter became a lawyer; his son, an economist.

A turning point in Kenya came in 1991, when there was an attempt to end one-party rule. Many of those in high-level positions were viewed as arbitrary appointees of the government who had not been subjected to confirmation hearings by a multiparty parliament. When one-party rule was legislatively abolished, Charles Angwenyi, among many others, was forced out of his job.

Friends believed he was a victim of the dictatorial side of Kenya's government, but he told them he did not mind being out of the glare attendant on being a public figure, his decisions continually questioned. He settled comfortably into a position as a professor at the University of Nairobi.

Steve Machooka retired from the Lake Basin Development Authority in 1999, and died of a heart attack on his Kitale farm in 2002. "His death affected a lot of people," his nephew recalled. "He helped communities all over the region become water-independent, built agricultural farms, and donated to the schools."

Haron Andima and his wife had a rough time in academia in the United States, moving from position to position until he received tenure as a professor in the new field of computer sciences and information technology at Bronx Community College, where he readied inner-city young men and women for jobs in that field. His wife took a similar position at Long Island University. They and their two daughters went back and forth to Kenya every few years to visit; the Andimas bought a vacation home in Mombasa, and Haron maintained his Kenyan citizenship for many years. He finally applied for and won American citizenship so he could cast a vote in the 2004 national election.

7

THE AIRLIFT *and the* PRESIDENTIAL ELECTION *of* 1960

In the midst of the controversy over how the 1960 airlift would be funded and by whom, Jackie Robinson engaged in a principled but heated argument on civil rights with Barry Gray, the man later known as "the father of talk radio," on Gray's syndicated radio program, which originated in New York City. Gray, whom Robinson referred to as a "long-time friend," had been very outspoken about many things in American life, and in the early 1950s had been thought of as quite a liberal. By 1960 he was edging toward becoming the quite conservative commentator that he would be in his later years.

On this August Saturday night broadcast, Gray took Robinson and other African-American leaders to task for concentrating on civil rights during this election season to the exclusion of more important issues; this was a "blind spot" in their worldview, Gray charged.

Robinson refused to back down. "It is very easy to tell others to stop rocking the boat . . . when you are comfortably riding inside and the 'others' are struggling to get on board," he put it when paraphrasing his on-air remarks in his next column. "Those civil rights that Barry and a lot of letter writers think are so unimportant just happen to be the ticket of admission to the starting-line." Robinson reported in that column that two African-American children had been taken to a Chattanooga hospital on Saturday night after their home had been bombed, and that in Fayette County in Texas, many more black children were starving because local white merchants would not sell their parents bread, milk, or other necessities now that the parents had dared to try to register to vote. Civil rights, Robinson summed up on the air and in his column, was "the very basis of our democracy" and therefore the most important issue in the coming election, whether or not white Americans understood the matter.

The Robinson-Nixon-Kennedy flap over funding the airlift—and its echo in the Robinson-Gray controversy over what issue was of principal importance to blacks and what was of secondary importance—had an impact on Robinson's relationship to the Nixon campaign. Earlier, Robinson had been happy to appear with the candidate and to hold his own pro-Nixon rallies. But after the airlift-funding fiasco Robinson could not escape the feeling that Nixon had been using him. Nixon, Robinson would write in a chapter of his 1972 autobiography, was "capable of deep personal goodwill and grace in one-to-one relationships," but such behavior occurred "particularly if he believes you can be useful to his goals." As the campaign wore on, Robinson understood that his own goals—and the AASF's—were not Nixon's. His wife, Rachel, pleaded with him to stop campaigning for Nixon, but as yet he did not.

In late August 1960, as the presidential campaign continued to heat up and the Kennedy Foundation advisory panel made arrangements to visit Kenya, the Phelps Stokes Fund released its report on the July conference. Now those conferees who before and during the conference had been dismissive of the AASF's approach applauded it and the Kennedy Foundation's involvement in the airlifts program, labeling them "a sharp answer" to the Eisenhower administration's modest postindependence educational grants to Guinea and the Congo. The conferees also adopted the AASF's larger view by calling on the government to, in effect, adopt the AASF strategies and philosophy, asking for "action by the United States Government on a broader—perhaps regional—scale" that would encompass bringing students to the United States from both independent and "dependent" countries.

That conclusion was being circulated to players such as Sims and Hagberg as the Kennedy Foundation advisory panel prepared to fly to visit Kenya and then to return—not with the students, as had originally been planned, since that would take up valuable space on a charter plane, but separately. Shriver told Montero that the panel's mission was "to observe the processes by which the students were selected . . . and to keep the Kennedy Foundation informed about the placement of these students in American Institutions, their progress and their welfare. We are also interested in what happens to these students when they return to Africa." The group would contain one longtime AASF critic, Albert Sims of the IIE; one semi-critical veteran who knew the Nairobi ropes, Gordon Hagberg, now representing the African-American Institute; a definite friend, Dr. Aaron Brown of Phelps Stokes; and a relative neutral, Father Gordon Fournier of the Foundation for All-Africa, the foundation for which Robert F. Kennedy currently served as honorary president. No one was designated as the leader, which would later cause some problems. Montero had been scheduled to go with them but quickly discovered upon attempting to obtain a visa that he, as were Scheinman and Peter Weiss, was now on a colonial blacklist and would not be granted entry to Kenya. Learning this on a Thursday, Montero immediately asked Ted Kheel to go in his stead. Kheel agreed. At a party that evening, Kheel told Milton Gordon what he was about to do, and Gordon asked if he could accompany the group, which he did.

The plane was to leave that Saturday, and the sequence of inoculations against various diseases prevalent in Africa took more than two days, so Kheel was supplied with an injection kit to take with him on the airplane, which he stored first in a refrigerated compartment, then in an overnight hotel in London, and finally in a hotel in Nairobi—and never did use. Articles in the major U.S. newspapers announced the advisory committee trip and kept the Kennedy connection to the airlift in the headlines.

In Nairobi the group's official schedule included visits to the AASF office, the Kenyan Ministry of Education, the Kenya Educational Trust (the entity collecting money for the students), and the U.S. consul general. Mboya almost always accompanied them on these visits, and also took the group on side trips to student fundraising events in the countryside. During their time at the labor federation headquarters, they witnessed some of the orientation about the United States for the September 1960 students. Kheel later wrote about this in an AFL-CIO publication: "Obviously, [the students] had to be told about segregation and the rebuffs they might receive. I felt very ashamed during this discussion. But so great was their sense of adventure and their desire to learn in order to return to help their country that no amount of hardship could possibly discourage them from going."

One evening Mboya drove the group to a village fifty miles from Nairobi. The roads were poor, and Mboya pushed his old BMW so

fast that en route—and while everyone was discussing points of political philosophy that did nothing to calm the situation—Kheel
asked Father Fournier to say a prayer for their safety. At the village
compound they met a ninety-two-year-old Kikuyu chief who spoke
no English and was surrounded by his wives and his three hundred
children. All were illiterate but, Kheel recalled, they asked pertinent
questions about the education being offered in the United States. At
another outing to the Machakos district of Kenya, where even
Mboya did not speak the local language, Kheel watched as five thousand Africans sat for more than four hours listening to speaker after
speaker explain why they should help twenty students from their
area go to college in the United States. A third fundraiser was a livestock auction held at Githunguri, the site of the Kenyatta teachers
college that had been long since shut by the colonial government.
Here Kheel made the highest bid for a goat, which he then donated to the cause. He photographed old women and small children contributing pence and shillings so that their neighbors' sons
and daughters could attend college in a faraway land. These fundraising activities, Kheel wrote in his letter to the Kennedy Foundation, were "as moving and inspiring as anything I have ever seen.
Words cannot do justice to the reverence these people showed for
education and . . . what [the airlift] meant to Kenya." Hagberg added
in his own letter to Shriver, "The willingness of Africans to sacrifice
to achieve education for their children is truly impressive."

On a flying visit to Tanganyika, Kheel and the others met with
Julius Nyerere one day after he had been sworn in as the new country's leader of a biracial cabinet; all those on the panel were impressed by Nyerere's abilities and his commitment to education.

The individual reports submitted by Kheel, Sims, and Hagberg to
Shriver would form the basis for the advisory committee's work during the fall of 1960, which would lead to a substantial evolution of the
airlifts program during the Kennedy administration. Although the
authors of the reports did not suggest a serious transfiguration of

the AASF and the airlifts, their well-reported and well-argued papers became a turning point in the eventual superseding of the AASF.

Kheel summed up his and the group's experiences for Shriver—previously conveyed by phone before the written report: "We saw evidence of a hunger for education not only on the part of the leaders, but among people who themselves are illiterate, that is as deep and determined as craving for food or thirst for water." He waxed enthusiastic about what the airlift would do for the individual students and about "its symbolic value as a dramatic and inspiring method of providing assistance to Africans." He warned, however, that Africans "are so determined on obtaining the education and training they need [that] they will seek it elsewhere unless supplied by us." Hagberg's report echoed Kheel's on this point, as well: "If we Americans do not help [the Africans] satisfy this hunger they will assuredly turn elsewhere." The "elsewhere" referred to by Kheel and Hagberg was the USSR and its Communist satellites.

During the advisory panel's meeting with the colonial minister of education, the Briton tried to insist that the AASF program be limited to those students who could demonstrate that they had the "whole cost" of college paid for in advance—meaning several years' worth of scholarships and fees. That requirement, of course, would severely restrict the number eligible to come to the United States. Hagberg later reported to Shriver some further colonial objections to the AASF's methods:

> That the airlift was an irresponsible enterprise, using haphazard selection methods and tending to disrupt the educational pattern planned by the government, that there was no effort to cooperate with or even inform the [Kenya] Education Department of what was going on . . . and that the sending of many unqualified students to colleges in the U.S. was a waste of money that might better be used for building up the educational facilities in Kenya.

After detailing these objections, Hagberg was quick to point out to Shriver that Mboya had a good answer to each of the minister's points. Like Sims, Hagberg was beginning to be converted from a rigid critic of the airlift program to a man convinced by the students' enthusiasm, fervor, and potential that something must be done for them, even if that entailed rewriting the rules for foreign-student selection and for the American educational institutions that would teach them.

Kheel's report to Shriver reinforced Mboya's and Nyerere's basic answer to complaints about various shortcomings of the airlift: that even if the airlift was not sending the top students to America, and even if the colleges they attended in the United States were not the most prestigious, the whole program was still salutary because it would produce a substantial number of individuals educated enough to help the new countries as they emerged from colonial rule. The 1960 airlift would include students from Uganda, Zanzibar, Northern Rhodesia, Southern Rhodesia, and Nyasaland—all territories, like Kenya, that were not yet self-governing but that soon would be.

After Kheel and Gordon returned to New York, Hagberg and Sims remained in Africa and separately visited other countries. Hagberg spent more time in Dar es Salaam, Tanganyika, conferring with various men in the ministry of education, and with the president of Makerere in Kampala, Uganda. Sims went with him to those stops, and separately on to the Rhodesias and Nyasaland. Kheel, Hagberg, and Sims all submitted laudatory reports about the program to Shriver, though Sims had more bones to pick with the AASF than the others did. Sims's ultimate conclusion: "The total U.S. effort [for scholarships to East Africans] needs to be expanded substantially in our own interest as well as that of the Africans."

The executive vice president of the IIE, a State Department contractor agency highly invested in the status quo, Sims was also quite experienced in international affairs. At the end of World War II he had served on the group that divided Berlin in four, and then joined the State Department, rising to chief of the precursor agency of the United States Information Agency before leaving to become executive vice president of the IIE. In his report to Shriver, Sims pulled no punches, decrying the AASF operations in Nairobi as "a haphazard, free-style affair saved only by the dedication and extremely hard work of the zealous staff." "There is a need for a more orderly system," Hagberg agreed in his report, as Kheel did in his. Sims also felt that Mboya was too much in control, but admitted that if he had not been, very little of a positive nature would have been achieved. Sims wanted the Kennedy Foundation to put more money into a program for supporting the airlifted students once they were in the United States, and for four years rather than just for one year, at a cost of $200,000 to $300,000.

Sims's report revealed that this important critic had finally bought into the AASF premise of needing to bring large numbers of East Africans to the United States to study, immediately. His critique also had a perhaps unintended effect: Shriver was so impressed with its breadth, insight, and fairness that he began conversations with Sims that would lead him to hire Sims as the first executive director of university relations for the Peace Corps.

Privately, Kheel wrote to Scheinman, Montero, and the Weisses, exhorting them (and himself) to put the AASF's activities on a more formal basis so it would be eligible for funding from other large foundations. Needing to airlift and succor hundreds of students each year, the AASF could no longer afford to be a catch-as-catch-can organization. Though not stated overtly, Kheel's implication was clear: If the AASF did not put its house in order, the Kennedy Foundation would not be so eager to jump in next year, and the airlift, if it continued, would be taken over by other organizations.

In mid-September 1960, 289 East African students (236 men, 53 women—an even higher proportion of women than in 1959) came over in four planes, on several dates. This was a large-scale affair, requiring the services of dozens of volunteers and chaperones, name tags, ID cards, and phone numbers for students to call if they became lost, since, as Montero's letter to the students advised, "There are a great many of you, and New York is a large place." The three-day orientation, coordinated by Cora Weiss, had grown in complexity since the previous year's. In addition to visits to the United Nations and other sightseeing trips, there were addresses by Representative Diggs, several college presidents, 1959 airliftees, and Mrs. Chester Bowles; presentations by the British Embassy and Undersecretary of State Snyder; panels that included Bayard Rustin and ten African-American student sit-in leaders; and entertainment by the casts of shows on Broadway. Eunice Shriver, Senator Kennedy's sister and the wife of R. Sargent Shriver, Jr., was an interested observer of the orientation. Malcolm X and other African-Americans of note held personal chats with many of the students. The presence of these dignitaries testified to the importance of the airlift to the African-American and white liberal communities.

The night before the East Africans left New York City for their college destinations, two young men from Kenya wandered up to Harlem, where they were importuned by a street orator, who asked them to come up to speak. "I just climbed on the table and told them about Africa," one later told a reporter. "The people in the crowd knew all the African leaders. They were against Tshombe and Kasa-vubu and Mobutu and for Lumumba."

The students soon dispersed to 145 colleges in forty-one states in the United States and all across Canada, as well as to thirty-six high schools. By way of comparison, David Henry's coalition of two dozen universities awarded a total of twenty-four all-expenses-paid scholarships to Nigerians only, to start in September of 1960; the number of Nigerians studying in the United States was three times the number from all other countries in sub-Saharan Africa. The State Department program had brought over about one hundred and fifty students from various countries, double the previous year's contingent of seventy-five, but it was still well shy of the numbers served by the airlift. And no other program had brought over such a substantial group of women. Although East African society was quite patriarchal, and there were very few secondary schools for girls, the AASF's African leaders worked diligently to transport women to the United States for higher education, in the expectation that they, too, would become future leaders. And they did. Muthoni Muthiga, for instance, after graduating from Fairleigh Dickinson, went home to a career in education, eventually becoming dean of students at the University of Dar es Salaam, and then, in later years, working in business, first in human resources for the large Kenya Breweries Corporation, then as the head of her own public relations firm. Miriam Khamadi would return to a career in teaching at high schools, universities, and public health clinics. Margaret Waithira Giithara became a long-serving civil servant.

Typical of the wide media coverage of the 1960 airlift and its students was an illustrated article in Canada's leading magazine, *Maclean's*, that told the story of thirteen men and one very shy young woman, posed in New York with ceremonial fly whisks, being chaperoned by a Kenyan graduate student from Acadia University on their way to a half-dozen colleges across Canada. The article did not report that some of the students had almost been left off the charter in favor of students going to American universities; a Kenyan student in Toronto had appealed to friends in that city for additional funds that allowed four of the Kenyans to make it onto the planes. These four, acutely aware of their good fortune and their responsibility to pass it on, began a Canadian African Students Foundation that in future years would bring to Canada additional Kenyans and students from other countries—sixty-three of them in 1961. The AASF in New York was thrilled, and hoped that the Canadian ASF program would become a model for other regional groups.

A delegation of airlifted students presented Senator Kennedy with a traditional African three-legged stool. A photo of this was taken and widely distributed to the African-American press. The national media coverage of the arrival of these students, and complementary reporting on a local level when they reached their collegiate destinations, kept the airlift effort—and the Kennedy connection to it—in the news all during the fall, as the presidential election approached.

The 1960 airlift's doubling of the number of East African students in North America meant headaches for Kenneth D. Luke, the British adviser to them, and he blamed those headaches on the AASF. Many years later, in his autobiography, Luke would still be incensed about it, charging that the AASF

> was only interested in getting Kenyan students across the Atlantic and into institutions of higher Education of any kind . . . [and] not greatly concerned about supporting these students, believing, quite rightly in many cases, that the institutions which admitted them would find financial assistance for them from some source or another rather than refuse to continue to support them.

In 1960 Ted Kheel found Luke's attitude grating and his report inaccurate and deleterious to the AASF's activities, and challenged Luke in letters in September and October. Kheel assailed Luke's "implication" that a higher percentage of the airlift students were in dire financial straits than other students from Africa. As an example of their need, Luke had cited the African-American Institute's recent grants to African students, twenty-four of which had gone to airlifted students, and he labeled them "emergency" grants to relieve financial pressure. Kheel checked with Hagberg, who had made the grants, and learned that these were regular merit grants and not emergency aid—and that Hagberg had previously told this to Luke. Only two students from 1959 had dropped out and gone home, and

Barack Obama, Sr., and Barack Obama, Jr. (1971).

Tom Mboya welcomes airlift students aboard the first charter plane in Nairobi (September 7, 1959).

The group of eighty-one East African students after landing in New York and before dispersing to colleges throughout the United States and Canada.

Dr. Martin Luther King, Jr. *(left)* and Harry Belafonte *(right)*, in a photo from 1960. Belafonte, an early supporter of Dr. King, signed the 1959 airlift appeal for funds, along with Sidney Poitier and Jackie Robinson.

Jackie Robinson, counseling the East African students at an orientation session in New York (September 1959).

William X. Scheinman, cofounder of the airlift, counsels a student (1959).

Left to right: Frank Montero, George Houser, and Scheinman. Houser led the American Committee on Africa. Scheinman and Montero, board members of ACOA, were the chief officers of the African American Students Foundation (AASF), sponsor of the airlifts.

Tom Mboya *(center)* and AASF executive director Cora Weiss with unidentified student at Fairleigh Dickinson University. Because many East African students were uncomfortable at colleges in the South, Mboya and Weiss convinced the New Jersey university to accept some as transfer students.

LEFT: Senator John F. Kennedy and Tom Mboya (Hyannisport, July 1960), after discussions that led to support of the 1960 airlift by the Joseph P. Kennedy, Jr., Foundation. On the left, behind Kennedy, is Mboya's brother, Alphonse Okuku Ndiege.

BOTTOM: The advisers to the Kennedy Foundation arrive in Nairobi to review the airlift operations (1960). *Back row, left to right*: Albert Sims, Institute of International Education; Gordon Hagberg, African-American Institute; Theodore Kheel, secretary-treasurer of AASF. *Front row, left to right*: an unidentified man, Dr. Aaron Brown of the Phelps Stokes Fund, Tom Mboya, and Father Gordon Fournier of the Foundation for All Africa.

Both 1960 presidential candidates knew that the African-American vote would be crucial to winning the presidency.

LEFT: Senator Kennedy campaigns in Harlem with Congressman Adam Clayton Powell, Jr. (October 1960). Partly visible on Kennedy's left is Mrs. Eleanor Roosevelt.

BOTTOM: Vice President Richard M. Nixon campaigns with Jackie Robinson in New Jersey (1960).

Senator Kennedy receives a ceremonial stool from East African students (September 1960).

Luminaries counsel the students at the 1960 orientation in New York.

LEFT: Malcolm X, of the Nation of Islam.

RIGHT: Playwright Lorraine Hansberry, whose play *A Raisin in the Sun*, starring Sidney Poitier, had recently been on Broadway.

At the reunion of the "airlift generation" in Nairobi (December 2007).

LEFT: Two distinguished airliftees, Ambassador Pamela Mboya *(left)* and Wangari Maathai *(right)*, winner of the 2004 Nobel Peace Prize.

BOTTOM: Peter and Cora Weiss flank Pamela Mboya.

those two had done so for personal reasons rather than from lack of funds.

Montero and Kheel attended meetings of the Kennedy Foundation advisory group, reporting that since the 1960 students had arrived at their colleges and high schools, fifty had contacted the AASF offices to express their gratitude, along with a dozen who needed document assistance for their admissions procedures, and two who immediately wanted to transfer away from schools in the South. The cost of air and ground transportation had exceeded $115,000, using up the Kennedy Foundation's allotted $100,000. More money would be required in the future, and at these advisory panel sessions the major concern was how to provide the students with adequate stipends and other kinds of support to maintain them through to graduation. The panelists edged toward a structure in which other entities—in particular the IIE (Sims) and the African-American Institute (Hagberg)—would work with the AASF to keep in touch with the students and assist them while they were in the United States.

In the later lore of the 1960 presidential campaign, because the election was so close, the votes that put Kennedy over the top were attributed to various groups and incidents. Theodore White's *The Making of the President, 1960* suggests that the Kennedy campaign's calls on behalf of the jailed Martin Luther King, Jr., were of great importance in Kennedy's victory. This claim was repeated and embellished in *Of Kennedys and Kings*, by Harris Wofford, who had a large hand in making certain those calls were made by the candidate and his brother, and it is prominently featured in Taylor Branch's bestselling biography, *Parting the Waters: America in the King Years 1954–63*, and in *Walking with Presidents*, Alex Poinsett's biography of Louis Martin. But the story of the African-American vote in 1960 has more than one strand, and the remainder of this chapter documents how Kennedy's support of the East African airlift figured in it.

At the UN General Assembly that fall, seventeen new African nations took their seats. For this and other reasons, including the continuing problems in the Congo, Africa was much in the news; Kennedy during his presidential campaign referred to Africa several hundred times in speeches and question-and-answer sessions, far more than he did to civil rights. "For Kennedy," scholar James Meriwether writes in a recent article, "Africa was the newest frontier, one where he could burnish his Cold War credentials by extolling the need to ensure newly independent Africa was on the side of the West while simultaneously laying the groundwork for being seen as a candidate sympathetic to black Americans."

In his speeches, Kennedy continued to stress his sympathies for Africa, to castigate the Eisenhower State Department for having only a handful of black personnel among its hundreds of U.S. employees in embassies in Africa, and to propose that the next president launch "an American program of 'Education for African Freedom.'"

Meriwether points out that Kennedy advertised much more than Nixon in the black press, and contends that Kennedy "deftly used Africa" in several different ways: dispatching W. Averell Harriman—a large individual donor to the AASF—to the continent for a fact-finding tour; taking up the cause (previously championed by Nixon) of underrepresentation of African-Americans in the U.S. diplomatic corps; and contrasting the Eisenhower administration's contention that it was focused on countering Soviet and Chinese influence in Africa with its refusal to help bring the East African students to the United States to study. Meriwether argues that Kennedy's use of Africa as a wedge issue was politically shrewd, because while white voters might not care much if several hundred Africans attended U.S. colleges, black voters did, and "the airlift offered [Kennedy] a way to support Africa without explicitly engaging the more controversial matter of exactly when African independence should come."

The black press actually started off with a negative impression, not necessarily of Kennedy but of the Democratic Party, which owed those newspapers a debt of between $50,000 and $100,000 for the 1956 campaign. At the insistence of Louis Martin, the African-American journalist who had become the campaign's civil rights point person, this debt was paid off by the Kennedy campaign, which also undertook to buy regular advertising space in the African-American community's newspapers, mostly in big cities, and in *Jet* and *Ebony*.

Kennedy had not been the candidate of choice for many African-Americans because they were mistrustful of his Catholicism; the ministers of most African-American churches were Protestants, and Martin Luther King, Sr., for one, had used Kennedy's Catholicism as part reason for remaining within the Republican fold. His son in 1960 held deliberately to a nonpartisan stance, believing that to publicly embrace one or the other party would not help the cause of civil rights.

Within the black community in 1960, support for civil rights was intertwined with support for Africa, Africans, and the airlift. This had become obvious even to Senator Scott, who, in an explanatory letter to the *Amsterdam News* after the flap on the Senate floor, tried to reassure its readers that his "interest in helping to bring students here from Africa will continue, as will my efforts in connection with civil rights legislation."

On October 12 Kennedy, along with Adam Clayton Powell, Hubert Humphrey, Eleanor Roosevelt, and other Democratic leaders, spoke at a Harlem conference on civil rights, and continued a major theme of his campaign, tying together the need to educate future African leaders in the United States with the need to wipe out discrimination in America.

During this stop in New York City, Kennedy sat with Harry Belafonte in a room in Harlem and they were filmed as they spoke about civil rights and other African-American concerns. Earlier in the year, Belafonte, as Jackie Robinson had, had found the candidate ignorant of black concerns; by now, however, Kennedy had become both knowledgeable and outspoken on African-American issues. Belafonte endorsed him, and a television ad showing them together was run in some Southern cities to significant effect before it was pulled off the air. The explanations for its removal ranged from station owners being concerned about white objections, to the Kennedy campaign being worried about losing the white Southern vote if the ad appealed too strongly for the black vote. White backlash was a major concern for Kennedy, who needed to win some Southern states in order to succeed in the election. Part of the way that Kennedy could achieve both objectives—hold the Southern whites and win important black votes—was to focus on the African students matter rather than solely on the more superheated, more contentious, and less easily solved issue of civil rights. The Kennedy campaign issued several versions of a brochure on "moral leadership" that included a photo of the candidate and Mboya, and a paragraph about Kennedy's position on African affairs.

In mid-October Jackie Robinson was still campaigning for Nixon when the Republican nominee for vice president, Henry Cabot Lodge, Jr., said flatly in a speech that Nixon would have an African-American in his cabinet. This happened in the midst of the National Conference on Constitutional Rights in Harlem, and, Louis Martin remembered, "It hit like a bomb. Of course everybody said, 'That's just cheap politics.'" The press asked Nixon if Lodge's statement was accurate, and the vice president, instead of agreeing with Lodge, said that candidates for the cabinet would be judged on their merits, implying that Lodge spoke only for himself. "This did not sit well with me," Robinson recalled in his autobiography. At the time Robinson continued on the campaign trail, though now with serious misgivings. That Kennedy and his vice presidential candidate, Lyndon Johnson, said the same thing as Nixon had—cabinet aspirants were to be evaluated only on their qualifications—did not lessen Robinson's doubts about Nixon.

Nixon's repudiation of the Lodge remark also did not sit well with Martin Luther King, Jr., or Harris Wofford, according to King biographer Taylor Branch: "Wofford and Martin winced at the underlying reality that this was really a pitch to white voters. Lodge had given Kennedy and Johnson a safe way to attack the Republicans for excessive sympathy for Negroes." King and Kennedy were being pressed to meet publicly, but when King insisted that he would also have to invite Nixon to meet with him, Kennedy backed out. Nonetheless, events impelled them toward one another.

On October 19, a day after King's father had joined with other Atlanta Baptist Union ministers to endorse Nixon, King was arrested as he prepared to sit in at a downtown Atlanta lunch counter. He spent a night in jail—his first ever—because he would not post bond since the other "trespassers" had been unable to do so. A day later he was rearrested. He had previously been convicted and given a suspended sentence for a traffic violation, driving in Georgia with an out-of-date Alabama license while taking a white woman friend, the writer Lillian Smith, to the hospital. Now, because of the new arrest connected to the sit-in, he was considered to have violated the conditions of his suspension, and a judge, ignoring many legal precedents, sentenced him to four months of hard labor in a state prison.

This created a crisis not only for King but also, because of King's celebrity and status, for the presidential candidates. Robinson, Belafonte, and other supporters of King put pressure on both Nixon and Kennedy to help in some way. Robinson was then at a Midwestern hotel with the candidate and his campaign associates. One of them, William Safire, later remembered Robinson arguing adamantly that the vice president "must call Martin, right now, today." After seeing the candidate and making the case, Robinson returned with tears in his eyes and told Safire, "He thinks calling Martin would be 'grandstanding.'" Nixon convinced himself that this was a "local matter" involving the state of Georgia, so he could not directly importune the governor or provide legal assistance to help overturn the judge's ruling.

On the other hand, Senator Kennedy's brother Robert was convinced that the judge's ruling had been quite improper, and Harris Wofford was equally convinced that the candidate could pressure the Democratic governor to do something without losing the support of Georgia's white voters.

Coretta Scott King, six months pregnant and quite worried about her husband, called Wofford for additional help, and he managed to get through to Kennedy and ask him to call her directly. Kennedy did.

Robert Kennedy, learning of this call, turned to Louis Martin and said, "Do you know that three Southern governors told us that if Jack supported Jimmy Hoffa, Nikita Khrushchev, or Martin Luther King, they would throw their states to Nixon? Do you know that this election may be razor thin and that you have lost it for us?" But a few hours later, Robert Kennedy changed his mind and called the judge who had sentenced King to jail, and asked him to release King. The judge did so.

These calls were carefully publicized, at Louis Martin's insistence, only to the black press, because he felt that if the information was generally released the Republicans would try to use it somehow against Kennedy, perhaps by stirring a white backlash. "Daddy King," Martin Luther King, Sr., made an unusual statement, carried by the black press: "I had expected to vote against Senator Kennedy because of his religion. But now he can be my president, Catholic or whoever he is. It took courage to call my daughter-in-law at a time like this. He has the moral courage to stand up for what he knows is right. I've got all my votes and I've got a suitcase, and I'm going to take them up there and dump them in his lap."

Jackie Robinson did not switch his allegiance, but he did use Nixon's refusal to call King as his reason to stop campaigning for the vice president, although he did not make a public announcement about it.

Rather, "I clung to the hope that Nixon would follow through on the things he had indicated were important to him . . . after the pressures of the campaign were over."

The phone calls on behalf of Martin Luther King, Jr., were now publicized by the Kennedy campaign throughout the African-American community, in two million copies of a "blue book" pamphlet that were widely distributed in black churches on the Sunday before election day. However, this last-minute effort, Louis Martin later wrote, was "the icing on the cake," since Kennedy had already "won the endorsement of the black leadership and the rank and file." Those endorsements had been earned through Kennedy's several months' worth of campaigning for civil rights, including his (and Lyndon Johnson's) support for a civil rights plank in the Democratic platform that many African-American leaders characterized as ideal, but above all by Kennedy's actions on behalf of the East African airlift. His willingness to take action, not just to offer verbal support or promises, in the matter of rescuing the 1960 East African airlift was widely appreciated in African-American communities.

The 1960 election was one of the closest in American history. Kennedy won the popular vote by slightly more than 112,000 out of 68 million cast. Voter turnout overall was among the highest ever, at 63 percent of those eligible.

African-American eligible-voter turnout, which in previous elections had been low, increased in 1960, though because of inadequate record keeping it has not been possible to put a definite percentage figure on this increase. It is known that while in 1956 the African-American vote was 61 percent for Stevenson and 39 percent for Eisenhower, and that Eisenhower's percentage of it had increased over that in 1952, in 1960 Kennedy reversed that trend, winning close to 70 percent of African-American votes cast.

Sampling studies of African-American voting patterns showed that voter participation among African-American groups such as inner-city mothers was around 65 percent in 1960, in line with the

overall voter turnout. But the countrywide African-American turnout percentage mixed together the high participation in the North
and low participation in the South. Because of vote-suppression activities, the participation of African-American voters in Alabama,
Mississippi, and South Carolina was below 15 percent and the average
African-American turnout in the entire South was only 30 percent.
This suggests that in the North, African-Americans' voting percentage was well above the national average of 63 percent.

In a half-dozen states critical to Kennedy's Electoral College victory, Kennedy's winning margin was around 1 percent, and it was in
these key states—Illinois, New Jersey, Pennsylvania, Maryland, Delaware, and Missouri—that the African-American vote proved to be
Kennedy's edge. All these states were home to large cities containing
substantial African-American populations—cities also served by influential African-American newspapers that had been reporting
positively for months on Kennedy's involvement with the airlifts.

African-Americans living in large cities of the toss-up states voted
heavily enough for Kennedy to secure his victory in those states, and
the standard prior explanation—that this was due to his and his
brother's phone calls to help Martin Luther King, Jr.—must be re-
vised to include the understanding that his support for the 1960 East
African airlift was equally if not more crucial to his election as president.

Barack Obama, Sr., because of his sterling record at Hawaii,
received two offers of scholarships for a doctoral program in
economics in 1962, a full one from the New School in New York and
a partial one from Harvard University. He chose the latter, and also
chose to leave behind his wife and infant son, since he would not
have enough money to support all three in Cambridge. Mboya had
learned of Obama Sr.'s new marriage, and counseled him by mail not
to abandon his son while moving on. Nonetheless, Obama Sr. moved
to an apartment above Central Square, in the heart of Cambridge,

and became a Harvard campus figure—hanging out in cafés, smoking cigarettes, arguing intensely, and forging a relationship with Ruth Nidesand, a white teacher. Frederick Okatcha, an airlift graduate who today is a psychology professor at Kenyatta University, knew Obama Sr. in those years and recalls, "He had personality and self-confidence. The fact that he was brilliant and well-educated meant he had everything [with which] to impress the girls, despite a different cultural background." Olara Otunnu, who also knew him during his Harvard days, recalled his "incredible charismatic presence, very outgoing, charming, talking—would walk into a room and start joking with everyone, a compelling personality."

Ann Dunham filed for divorce in Hawaii, citing abandonment by her husband. Obama Sr. returned to Kenya in 1965, having earned a master's degree from Harvard and mostly completed a doctorate in econometrics, a subspecialty of economics. Since Kenya had been independent for two years, most government positions were already filled, and he took a job with an oil company. He penned a tough critique of a government white paper on African socialism, a paper issued under the imprimatur of Tom Mboya, then the minister of economic planning and development. African socialism was different from ordinary socialism, Mboya had written elsewhere, quoting Julius Nyerere of Tanganyika in regard to understanding socialism "only as cooperation," and citing another African leader who defined African socialism as "the merciless fight against social dishonesties and injustices." Kenyatta had specifically said that Kenya's brand of African socialism would not include nationalization of key industries. "Sessional Paper No. 10" had been prepared as an answer to the formation of the Lumumba Institute by Odinga and his Soviet friends, and that institute's strong advocacy of leftist economic policies. Mboya's paper had more capitalism in it than traditional socialism.

The Mboya paper was issued on April 29, and Obama Sr.'s article was published in the *East Africa Journal* in July. Today the brilliance

of the Obama Sr. critique is still clear. He poses the correct questions to be asking in the opening years of the republic. "How are we
going to remove the disparities in our country, such as the concen-
tration of economic power in Asian and European hands, while not
destroying what has already been achieved?" This was the most important issue, he asserted, because if the country's income was not
redistributed so that the poorest people of Kenya were able to earn
more money and raise their standard of living, Kenya's self-rule
would become almost meaningless.

> We need to eliminate power structures that have been built
> through excessive accumulation so that not only a few indi-
> viduals shall control a vast magnitude of resources as is the
> case now. . . . The [government] paper says that the principle
> of political equality eliminates the use of economic power as a
> political base. It is strange that the government can say this
> when, wherever we go, in America, in Africa, in Europe, the
> dollar, the pound and the mark have been used as political
> weapons despite professed ideologies.

The best, easiest, and fairest way to redistribute income, Obama
Sr. insisted, was to put land ownership into tribal and individual African hands. The government had been reluctant to do that, contending in its white paper that there were technical problems in promoting
land ownership by tribal cooperatives or by African individuals who
did not have bank accounts. But, Obama Sr. warned, if a readjustment
of the income disparities was not somehow achieved, supposedly
classless new Kenya would continue being the same superrich and
superpoor society as it had been in the hated colonial era. His cogent
and insightful article pointed to a way for Kenya to utilize long-
standing traditions of communal tribal ownership of land as the route
to Africans accumulating wealth and therefore true equality.

In political terms, the Obama Sr. article assisted Mboya because it advocated solutions that Mboya agreed with but that he had been unable to completely promote within the government. With this well-reasoned, outside critique in hand, Mboya was able to press Kenyatta and the rest of the cabinet for more action to address wealth inequalities in Kenya. The paper also served as a reason for Mboya's hiring of Obama Sr. for the Ministry of Economic Planning and Development. Obama Sr. was already disdainful of Shell, according to a telling passage in his article: "Many highly qualified Africans are employed by commercial firms and are given very pompous titles. This is done only for publicity. If one were to go into the workings of these companies, one would find that [the Africans] actually have no voice in the companies which gave them those high titles."

Inside the government, Obama Sr. helped formulate policies that increased "Africanization," such as new rules that permitted only Africans to operate many rural businesses (for example, small plantations), that pressured foreign-run companies to increase the number of their African management employees, and that encouraged and enabled rural individual land ownership. In his work Obama Sr. had the confidence not only of Mboya but also of Vice President Oginga Odinga. According to stories of those who encountered Obama Sr. professionally at that time, he enjoyed being the representative of the ministry in various councils. Ruth Nidesand had pursued him to Kenya, and they married; Obama's children by his Kenyan wife came to live with them, and several other children were born from this union. The days at the Ministry of Economic Planning and Development, according to friends, were the halcyon days of Obama Sr.'s life. He would come back to Kogelo with food for every family in the village, and helped some of its residents obtain government jobs.

All too soon, though, he found himself frustrated by the bureaucracy and in the midst of a political upheaval that affected his position and clout. Odinga attempted to form an opposition party. A resolution was passed that stripped him and twenty-one other members who had previously been elected on a KANU ticket of their seats; Odinga also lost his vice presidency. His removal from the government jeopardized the positions of Obama Sr., as well as Odinga's other Luo protégés.

This 1966 uproar had additional consequences. Mboya's former deputy at the Ministry of Economic Planning and Development, Mwai Kibaki, became minister of commerce and industry, taking the place of one of the MPs forced out of the government. The two ministries' responsibilities overlapped, and according to Otunnu, this was not good for Obama Sr., because, Otunnu says, Obama Sr. and Kibaki had been at odds for years. They had clashed professionally because Obama Sr. had little respect for Kibaki's degree from the London School of Economics. (Others dispute this story, saying that Kibaki—today Kenya's president—and Obama Sr. were actually good friends.) Another problem for Obama Sr. was the rise in the ministry of Philip Ndegwa, who had also been trained as an economist at Harvard as well as at LSE. Ndegwa became the chief planning officer and permanent secretary of the ministry, while Obama Sr. remained without additional bureaucratic titles or the associated power. In such situations, Okatcha observed, Obama Sr.'s brilliance would work against him, since "[i]n developing countries, it is always the brightest people who suffer the most. They are regarded as rebels."

Events beyond Obama Sr.'s control continued to contribute to his difficulties. In 1969, Mboya—who, as Odinga had, had begun to take policy positions in opposition to Kenyatta—was assassinated on a busy Nairobi street, in front of a pharmacy. By chance Obama Sr. was there when it happened. Just moments before the fatal shots, he had had a short, joking conversation with Mboya on that street.

A few months later, Obama Sr. testified at the trial of the alleged assassin, and later came to believe that because he had come forward to testify at the trial he was targeted by Kenyatta and his inner Kikuyu circle, who were accused—in the press, though not in the courts—of having had a hand in the death of Mboya.

In these perilous circumstances, Obama Sr. continued to criticize the government, to publicly contradict Kibaki, Ndegwa, and other high officials in the several finance ministries, and to expose fraud. "He had no fear," Otunnu remembers. If Obama Sr. appeared to some as arrogant, Otunnu and Okatcha viewed his attitude differently. "He would listen carefully to your arguments and then tear into you with facts and figures," Okatcha recalled. "He could be very forthright and that could be annoying to some people." Otunnu and Okatcha also agree that Obama Sr. would have been better and more happily situated in academia, but inside the government and able to affect policy was "the place to be" at that moment in time, as Otunnu points out.

In the early 1970s, Kenyatta personally threw Obama Sr. out of the government. Shortly, Obama Sr. was involved in a car accident that killed his passenger and crippled him permanently. He told friends that people out to get him had staged the accident, an allegation that could not be proved or disproved.

Partially recovered, he made a monthlong visit to see Barack Jr., age ten, and his former wife, who in the preceding decade had married and divorced again. It was an intense reunion, but after it father and son never again saw one another.

A last good period for Obama Sr. began after the deaths of Kenyatta and of his father, Onyango, in 1978–79, which resulted in his obtaining a position in the new Daniel arap Moi government, in the Department of Tourism. Kibaki continued to lead the Ministry of Finance and was now, in addition, vice president under Moi. Family members in Kenya recall this as the time when the Obama Sr. family had money and social status. Nonetheless, old friends like journalist Philip Ochieng, another airlift graduate, saw some deep crevasses behind the happy exterior, problems that occasionally pushed Obama Sr. to drink too much; Ochieng has written that his "drinking buddy" was excessively fond of scotch, as Ochieng adds that he himself was in that era, though that did not detract from his friend's

talents or effectiveness in the ministry. Otunnu, then Uganda's ambassador to the United Nations, worked on several matters with
Obama Sr., and recalls how avidly he followed the UN's activities.
"He was a major public intellectual," Otunnu insists. But he and others who knew Obama Sr. in those years, such as Okatcha and
Ochieng, characterize the Obama Sr. of the 1980s as frustrated, and,
as Otunnu puts it, "set on a descending path that led to the fatal accident in 1982 . . . aggravated by his own flaws."

8

CARE *and* FEEDING

Anticipating a Kennedy administration in late 1960, Frank Montero and Cora Weiss collaborated on a draft of a national plan for the United States to deal with foreign students. It was as blue sky as could be. They called it a "placement" program, meaning that students would be placed in bunches in selected colleges rather than being awarded scholarships as individuals. Placements would entail consultations between a particular college, the foreign country or area from which the students would be chosen, and the U.S. government. Kenya, say, would be given one hundred scholarships by various U.S. colleges, and Kenyan educators would decide which young Kenyans would fill the various collegiate slots. The placement program would be restricted to serving those areas of the world that lacked adequate college-level educational facilities. It would not obviate the traditional exchange programs, which, Montero and Weiss thought, should continue to be made available to the sort of students who sought "to broaden their experience" by attending a U.S. college. Placement students would follow a different educational course, a curriculum tailored to the needs of their home areas, an accelerated program of studies that would "avoid extraneous and unnecessary courses peculiar to American cultural patterns." Colleges would contribute the tuition payments; the U.S. government would provide money for room, board, and books; and private agencies that raised funds from the general public would pay for the students' travel, clothing, and incidental expenses.

It was an ambitious plan based on AASF's successes, but because the atmosphere for the airlifts was changing, the plan's chances of being adopted were low. From the fall of 1960 onward, partly because the Kennedy Foundation insisted, and partly because of the AASF's established ties to the East African students already in the United States, the foundation shifted its efforts to the task of what Cora Weiss refers to as the "care and feeding" of the airliftees. Around this time, Tom Mboya called her the "mother confessor" to the students. The AASF carried on its "mothering" even as the establishment was attempting to undermine, transform, and eliminate the foundation. That dual story is told here and in the following chapter.

While Montero and Scheinman concentrated on fundraising and on finding a way for the AASF to continue, Weiss and Mary Hamanaka dived into the care and feeding of the students— fielding telephone calls, answering letters, and receiving the visits of the East African students who came to New York on vacations or to seek summer jobs. Nearly five hundred students had been assisted by the airlifts program or by Scheinman individually between 1956 and 1960, and from 1960 to 1962 the New York AASF worked individually with nearly all of them in one way or another. The AASF provided counseling on subjects ranging from summer jobs to academic transfers, dating, loneliness, discrimination, and lack of funds.

Brief notations in the files summarize the consultations given by Weiss and Hamanaka: "Medical aid given, placed in summer job." "Considerable correspondence re financial assistance." "Extensive counselling . . . to help in adjustment to American student life." "Guided to self-help. Advised against coming to NYC [from Idaho] for summer employment." "Special clothing sent, provided eye glasses." "Extensive assistance and counselling." "Extra assistance given upon arrival." "Employment arranged at summer camp after much discussion." "Money needed for incidentals." "Financial difficulties discussed by mail and aid given." "Transferred . . . after considerable discussion." "Possible schools suggested for brother proposing to come to USA." "Guidance from older students arranged." "Substantial financial aid given for medical needs after full discussion." "Possible source for financial aid suggested." "Winter clothing sent." "Extensive help and guidance given for adjustment." "Transferred . . . after much counselling." "Guidance during Xmas vacation and adjustment problems."

A Kenyan student at a high school in Kansas had a predicament that was not of his making: A local fund back home, which had given him three hundred dollars, had written his father to ask for it back, not because the son had done anything wrong but because the money was needed desperately there. The alternative was for the father to sell his acre and a half of land. Cora Weiss sent the high school student some money and wrote to Dick Oloo, Mboya's assistant in Nairobi, for help in rectifying the situation.

In that December 1960 letter to Oloo, Cora Weiss estimated that she had already been in touch with 60 percent of that year's students, almost all of the communication initiated by the students; by spring, the percentage that she had dealt with was even higher. "Your kids don't give us a moment of rest," she wrote to Mboya, and summed up the students' worries: inadequate financing, inadequate preparation for life in the United States, wrong choice of schools—she strongly urged that Nairobi send no more students to Philander Smith, or Northeast Missouri State Teachers College, or to a few other schools that had many Kenyans on campus. Many of the Philander Smith Kenyans, she noted, were seeking to transfer out, and at that school as at the others on her do-not-apply list, "the students have nothing but complaints about the academic standards, difficult living conditions . . . discrimination [in Little Rock, and] . . . lack of employment possibilities," and "they also found that the little scholarship help they were given has become even less and is but a token assist in view of the total college expenses."

But she was also able to report some of the "successes." A Northern Rhodesian, Preston Mwenya, was thought of as the brightest student on the Roosevelt University campus. Regina and Lucia at Skidmore were doing well. After an accelerated two-year course, Florence Mwangi was graduating from Smith and heading to the Albert Einstein College of Medicine in New York. Joseph Obudo was president of the freshman class at Lake Forest in Illinois. Sam Okongo was heading to Brandeis for a master's in biology. In Alaska, "Simon Odede has melted icebergs with his charm."

Pamela Odede came to New York for a meeting, and Cora Weiss brought her to be the featured guest on the first broadcast of NBC's *Today* show anchored by John Chancellor. Pamela took one look at the studio's set, which featured a backdrop of mud huts, and was offended at the characterization of Africans. She almost walked off, but Weiss convinced her that the nationwide publicity for the cause was worth enduring a slight. On the air, "Pamela's tact was admirable. It foreshadowed her later career as an ambassador," Weiss recalled.

Frequently, students presented more than one problem for AASF to solve; Frederick Okatcha at Central Missouri State College was industrious enough to cadge an interview with former president Harry Truman, but still needed the fifty dollars AASF sent to get through the semester, and assistance in dealing with the British consulate office in Kansas City. The dean of his college had offered to allow him to attend summer school without tuition, but he felt that he must turn down the offer because he needed to work and make money to see him through the next couple of years. Okatcha had his plans all laid out: complete his bachelor's at the present college, then spend a couple more years at Michigan State, earning an advanced degree in psychology. He had been attending services at the local Episcopal church (according to an article in a local paper that he sent along to Weiss), had joined the psychology club and the international students club, and had been made an honorary member of the local Lions Club in Warrensburg, Missouri. "I do not plan to enter politics since by the time I go back [to Kenya] we shall be independent. But if I was to join politics, I would make a fine politician. Even people in Warrensburg said this," he wrote to Cora Weiss. She arranged a summer job for him, facilitated his early transfer to Michigan State, and squeezed out two more checks for him over six months. Shortly, he had his sights set on Yale for his doctorate. In New York, going for a drink to the West End bar, a hangout for expat East Africans, Okatcha became reacquainted with Barack Obama Sr., who was on his way to Harvard.

Perez Malende Olindo, now also a Warrensburg student and Okatcha's roommate, was serious and talented. Everyone at the college who came in touch with him was impressed by him and tried to help him. He was trained as an audiovisual technician so he could earn money to supplement his savings. He also needed the sixty dollars that the AASF could send him and the five- and ten-dollar payments that he collected for doing household chores for various professors. Then, as Olindo later recalled, something very strange and worrisome happened. I received a letter from a judge of the United States Tax Court! Since all foreign students entered America on student visas, which precluded the taking up of any paying employment during our stay in the United States of America, I immediately thought that the American government had discovered that I had been working on campus . . . at the Audiovisual Department! I feared that this would be the beginning of my repatriation back to Kenya!

Judge Russell E. Train was one of the United States' leading environmentalists and would later become head of the Environmental Protection Agency; his inquiry to Olindo had nothing to do with visas and everything to do with furthering the young man's career. It soon led to Olindo's becoming the first African recipient of a scholarship from the African Wildlife Leadership Foundation, a group underwritten by contributions from American importers of African flora and fauna. "I felt that the God whom I worship had touched me!" Olindo later recalled. The scholarship could be used for his current college, the foundation told him, but they gently suggested that he transfer to an institution that offered more wildlife-conservation-focused classes, Michigan State University, where he could train under Dr. George Petrides. Olindo was ecstatic at the idea.

The dropout rate for the East African students in U.S. colleges was relatively low compared to that of the American-born college students, perhaps 2 percent, most of the dropouts returning to Kenya because of personal or family problems. Now and then, Cora Weiss had to arrange their return transport. Her saddest task was occasioned by a roadside "accident" near Lincoln University; one of the half-dozen East African airlift students at Lincoln, Naftali Gichaba, was killed by a passing automobile. His friends believed that there should have been a more thorough investigation into the circumstances, but this notion was not pursued by the authorities. Accompanied by Haron Andima, who had met Gichaba at the Krims' house, and by other Kenyan students in the New York area, Cora Weiss had to arrange for Gichaba's body in its simple pine box to be put into the cargo dock of a plane to Kenya, where the young man would be buried. An image of the plastic flowers that Kenyan students brought to accompany the pine box remains indelibly fixed in her mind.

While the New York office of the AASF was busy with its care and feeding, and as the Nairobi office was dealing with nearly a thousand requests for transport from East African students in 1961, a challenge to the AASF's basic principles and methods arrived in the form of an IIE "Survey of the African Student." During 1960, drafts of a preliminary study had gone back and forth from the IIE to the AASF, and in early 1961 a ninety-thousand-dollar IIE grant to a Michigan survey organization got the survey rolling. The results and the interpretation of those results became bones of contention between the AASF and the other organizations in the foreign-student-aid field, and provided a rationale to the others for putting even more pressure on the AASF to change its ways or get out of the picture.

The numbers gleaned by the survey were of intrinsic interest. Of the 60,000 foreign students at U.S. educational institutions, about 1,500 from sub-Saharan Africa (excluding South Africa) were in the United States, attending some 366 colleges. An impressive two-thirds of these 1,500 students filled out the 65-subject multiple-choice questionnaire, and the polling organization did follow-up interviews with 208 students and 112 administrators on 43 campuses. Questions ranged from "Do you live with a white person?" to "How much information did you have about the U.S. before selecting the U.S. as a place to study?" and "How satisfied are you with the education you have been receiving in the U.S.?"

A quarter of the sub-Saharan students came from Nigeria and another quarter from Kenya—the latter almost all as a result of the airlifts. Most of the students were male, single, and older than the usual American college student, had attended church-related schools in their native countries, and had learned English in secondary school.

A high proportion of those interviewed reported having academic difficulties, but many of these were in their first year in the United States, and students who had been in residence longer reported better grades in their classes. Socially the Africans also had difficulties, the most puzzling to them being the indifference of African-American students in both historically black and integrated colleges. Three-quarters of the respondents answered that they had been discriminated against on a regular basis, though more often off campus than on campus, and by people other than course instructors. Most had found racial discrimination "worse than expected." Nearly all were planning to return home after graduation; a third believed they would become teachers, no matter what their academic emphasis, and a fifth thought they would go into the civil service. They admired American "friendliness," "industriousness," "informality," and "interest in the individual." Students with more American friends rated the United States higher in their esteem than those with fewer or with no American friends.

The AASF objected to certain sections of the interpretation as slanted, inaccurate, or simply insensitive. One was the IIE's assertion that there was "no relationship between the extent of a student's financial problems and his grades." Letters in the AASF file said just the opposite: Students who had to spend many hours working at outside jobs to provide themselves with needed cash complained that the time thus spent cut into their study hours and negatively affected their grades. A second objectionable IIE assertion was the opinion that some students' confusion as to which courses to take could be traced, in part, to "the absence of a definite plan at home for the specific use of a U.S.-trained individual after his return." This was sheer nonsense. In Ghana, Nkrumah had jobs waiting for every Ghanaian who had graduated from an American college, and the East Africans had all been guaranteed jobs upon their return by Mboya, Nyerere, and similar leaders—contingent, of course, on their sponsors being in power at the time of the return.

In sum, the IIE survey was interesting but premature insofar as the experiences of the majority of the East African airlifted students were concerned, since the bulk of them were still in their first year at an American academic institution. Just how wrong the report was, in terms of underestimating the potential of the students and their ability to absorb the education being given to them, would not be known until more time had passed—a few years in the case of some of the students, decades for others.

Miriam Khamadi, the Butere school graduate who arrived in the United States in 1960, was a good example. Although she was attending the small Quaker institution William Penn College, in Iowa, within a few years she had her poetry published in the *Beloit Poetry Journal* in an issue that also featured Raymond Carver, later a noted short-story writer. Upon returning to Kenya, under her married name, Miriam Were, she taught science and health at secondary schools and simultaneously took an advanced degree in education at Makerere. In 1968 she decided to leave teaching and study medicine because, she later wrote, "too many students in her classes were sick." After receiving a medical degree from Nairobi University, she went on to take another medical degree from Johns Hopkins, as well as a master's and doctorate in public health. Returning once more to Kenya, she became a foremost AIDS researcher and activist, and an advocate for better health care for women throughout the African continent. Her work in these areas has won her commendations from Great Britain, Japan, Italy, and other countries, as well as numerous citations for excellence from Kenya. She is also the author of four novels and a biography of an earlier women's health advocate in Africa.

Typical of the underassessment of potential that characterized the IIE study—and, for that matter, the evaluations of Kenneth D. Luke and others who looked askance at the airlift students in those years—are the accomplishments of the various students who began at Philander Smith in Little Rock. Most of them transferred and, once in other environments, thrived. Peter Muia Makau went to the New School in New York, where he remained for years until obtaining a PhD in economics, after which he returned to Kenya and worked as an economist, taught at Kenyatta University, and wrote influential papers about Kenya's investment and banking practices. Joseph Maitha ended up at the University of Buffalo for a doctorate; like Barack Obama, Sr., Maitha studied the then-new field of econometrics, applying its analysis to the coffee industry in Kenya. The first African fellow of the U.S. National Bureau of Economic Research, sponsored by the Rockefeller Foundation, Maitha specialized in production economics. In Kenya, he became acting dean of the faculty at the University of Nairobi, then the chancellor of Kenyatta University as well a director of the African Development Research Foundation. George Samuel Okello-Obong won his doctorate at the University of Kansas, also in economics, and later worked as an economist for the United Nations. Haron Andima also continued through to a doctorate. Today, when asked about his and the others' starts at Philander Smith, he shrugs and says, "We did what we had to in order to go up and out."

That attitude characterized many East Africans who began their American schooling at institutions not primarily known for academic achievement. About two-thirds of them would transfer at least once before gaining their bachelor's degrees.

Many moved on with the AASF's help. Sam Okello Onyango transferred from Morgan State to Brooklyn College, where he completed his bachelor's degree in economics, then a master's in mathematics, and joined the faculty. He was "thorough, demanding, and endlessly available to students," a colleague later recalled. Gerald

Mahinda transferred from Voorhees Junior College, a historically black school in South Carolina, to Trinity University in San Antonio to study accounting, on his way to a career in the upper ranks of business. Joseph Kapela, whom the AASF had already assisted in transferring from another historically black school, Alcorn A & M in Mississippi, to Wisconsin State, transferred a second time to Kansas State, where he found a home on the college's soccer team, which featured fifteen players from fifteen different nations. Oliver Mbata transferred several times as well, from Alcorn to Foothill to the University of Wisconsin and then to Oregon State for a master's degree in agricultural economics. Johnstone Muthiora moved steadily eastward from California Polytechnic State University to other schools until he received his doctorate in political science from a Washington, D.C., area college. Boniface Nyaggah, who had been at a junior college in the San Francisco area, did well enough to transfer to Berkeley and set his sights on a doctorate in history. Kamuti Kiteme completed his studies at Fairleigh Dickinson, then took a master's in education at Bank Street College and a doctorate at Yeshiva University before joining the faculty at the City College of New York, where he became a mainstay of the African studies program until his retirement, after which he returned to Kenya to continue helping students there.

Augustine Ingutia, known as Gus, was one of the students sponsored by Martin Luther King, Jr., for his early college days at Atlanta University. Ingutia had known about King before coming to the United States, found out more about him in Atlanta, and wrote him that he hoped one day to be in the audience to hear one of his sermons. "We—all that believe in equal human dignity—will unite behind you, whether we be in the troubled Africa, Europe, Asia, or in the segregated South." The AASF helped Ingutia transfer to a college that more suited his restless intellect. He still needed money, though, writing that when the snow disappeared in Wisconsin, so did his earnings as a snow shoveler. His clothes were so tattered, he wrote, that he felt "ridiculous" in standing before a professor in class, but felt he could not buy new clothes "lest I be left with [not] enough to buy a sandwich or a hot dog. . . . I am actually a very hardworking student both academically and manually and this is why I am still surviving." He asked Cora Weiss not to be "exasperated" with his list of problems, because "I am like a patient who is explaining my illness status to a physician." Ingutia's graduate thesis was a sociological and demographic analysis of the Kenyan population, but as he continued in the United States he felt a great kinship with African-Americans and with union-organizing efforts. A follower of Odinga, Ingutia could quote as easily from him as from the Bible, a friend later said. Unable to find academic employment in the United States, he moved to Ontario, Canada, and began to work his way toward tenure at Seneca College. Eventually, he recruited his brother, a lawyer, to follow him to Ontario.

When the airlift students found or transferred to an amenable venue, they usually did well there academically and in their later careers. James Reuben Olembo, an agricultural economics student from the extreme western province of Kenya, attended Purdue, emerging with a doctorate in agriculture. Then he returned home to teach and to help found, in 1972, the United Nations Environmental Programme, one of the UN's most successful international assistance efforts. Olembo stayed with UNEP and rose to the rank of assistant secretary-general. He and his wife, Norah K. Olembo, who had trained first in Great Britain, became Kenya's reigning experts on biodiversity, and worked with villagers in remote areas to diversify their crops in order to gain income and stability.

Similarly, Michael George Okeyo took his bachelor's and master's in public administration at Berkeley before joining the Kenya diplomatic corps, where he rose up the ladder in various embassies around the world, and at UN headquarters in New York, until being appointed as Kenya's ambassador to the UN in the 1980s. Zackary Onyanko took three degrees in economic planning at Syracuse

University before returning to Kenya and working directly for Jomo Kenyatta as one of the youngest ministers in the new government. Elected to Parliament in 1969, "Dr. Z," as he was known, also served as the leader of several different ministries until his death in 1996.

In addition to speaking or corresponding with students, the AASF conducted quite a bit of correspondence with collegiate officials, deans, provosts, and foreign-student advisers. Before the Christmas holidays in 1960, an inquiry letter from Cora Weiss was sent to hundreds of colleges, asking if arrangements had been made to assist the East African students who were likely going to remain on campus during the break, and suggesting that the schools help these students to spend time with American families. The letter produced a flood of responses, almost all reporting that the schools had made or would now make such arrangements.

In more than a dozen instances, these letter exchanges between the AASF and the colleges spurred the institutions to keep in closer touch with foreign students about future holiday seasons. As a result, various professors and their families each took charge of a visiting African so that he or she would not be alone and without meals in an otherwise-empty dorm. Barnard's foreign-student adviser got the message, reporting that their East African student, Hamida Butt, would stay in her dorm but would be spending a lot of time in the library, studying—a "wise" decision, "because her academic program has been rather difficult for her and she is, of course, anxious to make a good record this term." The chaplain at McGill, in Toronto, surprised the AASF with his report that he had recently presided at the marriage of the student under his charge to "a charming bride also from Kenya." The president's office at McMaster University in Ontario reported to the AASF more offers of hospitality from the community than there were foreign students available to accept them. "Lucia Muthusi is spending ten days of her holidays with a

Skidmore student and the remainder with a family in Schenectady," the Skidmore dean reported. Lucia's roommate, Regina Katungulu, came to the Weiss home, where she had previously stayed during an illness. While in New York Regina met Philip Ndibo, another air-liftee, and they fell in love and planned to marry once they returned to Kenya. From Mount Hermon, the prep school that Montero had once attended, came word that the Kenyan there would remain on campus during the holiday break and do paid work: "In this way he will be able to earn some money and be with people who have an in-terest in him." Similar letters about East African students doing paid work through the holidays came from dozens of colleges, along with admiring words about the students' industry and persistence.

Having an African on campus was increasingly taken as reason for a school to widen its horizons. The provost of Xavier College in Cincinnati, after assuring Cora Weiss that his two charges would be well cared for, told the story of how, after a visiting lecturer had made snide remarks about the "African turmoil," the two East Afri-cans at Xavier complained to their dean, who arranged for them to present their views "at an exactly similar student convocation" and to have that presentation covered on the front page of the *Cincinnati Enquirer* and on local television. "Most of all," the provost summed up, "we were delighted to have them experience at first hand the freedom of American ways."

Other interchanges presaged arrangements for future years; Ithaca College reported (without being asked) that it was going to award two additional scholarships for Tanganyikans the following year, and hoped that AASF would be able to transport the recipients.

The students were chronically short of funds. Cora Weiss spent a lot of time doling out small amounts of AASF money—in response to urgent pleas—$25 here, $50 there, almost always less than $100. By June 1961, she reported to the AASF board, some $37,000 had been spent in this manner since the fall of 1959. She was also able to report that of the 500 East African students airlifted to the United

States, AASF had been able to place 186 of them in summer jobs in 1961 through the assistance of friends in various cities, with the help of organized labor—Maida Springer unearthed a few jobs in the hotel unions—and by nudging college administrations to assist their charges.

In 1958 John Marangu had been a student at the religious-run Kaaga boarding school in the Meru area, on the slopes of Mount Kenya, when Leah walked into his life—literally, having hiked the twenty miles from her home to attend the secondary school. Her father, a Methodist preacher, had been the most educated man in his community, she recalled, but he had only a third-grade education and her mother was adamantly opposed to Leah being educated. "The more I tried to go to school, the more I was challenged by my mother," she would later tell an American lecture audience. "I had to go to school either in the morning or in the afternoon and spent the rest of the day fetching firewood or water." Nonetheless, when the examinations were given, she was one of only two students to excel, beating out those who had attended school for the full day. Her mother still opposed her further education, so she took training and worked as a nurse, organizing maternity clinics and doing other jobs to accumulate the money for her schooling. Only then could she walk the twenty miles to Kaaga, which was run by the Nazarenes, another Protestant sect.

Leah and John married, and John won a place on the 1960 airlift to attend Olivet Nazarene University in Illinois. Leah worked as a nurse in the Meru area until she could win a place on the next airlift and join him. Good students, they completed their bachelor's degrees at Olivet and went together to study at Iowa State, he in genetics, she in home economics.

She later recalled that John would frequently attend to the children, and even cook, so that she could go to her classes and study. "For an African man this was very hard because many don't believe

in going into the kitchen," she explained. The couple also had to
fend off criticism from fellow Africans that Leah was pursuing degrees in an unseemly attempt to compete with her husband.

In the 1970s the Marangus taught in various American universities, including Michigan State and NYU, until 1977, when they
were both recruited for a new college in Kenya, Kenyatta University,
where both became heads of their respective departments. Leah was
the first woman in Kenya to lead a department of a major university,
and then the first woman to head a "parastatal," the Jomo Kenyatta
Foundation. She also founded the Home Economics Association of
Kenya and became a well-known advocate for women and girls. Her
motto was: "A Kenyan woman looks at herself, appreciating who she
is as a woman, not imitating the male aspect of being. We must not
apologize to be women."

After a Fulbright scholarship and another stint at teaching in
U.S. colleges in the late 1980s, she returned to Kenya and took charge
of the development of the country's textbooks. While Leah was
filling that position, she and John helped found a new university,
the African Nazarene University, an hour's drive from downtown
Nairobi. Leah and John assisted in the design of the building and its
landscaping, an oasis of flora in an expanse of grassy savannah. ANU
provides an alternative to the secular universities in Kenya. She is
ANU's vice-chancellor, the equivalent of president of the university,
the first woman to head a university in Africa. Kenya also awarded
her its highest civilian decoration, the Silver Star.

9

A LOGICAL EVOLUTION

The African American Students Foundation has no desire to perpetuate itself. Just as soon as more powerful public and private interests in this country accelerate their programs, the Foundation feels it will have fulfilled its role" and would cease operating, a 1960 policy statement avowed. That was why, on the eve of John F. Kennedy's taking office as president, the AASF had been willing to make the logical evolution to focusing on the care and feeding of students already transported to the United States. The board fully expected that the U.S. government would soon take over the program and handle the flood of African students seeking higher education in America.

Kennedy's victory was accompanied by solid Democratic majorities in the House and Senate, and did bring to Washington a new liberalism and a sense of hope that engendered many new programs and ideas. The Peace Corps was one, and a main area of opportunity for it was Africa. Democratic Senator Frank Church, a Kennedy supporter, made a fact-finding tour of Africa and came back to stress to the Senate the "urgent need for education in Africa." A high-ranked officer in the U.S. Office of Education agreed, suggesting that American universities ought to be training ten thousand African students per year and "should establish a revolving loan fund for 'educational investments' in Africa," something Kennedy had advocated in prepresidential speeches and that the AASF enthusiastically supported. The State Department, under Kennedy, was in hands presumed to be more friendly to third-world countries, including those of newly appointed Undersecretary of State Chester Bowles.

The AASF kept up the pressure by noting publicly that while State was making available the scholarships that Eisenhower had promised to Guinea, the first thirty-five—the only ones awarded in the program's first year—were being given to students chosen not by Guineans but by the African-American Institute, which arrangement, the Guinean educators let the AASF know, displeased them. And East Africa and Central Africa were still not in the State educational scholarship program to any significant degree.

Partly because of the expectation of support from the Kennedy administration, and partly because the airlifts had become a large operation that cried out for greater regularization in its handling, in the early days of 1961 pressure built on the AASF to change its ways. The AASF would have to either agree to some alteration in its seat-of-the-pants operation or yield control of the airlifts to mainstream organizations that would obtain their money from the government rather than from the private sector.

By early January 1961, the U.S foreign-student establishment had already begun to extend existing government and big-university plans for educating Africans. Some of their gains were at the expense of the AASF and of students from the East African territories still under colonial control. That month the African-American Institute, the Institute for International Education, the Phelps Stokes Fund, and the Dean David Henry "African Program of Cooperating with U.S. Colleges" drafted a statement on how they were going to cooperatively bring over lots of African students to be educated in the United States. The AASF had not been invited to their meeting, and decided not to make any immediate public comment about the draft statement until the foundation's African directors could evaluate it. The refusal to comment was because the details of the new program alarmed the AASF. Its emphases were wrong—the new program would overspend on bureaucracy while paying scant attention to the wishes of the Africans, sponsors and students alike. As Cora Weiss complained to a correspondent in Canada, the State-funded program to bring over the Guineans had already wasted so much money on administration and selection "that if we had this money we could bring over 500 students for the same amount." In the Dean Henry program's first year, it had awarded twenty-four scholarships, all to Nigerians. The AASF could applaud that these students had been chosen partly by Nigerians, that the Nigerian government had paid for their transport to the United States, and that the scholarships were renewable and all-expenses-paid—but twenty-four was still a small number, and Nigeria was only one country out of a large continent with many countries. Cora Weiss was equally upset at the Dean Henry program's use of $100,000 from the Carnegie Foundation merely for administrative purposes to run their million-dollar program, which aimed in its second year at bringing over only two hundred students from the entire continent of Africa. "We brought 280 students for $100,000 all inclusive," she observed. Moreover, she noted, the State programs made little sense in terms of proportionality—a few hundred proposed Guinean students from a population of two million, but none from Angola with a population of four million or from Mozambique with a population of six million.

To get a reading from the AASF's African board members, Frank Montero flew to East Africa right in the middle of the Kenyan election ferment in early 1961. Mboya, though busy trying to get himself elected, had arranged a meeting in Nairobi of the Pan-African Freedom Movement in East and Central Africa. At the meeting, Montero spoke with the movers and shakers of PAFMECA, the four who were African board members of the AASF—Mboya of Kenya, Nyerere of Tanganyika, Kenneth Kaunda of Northern Rhodesia, and Joshua Nkomo of Southern Rhodesia—as well as Hastings Banda of Nyasaland. All five told Montero that, having been exposed to the new State-backed initiatives, they still very much wanted the AASF program to continue. PAFMECA issued an official resolution reaffirming the need for more airlifts "in the wake of preparation for independence" of their member countries. Moreover, the South African United Front and the Union of the Peoples of Angola were requesting that their students be included in the airlifts program as soon as was practical.

Ten days after the Kennedy inauguration, the IIE, the AAI, Phelps Stokes, and the Dean Henry group invited the AASF and the United Negro College Fund (UNCF) to a meeting in New York to form the "cooperative council" that the IIE and the Dean Henry group had already attempted to establish by fiat. The UNCF was invited because it had applied to the State Department for money to assist African students at its member colleges, and the cooperative council hoped to subsume it under its umbrella. AASF was invited because it could no longer be ignored. Cora Weiss attended the meeting and reported back to the AASF board that each of the agencies, with the exception of the UNCF and the AASF, was already the recipient of a State grant—it was announced at the meeting that the IIE was receiving another $100,000, for example. She worried that the proposed cooperative council's objective was too vague and that it would become

> another organization which will get bogged down with the normal problems of committees, administration, and with the concern about creating more standards for evaluation of students. . . . It seems heavily influenced by the principles of the Dean Henry Program which in many ways are antithetical to the original guiding philosophy which has made for our successful airlifts.

Nonetheless, the AASF board understood that the AASF would have to join, but fretted that if these other agencies stepped in, they would not—perhaps could not, because of their ties to State—adhere to the AASF's cardinal principles of ceding to Africans the decisions on which students to transport, and to taking students from non-self-governing territories. The cooperative council wanted the selection decisions made by American universities, not by Africans who had obtained their own scholarships, and by those universities' American representatives in consultation with Africans of their own choosing. Also, many non-self-governing areas would be excluded from the program.

Montero visited Kenya, Tanganyika, Uganda, Zanzibar, and Northern and Southern Rhodesia, seeing nearly everyone associated with education and the airlifts, including parents of students that the AASF had airlifted in previous years. "Everywhere I went I was constantly besieged by young Africans who wanted to find a way of getting an American education," he wrote in a summary report. After conversations with Nyerere and other leaders, he estimated a "gap" of a thousand or more between the number of qualified students that the U.S. government (and its contractor agencies) was prepared to handle in 1961 and the number that were qualified and ready to come. Montero reported that he had been repeatedly told that if the United States was not ready to address that gap, it would "certainly be bridged by scholarship assistance from Iron Curtain countries which have tremendously increased their aid. It is in the areas [of Africa] where [the United States has] done the least that the Soviet bloc educational programs have had their greatest response."

The Soviet bloc was working harder than ever to sway Africans. A March 1961 *Christian Science Monitor* article listed more than fifty Soviet-bloc and Red Chinese projects being carried out during a single month on the African continent, including radio broadcasts in English and Swahili aimed at Kenya, Uganda, and Tanganyika, and caravans ferrying students from various African countries toward Moscow.

Summing up his official report, which he presented to the press in a news conference in New York upon his return, Montero quoted an "African leader" as imploring, "The United States must make a more determined effort to see African need through African eyes," and called on the Kennedy administration to implement a plan that Kennedy had proposed prior to the election—an American program to educate Africans, undertaken in partnership with African nations and leaders. Mboya wrote to President Kennedy directly, on May 2, 1961, asking for the government to underwrite the 1961 charters, because the airlift "remains the most significant and meaningful thing in all our relations with the United States so far," and, as he had in the past, raising the specter of the Communist countries stepping in to educate the students if the United States did not.

The Kennedy administration had to tread carefully in dealing with what was still the colony of Kenya, because events in the former Belgian Congo were affecting the political situation all throughout East Africa. During the second half of 1960 there had been a sobering tragedy. Prime Minister Patrice Lumumba had drawn closer to Moscow after his appeals for help from the United States went mostly unanswered. In July, when the mineral-rich province of

Katanga had attempted to secede, Lumumba's pleas had brought in UN monitors but also Soviet troops; neither contingent had been able to stem the killings, rioting, and looting that threatened to dissolve the country into complete chaos. The president of the Congo dismissed Lumumba and announced a successor as prime minister; Lumumba fought back, but was arrested by Colonel Joseph Mobutu's men as they completed a CIA-backed coup that swept up both Lumumba and his successor. In mid-January 1961, Lumumba and two political compatriots were shot to death by a Belgian-controlled firing squad. That an uprising in the Congo could unleash the forces of the USSR, the UN, a CIA-backed usurpation of a democratically elected regime, and a great deal of violence deeply affected both Kenya's progress toward self-rule and the incoming Kennedy administration's foreign policy toward Kenya.

The Congo chaos also had the effect of making the British more reluctant to release Kenyatta from his confinement even as Kenya's elections proceeded in February. The airlift played a part in those elections. Mboya was running for representative from the Nairobi East district, which contained many Kikuyus as well as Luos and members of a dozen smaller tribes. Since a great many of those who would be casting votes in this election were illiterate, each candidate was to have a symbol to enable the nonliterate to identify and vote for their choice. A particularly obese and obnoxious "European reactionary," as Mboya characterized him, drew out of the hat a hippopotamus, which Mboya thought was laughingly appropriate, but he himself was more fortunate, drawing out the icon of an airplane. It was the perfect symbol. "By this happy chance," he later wrote, "I was able to dramatize the work I and my colleagues had done for Kenya students" in the airlifts. The symbol also spurred him to hire a plane to trail election banners above his rallies. One read VOTE TOM NDEGE MBOYA, *ndege* being the Swahili word for "airplane," and another, UHURU NA NDEGE (freedom via airplane).

A nasty rumor had been circulated claiming that Mboya had

made a pact with London to become a leader of the eventual black-controlled government and to keep Kenyatta in prison; to deny this, Mboya had to issue a statement in which he also pledged not to participate in any new government unless it was led by Kenyatta. In early 1961, prior to the election of the representatives, Mboya attempted to lead KANU into a three-day national general strike in support of Kenyatta's release, but was blocked by the Odinga faction. After this infighting was resolved, the election was held and Mboya won easily, polling fifteen times as many votes as his nearest rival.

The settler party continued to hold power, though it did not represent the 65 percent of the population that had voted for Mboya and other KANU candidates. Accordingly, in May 1961 the KANU party announced the formation of a shadow cabinet. It included Mboya as the shadow minister for defense and internal security, Kiano as the shadow minister of finance, and Njiiri as a shadow undersecretary for information and broadcasting. It was expected that if a general election eventually put KANU in power, then these men would take up the actual cabinet portfolios. The press statement accompanying the list of shadow cabinet members, written by Mboya, decried the victory speech of the new governor, which "contained the usual pious hopes, intimidation and threats and a touch of blackmail [but] failed to realistically analyze the country's present dilemma." Kenyatta remained in "restriction."

In the early summer of 1961 the IIE-led cooperative council idea steamed ahead, with the heft of the State Department behind it—including the $100,000 of State Department funds that Kennedy had ordered released for the airlift. Shortly, the establishment press fell into line, praising the new program. In an editorial, *The New York Times* approved it as benefiting students from all over Africa and being "soundly based, carefully thought-out," and a welcome contrast to the previous "crash program . . . that contained more 'crash' than 'program.'" Although the AASF was not specifically named in the editorial, there was no doubt about the reference, and Scheinman began to answer the charges with a long letter culminating in a plea: "Rather than condemn the thousands of Africans and Americans who have produced more results (not publicity) than any other program, *The New York Times* and others might do well to inquire whether present Government programs are spending funds wisely, and in accordance with African wishes." This letter was not sent; instead, a less strident response by Cora Weiss found its way into the *Times'* letters-to-the-editor column. "No one could disagree with your editorial endorsement" of the new plan, she wrote, but she also pointed out that the new program constituted "education for the elite" and did nothing to ameliorate "one of Africa's paramount development problems . . . the failure to provide support for that tiny elite with adequate numbers of college and technical-school graduates." She asserted that the AASF had done more for Africans with one-sixth the new organization's budget, and that in addition it had accomplished things the new program would not do, such as locating summer jobs for the students and finding them living accommodations near those jobs. The help that African students needed, her letter concluded, must be furnished by "a variety of approaches."

The media barrage continued with a salvo from *Time*, which in previous years had also been very supportive of AASF efforts; now it called them "pell-mell" and contended that the Dean Henry program provided a "tidy contrast," lauding the notion of students in that program spending eight days crossing to New York on a transatlantic steamer, during which time they were given an intensive orientation course.

From the AASF point of view there were many things wrong with the "new cooperative program" of the Ivy League and top-tier universities. It provided opportunities for fewer African students than AASF had done, because the new program awarded only full scholarships. It excluded students who had obtained their own scholarships and in other ways did little for the cause of self-help, pushing to the background students who had scrimped and saved for their college expenses in favor of "the best and the brightest." It obviated the largesse of the second- and third-tier colleges in the United States that had granted hundreds of scholarships to East Africans, bypassing those in favor of sending handfuls of students to top-tier institutions with multimillion-dollar endowments that could each easily afford to grant a few scholarships apiece.

There was an additional problem with the establishment approach, one that the AASF did not stress in its letters to the editor (or in Mboya's articles, such as one in *The Atlantic*). The AASF's dedication to helping colonial territories toward independence necessitated, anticipated, and encouraged the eventual return home of all the airlifted students, knowing they would be needed in the early years of their new countries. But the Dean Henry program, like most foreign-student programs in the United States, would almost surely produce graduates who would opt to remain in the United States, with its wealth of opportunities for educated people. Mboya, Kiano, and Njiiri had extracted pledges from the Kenyan students to return home and help Kenya as a concomitant of accepting AASF aid to reach America. Scheinman and his colleagues in New York were equally dedicated to the principle of the mandated return of the students. The State Department and David Henry programs, U.S. based and funded, could not expect such promises.

Scheinman was "exhausted," he confided to friends, and had to cut back on his financial and time commitments to the airlift program. Montero was similarly depleted. Moreover, it had become increasingly clear that the Kennedy Foundation no longer wanted to be involved in the airlifts and preferred that they be managed by State, through the new cooperative council group.

That group, now named the Council for Education Cooperation with Africa (CECA), would operate from the IIE offices, and Al Sims would be its acting chairman. The AASF had managed to shoehorn into the new group's "statement of principles" the tenet that "U.S. study and training opportunities for Africans throughout the continent must be expanded . . . and that U.S.-sponsored exchange programs should be planned with due regard to African educational, social, and economic needs as defined by competent authorities in Africa." Another indication of AASF principles penetrating the bureaucracy came in a statement issued by the International Cooperation Administration (ICA), a State Department grantee organization that contracted with American universities for scholarships and other educational services. The ICA, in what the Ford Foundation labeled a "new departure," was officially recognizing that "general undergraduate education may be as important to the emerging African nations in this stage of their development as the training of steel mill technicians may be at a later stage."

However, the IIE had succeeded in establishing principles for CECA that the AASF had long fought against but now had to accept: that African applicants for U.S. scholarships "should be carefully evaluated with respect to their academic and personal qualifications by a group of persons well qualified in education," and that the conclusions of the evaluators should be made available to the U.S. colleges prior to their granting scholarships. In practical terms, this meant that the AASF could no longer prevent Sims and Hagberg from going to Nairobi to officially assist Mboya, Kiano, and Njiiri in allocating places for the 1961 airlift, using somewhat stricter evaluation procedures that had more in common with the Dean Henry program than with the AASF's.

At the AASF's insistence, Hagberg, who was now more sympathetic to the program, was made the leader of the selection committee rather than Sims. The three Kenyans of that committee, largely caught up in the ferment attendant on Kenyatta's release from confinement and the impending national elections, acquiesced in the whole process. Everything on the Kenya side of the panel was folded into the organization that Mboya and his associates had founded as the Kenya Educational Trust, which would now be called the Kenya Educational Fund (KEF) and would include CECA as a member. As evidence of the importance of KEF, when Kenyatta was finally released, his first public appearance was at a KEF fundraising rally at Nairobi Stadium with Mboya.

During their stay in Nairobi this time, Hagberg and Sims became advocates of the need to educate more than the "best and brightest," and of what the AASF had managed to do in the past. Nonetheless, the AASF in New York became so concerned about the priorities and practices of the new selection panel, and particularly about the deteriorating ability of the Kenyans to cooperate with one another and with that panel, that Cora Weiss was dispatched to Nairobi. Once there, as she expected, she was accused by Hagberg and Sims of meddling. But she also confirmed the New York office's fears that the tougher selection process was going to result in fewer students for the 1961 airlift. "I wanted the [Kenyans] to know that while we were cooperating fully in the present program we nonetheless did so with the regret that it was as small as it is and wanted [them] to know that we had fought unsuccessfully for a program considerably larger in scope," as she later explained in a letter to Hagberg. She traveled with Mboya and four other Kenyan men to an outdoor rally at which Mboya was to address a large gathering of Kikuyu women. The talk in the car was of politics and history. "One guy in the car was really being sponsored by Red China, another by Russia, and Tom by people in the United States," Weiss recalls. When they arrived at the village, they were taken to a room above an Asian's store, where a feast had been laid out; Weiss protested that they should skip the food and speak to the women, who had been waiting for them for hours, but the men (and the hosts) insisted on having the meal first. The crowd seemed not to mind. "It was an extraordinary experience," Weiss said recently. "Only one other white person was there, and he was from the British Special Branch. The women adored Tom and listened very closely to what he had to say."

While in Nairobi and Dar es Salaam she was able to institute a program, through the Reverend Dana Klotzle and the Unitarian Universalist Association in Boston, to secure high school positions and scholarships for a dozen East African students whose academic credentials were not yet at the college-admissions level. The Unitarians were going to pay for extras such as medical insurance and care during summer vacations. The number of students in the 1961 airlift was about the same as in 1960, but a larger proportion of them would attend high schools rather than colleges.

During the following year, the numbers rose a bit and there was even greater IIE, AAI, and State Department involvement in the selection process. By the spring of 1962, the AASF was sending out form letters to students already in the United States who were asking for aid, telling them, "[T]he Foundation is no longer able to assist students financially, as it has completely run out of funds." A list of other helping-hand organizations was provided along with the form letter.

In missives to friends, Cora Weiss reported, "[T]he other agencies in the field attacked us so violently and bitterly that they [have been] virtually successful in cutting off sources of financial help to us." Shortly, the New York AASF office was closed. Even so, she did not stop assisting students when and where she could; for instance, she wrote to her counterpart at Phelps Stokes to take over the care and feeding of Cyrus Karuga, the teacher who had spent five years in a detention camp before coming to the United States to study: "You will note from his file that we had had a long and loving interest in this student, whose wife is now enrolled at New Rochelle High School." "The students won't let go and although we no longer have funds or facilities to handle their real and serious problems, I manage to find a few jobs here and there to satisfy some of the requests," she told Mboya in a letter.

By late 1962, the airlift had almost completely been taken over by the State Department and its direct grantee organizations, and the

care and feeding of students in the United States had similarly devolved upon agencies other than the AASF. The 1962 airlift was
broader than the one in 1961, and by 1963—the last of the series in
which the AASF played a role—the program was broader still, and
filled with a new generation of East Africans, most of them born
after World War II rather than before it as most of the earlier airlift
students had been. The 1963 airliftees were also younger than those
in previous groups because they were able to go to the United States
closer to the time of their graduation from secondary school; previous airliftees had waited for years before having a chance to travel
abroad for a college-level education. Among the 1963 group were
George Saitoti and Mahmood Mamdani. Saitoti was an eighteen-
year-old Maasai who had already become a standout mathematician
when he headed for Brandeis University. In later years, Saitoti would
serve as executive chairman of the World Bank and International
Monetary Fund and, for thirteen years, as Kenya's vice president.
Mamdani, a Ugandan, began at the University of Pittsburgh and received a doctorate in government from Harvard University. A career
in academia brought him to prominence in the United States and in
Africa, notably as a historian of Africa and as director of the Institute of African Studies at Columbia University between 1990 and
2004. The author of many books, Mamdani is on *Foreign Policy* magazine's list of "100 top public intellectuals."

What had begun as an iconoclastic, private moral crusade by
a handful of committed individuals—Scheinman, Houser,
Montero, the Weisses, Kheel, Belafonte, Robinson, Poitier—had
metamorphosed, in just a few years, into a regularized mainstream
activity funded by the government and carried out by its grantor institutions. Was this as it should be? The Ford Foundation study argued that it was, since prior to 1961 "the universities' response" to the
"pressing need" for education of students from emerging nations had

been "largely sporadic and unplanned," so if wholesale education of young Africans was to become regular educational policy for American universities and the U.S. government, then it required a broader and more comprehensive program than any individual foundation or private group could provide.

As the AASF program drew to its inevitable close, more quickly than its partisans might have hoped, they could take comfort from knowing that during the AASF's few years, they had successfully addressed the urgency of East Africa's educational need, and had met it with requisite swiftness and with a great deal of care. Private and African-oriented, the AASF had detoured around the roadblocks thrown up by the colonial governments in East Africa and by the U.S. State Department and its grantee agencies, to enable an entire generation of young East Africans to seize the educational opportunities of their lives and to become a solid cadre of future leaders.

Trywell Nyirongo of Malawi, in southeastern Africa, was an unusually persistent young man. He wanted to be a medical doctor, and in search of an education he had tried schools in Uganda and in Kenya before being picked for the Klotzle program and airlifted in 1961 to the United States, settling in a suburb of St. Paul where he was the only black in the high school—in fact, the only person of color in a town of forty thousand. Though he did not know much English when he arrived, Nyirongo completed high school in a single year and even played on the school's football team.

He lived with the family of Whittier and Emily Day, two social workers, and their four children. One, Sarah, later recalled that Trywell would get only four hours of sleep each night because he had so much studying and catching up to do, and that he became an inspiration to her and her siblings. The Days had to take him to a barbershop in a larger city for a haircut, because he was black. However, fifty families in the Days' congregation, where Nyirongo attended services regularly, pledged fifteen dollars apiece each month for his college education. Still, after he graduated from college he was unable to gain entry to an American medical school.

Undaunted, Nyirongo found one in Iran, where to earn his degree he had to endure slights from the Muslim students; they would not even permit him to wash his bed linen with theirs, so he had to do it separately. He transferred to a medical school in Ghent, Belgium, and did well, even though, Sarah Day recalled, he had to learn Flemish to do so. When all ten medical schools she applied to rejected her, Sarah went to Belgium to visit Trywell, and he inspired her to continue trying. She did, and became a pediatrician. After completing a medical degree in Ghent and a graduate course in tropical medicine in Antwerp, Nyirongo returned to the United States to finish his residency at a St. Paul hospital and obtain a license to practice medicine in the United States. Then, finally, he went home to Malawi. "I always thought that the fact that he returned to Malawi after his training rather than stay in the States showed his deep levels of commitment and loyalty, as well as his true grit. Trywell is a great name for him," Sarah Day said in a recent interview. After working in a mission hospital for a year, in 1974 Nyirongo opened his own clinic, the Kasambala Medical Center, in N'ChenaChena. In the age of AIDS in Africa, the clinic became an invaluable resource for the area's fifty thousand people. To support the clinic, and Nyirongo's work, members of his old congregation and other Unitarian and Universalist churches and organizations made continuing contributions, and eventually helped bring his son to the United States for college and medical school, so he could be ready to continue the Kasambala Medical Center.

Epilogue

SONS *and* DAUGHTERS *of the* NEW FUTURE

The specially invited guests for Kenya's independence day ceremonies on December 12, 1963, included the Scheinmans, the
Monteros, the Weisses, the Belafontes, and Sidney Poitier, honored
for having done much to advance the cause of independence. It was a
joyous and momentous occasion, a nation of many millions, on its
own at last.

Six months earlier, on Self Government Day, June 1, 1963, the
seventy-three-year-old Jomo Kenyatta, elected as prime minister,
had taken control of the government from the British. Mboya was

appointed minister of justice and constitutional affairs, one of the
new government's most senior posts, but because of internal Kenyatta administration politics he was soon shifted to being minister
for economic planning and development. Immensely popular, Mboya
was openly talked about as Kenyatta's heir presumptive. By the time
of the independence ceremonies he and Pamela Odede had been
married for several years and had produced their first children; the
American guests joined the Mboya family at home for a private celebration that also included leaders from various other African countries.

Over the next decade, more than 90 percent of the 1959–63
airlift graduates returned home to Kenya, most of them because
they wanted to do so, the remainder because the Kenyan government actively recruited them for key positions in the ministries and
universities. Because the British were no longer in control of what
was and was not acceptable, the new government told the students
that American degrees would be as good as if not better than British
degrees as a credential for a returning Kenyan.

Back in 1959, in a letter to Jackie Robinson, Joseph Magucha had
thanked Robinson and his AASF associates for treating the airlifted
students as "sons of the new future" of Kenya. In the decade after
independence, those who returned home from North American educational institutions created that future.

George Saitoti would be a future vice president of Kenya; about
two dozen airliftees, including Sospeter Mageto and Arthur Magugu,
would hold ministerial and ambassadorial positions; and an even
larger number would be elected as members of the Kenyan legislative body, frequently opposed in such elections by fellow airliftees.
Nicholas Mugo was in public life in the early years after he returned
to Kenya; later on his wife, Beth Wambui Mugo, whose education in
the United States had begun at a high school before she went on to
college, became a member of Parliament and minister for public
health and sanitation, replacing Magugu, who had earlier held that

position. By the mid-1980s, nearly half of the members of the Kenyan legislature were American-educated graduates of the airlift generation. A large number had risen to the upper ranks of Kenya's universities as chancellors, deans, heads of departments, and distinguished professors. As one African educator put it, "The passage to America, besides the big number of students involved, carried academic revolution which broke with the British system." The returnees also filled the most important subministerial positions of the civil service, and founded clinics, schools, agricultural cooperatives, and similar infrastructure institutions. A cadre of eight hundred, they became the *asomi*, the American-educated elite guiding Kenya and enabling its progress in many areas.

Evanson Gichuchi, who had started in the United States at a community college and went on to receive advanced degrees before returning to Kenya and its foreign service, later recalled that when the students had left for the United States they were "ignorant schoolboys and schoolgirls," but they "came back a different breed," able to think for themselves. "Had it not been for the Airlift, [Kenya] would never have made it."

Serving as the founding brothers and sisters of Kenya and, to a similar but lesser extent, of Tanzania, Uganda, and other newly formed nations of East Africa, the airlift generation fulfilled the destiny envisioned for them by Mboya, Kiano, Njiiri, Nyerere, Kaunda, and Nkomo—and by Scheinman, Houser, Montero, the Weisses, Kheel, Belafonte, Robinson, Poitier, Martin Luther King, Jr., and many other Americans.

Collectively, the airlift generation's achievements have been remarkable.

E xposure to the United States and its go-getter, capitalist mentality deeply affected many airliftees. On their return to their homeland they bought property, invested in the many opportunities that were created by a new economy, and prospered. Simon Kairo came home from Huron College in South Dakota to become personal secretary to Kenyatta for two years, during which he also ran his three-hundred-acre family farm. In 1968, he took seventeen thousand dollars from that farm to buy five Volkswagen buses and open a safari business. Aiming, he told *Time* magazine, to disabuse tourists "of the myths of Hemingway and Robert Ruark—of the faithful, ignorant, black gun bearer and other noble savages of yesteryear," he brought tourists to the game parks but also to the homes of rural Africans for real African meals.

Joe Barrage Wanjui was always thinking about how to make money. Though at Columbia University, he wanted to transfer to a school that offered degrees in broadcast engineering, as "I am convinced that communications via radio and television is going to be very important in Africa," he wrote to the AASF. But he remained in New York and made his first money by selling goods to hippies around the Columbia campus. After a year working for Esso in New York he transferred to Esso in Nairobi, bringing with him a firm belief in real estate as the vehicle to wealth. "Joe B" parlayed his instincts and training into a career as one of East Africa's primary moguls, his rise paralleled by that of fellow airlift graduate Gerald Mahinda, who began in East Africa as an accountant for Guinness and became a tycoon astride several industries; and by that of Wilson Ndolo Ayah, a telecoms entrepreneur. All of these men moved in and out of government and ministerial jobs over the decades, and when they became wealthy, set up foundations to help young East African students further their education.

Those who had spent additional years in the United States acquiring advanced degrees went back to Kenya to become leading academics. They took up positions in Kenyan universities that had not existed when they had first flown over to the United States in 1959–63.

Owino Okong'o, for instance, has recently been teaching at the Great Lakes University of Kisumu, a school that is an outgrowth of the Tropical Institute of Community Health and Development, where he helps train health care personnel for the entire East African region. Okong'o took his undergraduate degree at Brandeis and graduate degrees at Boston College and the University of Vermont in medical physiology before returning to Kenya to teach at several universities. "I have taught undergraduate and postgraduate courses in medicine, surgery, dental surgery, pharmacy and public health," he wrote recently, and he is proud of also having worked with the World Health Organization on control of AIDS and other diseases, and of having conducted research on human anatomy.

Frederick Okatcha, the inveterate letter writer to the AASF in his undergraduate days, completed a doctorate in educational psychology at Yale before returning to Kenya and a position in what became the educational psychology department of Kenyatta University. Developing an interest in African learning systems and strategies, he wrote an important study on how Luos expressed their intelligence in other than literate ways, a study that provided new insights into how to teach the members of that and similar tribes. Okatcha also wrote about the toll taken on children's ability to learn by the typical mental and physical health problems encountered by rural Kenyans, and on the inaccuracy of standardized intelligence tests given to people whose frames of reference were not those of American or European test takers. In a study he conducted in association with European researchers, Okatcha found that children in outlying African villages who learned how to use natural herbs and medicines, which their elders considered a sign of their intelligence, actually did worse on IQ tests than the children who were believed by their village to be less intelligent.

Perez Malende Olindo, Okatcha's former roommate at Central Missouri State who had gone on to study zoology and wildlife conservation at Michigan State, was one of the first airliftees recruited to return to Kenya and to achieve a high position when he was chosen in 1966 to be the first African director of Kenya's national parks.

Richard Leakey, Kenya's leading European conservationist, later wrote that Olindo was responsible for creating "many of Kenya's finest national parks" between 1966 and 1976, the period during which the parks were administered as an entity outside of the government and the civil service. Olindo actively sought contributions to the parks and the conservation of wildlife from the United States and Europe, and this brought him into conflict with the Kenyan government, which did not want too much outside influence on Kenya's natural resources. In 1976, when the government decided to merge the national parks with the Game Department, Olindo resigned. Leakey writes that his friend did so in protest, believing that what Leakey described as the department's "infamous bureaucracy" would ruin the parks; other observers suggest that the government forced Olindo out because he was too close to American and European nature lovers who sought to preserve Kenya's wildlife and natural landscape.

Removing Olindo from the national parks directorship proved disastrous for Kenya, and after the death of Kenyatta Olindo was asked once again to lead the parks, now under the Wildlife Department. He restored them and went on to spearhead international efforts to save the elephants. At a pan-African wildlife meeting in Nairobi in 1988, elected as the chair, he had no sooner taken his seat on the dais for a conference about joining efforts against poachers than he had to leave by helicopter, as a report had come in that poachers had killed six white rhinos in a national park. After finally retiring from Kenya's top conservation posts, Olindo has recently taken a similar job with the Southern Sudan, "to help them rehabilitate their national parks and get their tourism off to a good start," he writes in an e-mail, adding that he has made a friendly bet with his successor in Kenya to see which of them can generate the most tourists for their country by 2012.

Florence Mwangi, after completing her studies in medicine at Albert Einstein in New York, returned to Kenya and became the first African woman physician in the country. She established a private medical clinic on the Athi River, where she was the only physician in an area of 300,000 people, many of them from the Maasai and associated ethnic groups. Later on, she set up mobile clinics to bring medical services to nomadic peoples.

Geoffrey ole Maloiy became the dean of the veterinary school at the University of Nairobi. It took him a while to get there, though. The Maasai lad who had electrified the New York press in 1959 when he told them of his hunting trophies, Maloiy had had his heart set on going to Harvard for a medical degree but initially lacked the qualifications and began at a school in the middle of Iowa; he transferred more than once before receiving his bachelor of science degree from the University of British Columbia in 1964 and a doctorate from Aberdeen University in Scotland in 1968. During the summers that he was still in school, he sometimes returned to East Africa; for instance, he taught at a technical college in Tanzania and researched drug interactions for a World Health Organization laboratory. He finally reached Harvard in 1965, and also worked for Raytheon, a defense contractor just getting into the manufacture of lasers, which, he was amazed to learn, could be used to "correct defects in the human body," as he later told an interviewer. He also became fascinated with DNA and its possibilities for medical research, pursuing his interest at Harvard as well as working in Boston area hospitals. "The American education proved very resourceful to me being a science person," he later recalled; there was "plenty of room for experimentation and a lot of practical work." In the mid-1970s, after some years at the University of Nairobi and at a simultaneous appointment in veterinary research at an outlying research station, he won a Fulbright scholarship that took him back to Harvard for an extended period, his travel partly financed—as it had been in earlier years—by the Aga Khan.

Maloiy also spent time as a visiting lecturer in Israel, in Germany, at the University of California at Davis, and at Duke, from which he received an honorary doctorate. He is the author or editor of many

texts on animal physiology and more than 170 articles on the meta-
bolic systems of African animals such as the deer, camel, and hyrax.
In a recent interview, he worried that the positive and enabling ex-
posure to the wider world that he had obtained from his years in
America has still not become the norm for Kenyans who complete
their education only in Kenya, and who in consequence are "lacking
in the curiosities required to bring about [intellectual] development,"
a lack that he plans to ameliorate by founding, with his colleagues, a
truly international medical research institute in Nairobi.

Johnstone Muthiora remained in the United States until he completed his doctorate, and then returned home to Kenya at the request of his old friend Kenyatta, the head of the government. He
became a lecturer in political science at the University of Nairobi,
very popular with his students. But Muthiora clashed with Njoroge
Mungai, the Stanford-trained doctor who was even closer to Kenyatta, had held the portfolio of minister for defense and internal security, and was a member of the leader's kitchen cabinet as well as
the founder of the country's African-led health care system. Muthiora had other ideas for health care, and in the early 1970s decided
that in order to have more standing to push them, he should run for
election to Parliament—in the district that Mungai represented. To
everyone's surprise, Muthiora won. But before he could take office,
he died under mysterious circumstances.

Not all the airlifted students had good experiences when they
returned home. Maina wa Kinyatti clashed with his professors and
fellow students at Michigan State University's African studies program and found it necessary to leave the school; he completed his
education elsewhere before returning to Kenya a decade later and
joining Kenyatta University. There he was known as a Marxist historian, and was a continual critic of the postindependence governments, assailing them as maintaining all the bad practices that the
Mau Mau had fought against. In 1982 his premises and offices were
searched and a copy of a pamphlet was found; although written by

someone else, it denigrated then-president Daniel arap Moi, and thus violated a recently passed law. Kinyatti was imprisoned in the same compound that had earlier held his father and brother. From prison he continued to write, even though he contracted an eye disease and lost most of his sight, composing poems and collecting Mau Mau songs. His writings attracted international attention, and that pressure eventually helped to force his release in 1988, after which he moved to Tanzania and then to the United States. PEN, an international writers association, gave him an award in 1988, and predicted that he would not be able to return to Kenya. A review of his 1994 book about the Mau Mau noted, "Maina demonstrates the clear similarities between the colonial government that tortured and jailed his Mau Mau activist brother and the post-independence government that did the same to him." He never softened his tone of criticism nor his embrace of Marxism, but the Kenyan government eventually allowed him to return, take up his teaching post, and continue to write his incendiary histories, the most recent of them published in 2008.

Philip Ochieng, aspiring journalist, returned from the United States after what he refers to as "four formative years" in Chicago, and soon gravitated to Dar es Salaam and the orbit of Julius Nyerere, the leader of Tanzania. Ochieng found a job and a comfortable intellectual environment as a reporter and columnist of *Daily News*, Tanzania's major newspaper. Within a few years he was writing weekly columns—"The Way I See It" and the satirical "Ochieng on Sunday"—that were influential throughout East Africa. Most of what he and his fellow reporters and editors wrote about was the need to support the programs of Nyerere, whom Ochieng idolized as "humble, brilliant, audacious in his simplicity." Nyerere's goal was "socialism and self-reliance," expressed in the nationalization of certain industries and "collectivization of peasant farming." In the early 1970s, as Tanzania under Nyerere drifted closer to Marxism, with Ochieng as a cheerleader, his reportorial colleagues told him, "If I was so revolutionary, I should go and revolutionize my own country. Fair enough. So I scrammed."

Ochieng's revolutionary impulses and embrace of socialism lessened over the years in Nairobi, as he became a mainstay of Kenya's journalism as a reporter, columnist, editor, resident intellectual, and government gadfly. Editor of the ruling party's newspaper, *The Kenya Times*, in 1988, he was nonetheless disgusted by that year's elections, writing that it was full of "layabouts, idlers, thieves, con men, and illiterates." "If I have faith," he more recently wrote, "it is only in man's natural ability to rid himself collectively of all the terrible thought-habits—greed, hatred, jealousy, cruelty, suchlike—which civilization has taught him."

Ochieng admired those who, as with his lifelong friend John Kang'ethe, would not knuckle under to the pressures of corruption and toadyism. Kang'ethe came home to work with the Central Bank of Kenya, eventually rising to the post of foreign exchange manager. But, Ochieng recently wrote in his column, his friend had an "inborn disdain for Pharisees and other hypocrites and pretenders," which got him into trouble with his colleagues at the Central Bank—in a way similar to how Barack Obama, Sr., clashed with his superiors at the Ministry of Finance, years earlier.

In a column after the 2008 election of Barack Obama, Jr., as president of the United States of America, Ochieng wrote, "From Martin Luther King to Barack Hussein Obama we learn one powerful lesson. Historic dreams are dreamed only when their realization has entered the agenda of history. But when it has done so, history is inexorable." Ochieng pointed out that he, along with Obama Sr., had been among the first beneficiaries of the airlift program organized on the Kenyan side by Mboya and Kiano and on the American side by such people as the Weisses, Frank Untermeyer of Roosevelt University, and

> black celebrities, including Harry Belafonte, Jackie Robinson, Sidney Poitier, Frank Montero and King himself.

This early collaboration between white and black is the point of my story. It is a cinch, however, that none of these individuals had even the foggiest idea that they were preparing the bedstead in which one of us—their black Kenyan beneficiaries—would plant the vital seed that would produce the 44th president of the United States of America.

The election of Barack Obama as president of the United States of America on November 4, 2008, was occasion for wide rejoicing in Kenya; a national holiday was declared, celebrating that a son of a Kenyan had reached such an exalted position. Some Kenyans also joked that the first Luo to become president of a country had to do so in the United States rather than in Kenya: The joke was a reflection of the bitter and often bloody ethnic violence that had roiled Kenya in recent years.

In much of the rest of the world, there was also rejoicing. Nobel Peace Prize winner Bishop Desmond Tutu of South Africa wrote that as a result of Obama's election, many people "have a new pride in who they are. If a dark-skinned person can become the leader of the world's most powerful nation, what is to stop children everywhere from aiming for the stars?" One of those children, a student from Botswana, told an interviewer, "Obama's victory has shown me that the American dream is real, you just have to dream. My heart is filled with joy." And a young man in Thailand observed, "What an inspiration. [Obama] is the first truly global US president the world has ever had. He had an Asian childhood, African parentage and has a Middle Eastern name. He is a truly global president."

In the United States of America, although the election of Barack Obama as president did not result in the declaration of an instant national holiday, the jubilation was immense. And the president-elect understood where it had come from, telling an enormous crowd in Chicago's Grant Park, "If there is anyone out there who still doubts that America is a place where all things are possible, who still wonders if the dream of our founders is alive in our time, who still questions the power of our democracy—tonight is your answer."

Olara Otunnu is stunned by how much Barack Obama, Jr., resembles his father physically and intellectually. Father and son, Otunnu says, have "the same tall frame and gait" and a similar "charisma, supreme confidence, and eloquence." Obama Jr., however, has "avoided inheriting any of [his father's] flaws." Otunnu adds that like Raila Odinga, the current prime minister of Kenya who is the son of Oginga Odinga, Barack Obama, Jr., has learned lessons on what to avoid from his father's excesses and wrong turns, and has "moved to a more refined sense of power."

Obama's election was the triumph for social justice and racial equality that so many citizens, black and white, had dared to imagine and had worked for during the previous fifty years. There was also a sense, to use a Churchill phrase, that Obama's election was not the end, nor even the beginning of the end, but that it was "the end of the beginning." After the two presidential terms of George W. Bush, during which the view of America in the rest of the world had sunk to a very low point, the election of an African-American pledged to dialogue, cooperation, and engagement with friends and enemies alike was a rebirth of hope and of great expectations for the future.

The course toward Obama's election in 2008 had been set not only by the presence of one particular East African in the United States, but also by the East African airliftees' participation in the civil rights revolution of the United States. While very few of them had directly taken part in sit-ins and other confrontations, they had nonetheless contributed to the cause, in various ways.

One way was by becoming academics in North American colleges and universities. Some airliftees remained in the United States and in Canada after they completed their degrees, often because they found themselves sought after by academia, which in the 1960s was beginning to want, as well as to accept, more "minority" faculty members. As they settled into various university systems, they also helped to steer those systems toward being more inclusionary. Sam Okello Onyango, a headmaster in Kenya before going to the United States, became a fixture at Brooklyn College, for thirty years teaching mathematics to generations of students. There he also functioned as the sparkplug of the college's "SEEK" program, which mentors students from "unusual" backgrounds, the disadvantaged as well as foreign students and those from urban ghettoes. He was several times voted "favorite teacher" by the Brooklyn campus before his death in 1997. Cora Weiss, who had known him from his student days onward, spoke at his funeral.

Boniface Nyaggah, who had worked his way to Berkeley, pursued his courses to a PhD in history and became a tenured professor in the California State University system, where he was known as Dr. Muogo Nyaggah, author of a text on the effects of colonial education in Africa; as he rose up the academic ladder, he took part in civil rights conferences and helped devise African studies programs.

Augustine "Gus" Ingutia moved from Wisconsin State to Seneca College, near Toronto, and its sociology department. He was also a faculty union leader. "It was his urgings and sense of humor that got us through the lean moments" of the 1960s and '70s, a colleague later recalled: "When we thought the problems at hand to be insurmountable, it was Gus's echo of 'let's try anyway' that sometimes kept us climbing. His was a distinctive, accentuated voice crying out for understanding that if change doesn't occur at the grassroots, black and poor people will never be free. We listened carefully to him." In 1976 Ingutia was chosen to lead a Canadian federal government study of the employment needs of black rural Ontario residents, and produced a report, his colleague recalls, "that caused the federal bureaucrats to run for cover" because it exposed how the parents of these black residents had had their land stolen from them during the 1930s. The report was buried because it embarrassed Prime Minister Pierre Trudeau, who had been claiming that

Canada was less racist than the United States. According to this former colleague, Ingutia was then "harassed and driven into seclusion and poverty by the State," until his death in a traffic accident in 1998.

Harrison Bwire Muyia, one of the three spokespersons for the 1959 airliftees, graduated from Wayne State, and then Michigan State, where his doctoral dissertation was on the World Health Organization. After receiving his PhD he returned to Wayne State and taught there until he moved to Wayne County Community College, in Detroit, whose inner-city student body has a high proportion of African-Americans.

Gilbert Odhiambo Ogonji, who began at Alcorn, earned a bachelor's from Hope College in Holland, Michigan, and then moved to Atlanta University for a master's in science and to Howard for his doctorate in genetics. After postgraduate work at Yale, he joined the biology department at Coppin State University in Baltimore, and developed a lifelong project of interesting K–12 students in the biological sciences, to go along with his interests in the genetics of the fruit fly and similar subjects. According to a recent article spotlighting teachers who have done a lot for the African-American community, "He advises and mentors students, participating in programs that motivate, and encourage minority students to pursue careers in the sciences and related fields."

A second way that the East Africans contributed to civil rights progress was by quietly opening doors.

Today, histories of the civil rights movement, mostly written by participants or based on their accounts, highlight the activities of African-Americans, who did the majority of the work in the 1960s and 1970s. Most such histories have little to say about the part played by the African students in that work, but this is understandable because, with a few exceptions, African students were not on the front lines in the civil rights revolution. The East Africans in particular could not be, lest they risk losing their positions in their schools, their scholarships—and their home communities' money that was helping to support them.

A glimpse into the role of the Africans emerges from a 1963 letter written by the then-chairman of the Cornell campus antisegregation committee. He confided to a friend that at Cornell, as at most other Ivy League schools, appearances were deceiving. The four African-Americans in each incoming Cornell freshman class of two thousand students, he asserted, were almost invisible on campus, but because Cornell had for the previous four or five years been accepting a dozen or more students from Africa in each class, "to the unsuspecting observer, the campus appears to be well-integrated."

The situation was similar on most of the "integrated" American campuses that had welcomed African students. Initially, they may have been accepted in order to provide protective coloration whose purpose was to delay the need to truly integrate the institutions, but during the course of their academic careers in the United States they came to fulfill other functions, in particular opening doors and clearing paths for African-Americans to follow.

They did so by dint of their principled behavior and hard work. As documented in earlier chapters, the East Africans were extremely well motivated and conscious of the need to be a credit to relatives, neighbors, and sponsors who had sacrificed to send them to college. Exemplars of correct behavior, they sometimes served as role models for other students of color, and to the college communities. A prominent white banker in Little Rock had taken Sam Ngola, a Philander Smith student, into his home, and Ngola had become close to the banker's family—esteemed enough for the banker to bring Ngola with him to a private tea with Governor Orval Faubus in 1960. The Arkansas governor was notorious for having resisted the integration of Little Rock Central High School in 1957. In Ngola's presence, the banker stressed to Faubus how disgraceful it was to have such sterling students as Ngola—ambassadors of their countries—treated in

Arkansas as second-class citizens. Faubus appeared to listen, and thereafter the racial climate in Little Rock did begin to improve, as did Faubus's standing with the increasingly numerous black voters of his state. Nonetheless, Sam Ngola chose to transfer away from Philander Smith, along with an entire contingent of East Africans who were unsatisfied with both the college and the segregationist climate in Little Rock.

Ngola and the several others from Philander Smith, as well as some airliftees from other Southern colleges, transferred as a group to Fairleigh Dickinson, in upper New Jersey, as a result of personal interaction between the university's president, Tom Mboya, and Cora Weiss. The East Africans were not the first young men of color on the Fairleigh Dickinson campus, but their presence as a group helped to push the school, which had only recently been granted accreditation as a university, to greater acceptance of African-American students in future entering classes. Sited near large African-American communities in Newark and Paterson, Fairleigh Dickinson became one of the first universities to matriculate significant numbers of students from inner-city communities.

In a half-dozen instances, airlift students were the first nonwhites to attend a university—at large schools like Brigham Young in Utah, and at small schools like Huron College in rural South Dakota. But although at Brigham Young the East African who attended felt ostracized to the point of transferring after his first year there, Simon Thuo Kairo was welcomed in Huron. While he attended the Presbyterian college, his wife, Nellie, and their two children were enveloped by the community, which provided nursery school scholarships, housing assistance, and friendship. The experience was mutually salutary enough for Huron to think more seriously about recruiting African-Americans for its classes.

Like Huron College, most of the other religious-affiliated schools that initially offered scholarships to the East Africans were Protestant. As a consequence of Mboya's arrangement with the Catholic archbishop in Kenya, and more so after Jack Kennedy's involvement in the 1960 airlift became known, additional American Catholic colleges and universities recruited East Africans and then African-Americans.

The inability of some schools to deal with the East African students' problems also brought about changes. According to letters received by the AASF, while some students at Northeast Missouri State College, like Perez Olindo, had very good experiences there, others, including Simon Kairo, did not. Part of the difficulty was attributable to the surrounding Kirksville community in which the college was located, and part to the way that some students were treated on campus. After Olindo, Kairo, and Okatcha transferred to larger schools and did well at them, the college re-examined its methods of dealing with black students. This, in time, led the college to enroll and succor African-American students, as well as to push Kirksville to become better integrated.

Airlifted students would tell Cora Weiss and Mary Hamanaka that their college administrators, surprised to hear that they had been refused housing or other service in supposedly integrated communities, had then personally intervened on the students' behalf. To test the depths of the discrimination, CBS radio reporter Ed Joyce took one of the airlift students, as well as a white student, around the New York area to attempt to rent a room; as expected, the East African student was turned down in many places where the white student was welcomed. On the campuses, the blatant instances of discrimination that airliftees reported helped push administrations to more intervention on the students' behalf with surrounding communities. In turn, the colleges' successes at obtaining off-campus rooms and better treatment for African students provided more reason for those colleges to believe that they could successfully accommodate African-Americans; previously, a major stumbling block to matriculating African-Americans was the fear, on the part of college administrations, of bad reactions from the surrounding communities.

Student letters and reports to the AASF emphasized that they had very few problems with their college instructors, or even with fellow students in classes or in dormitories, but that difficulties had cropped up in the larger college communities. When college administrators started using their economic and social clout within those communities to insist on better treatment for their students of color, barriers fell.

Under the gentle pressure of inquiries from the AASF, universities and colleges such as Bowling Green State University in Ohio asked their professors and trustees to sponsor individual East Africans and to personally invite them into their homes. Many agreed to do so. In later years these same professors and trustees would be the ones similarly sponsoring and taking into their homes African-American students.

A third way that the East Africans helped the cause of integration was by serving as guest speakers for American communities. Nearly every airlifted student in an American college who wished to do so had multiple speaking engagements in front of Rotary clubs, Elks clubs, Kiwanis clubs, church-affiliated groups, Boy Scout troops, library discussion groups, and high schools—as many as the student could handle, usually around twenty per year. The East Africans enjoyed these engagements because they were usually paid a small honorarium for their efforts—needed pin money—but also because the students took seriously their responsibility to educate Americans about Africa and about their own lives, hopes, and dreams. Topics on which they spoke repeatedly included the situation in various hot spots in Africa, tribal customs, colonialism, their previous educational experiences, and how the students liked the United States. One successfully completed speaking engagement frequently led to others. The students also gave interviews to college and local newspapers, and local television and radio stations. In many instances they were the first black speakers ever to address local groups. Their nonthreatening demeanor, intelligence, and thirst for learning helped to dispel generations of distrust of people of darker skin.

In many and varied ways, they paved the path for the communities surrounding the colleges to accept African-American students in future years. While the sit-ins and headlined confrontations stormed barriers and broke them down, the East African students also erased barriers, but in less confrontational ways.

Another accomplishment of the East African airlifts within the United States was their contribution to changing how foreign-exchange programs were administered.

Critics had initially charged that the airlifted students were not up to the standard of American universities; the students' tenacity and drive disproved this canard, as many reached the honors lists before they graduated, and a high percentage earned their way into competitive American, Canadian, and British graduate school programs. Another accusation was that the students were attending second- and third-tier colleges whose academic standards were far below those of the Ivy League; the students' subsequent professional success showed that such second- and third-tier colleges were as well suited to educating and assisting African students as the Ivies.

The students and the AASF shined a spotlight on matters previously taken for granted in the foreign-student exchange programs of the United States. Prior to the existence of the AASF, the selection of foreign students had been made by U.S. authorities; after the airlift program, much more of the selection process was put into the hands of Africans. Moreover, the type of students chosen by the Africans for foreign exchange also began to alter, to encompass more of them from rural areas and from nonmajority tribes.

Donna Shalala, who has served as the leader of three higher learning institutions, CUNY Hunter, the University of Wisconsin, and Miami University, believes that "the airlift helped inspire language and area studies programs on campuses," as well as spurring those campuses to extend opportunities to "significant numbers of foreign students," as she put it in an interview for this book. She also suggests a reciprocal accomplishment: "The airlift started a series of events; the combination of the airlift, followed by [the establishment of] the Peace Corps, created a great interest in Africa. A lot of Americans went to Africa as Peace Corps volunteers."

The AASF's programs did pioneer a large rise in the number of foreign students admitted to U.S. educational institutions. Once American colleges and universities had understood the capacities of the first batches of East African students, the positive impact they had on their American-educational-institution hosts, and the ease with which they were able to be absorbed into the daily life of their colleges, the institutions became eager to accept more than one or two at a time. The end result was that the Dean Henry program—the African Scholarship Program of American Universities—begun as an elite program, became a program for the masses in the AASF manner, expanding in the 1960s to include 250 American colleges and universities that annually awarded thousands of scholarships to Africans.

Though the AASF existed for only a brief period of time, and concentrated on servicing students whose countries had not yet become independent, its inclusive tenets and its insistence on having Africans take the lead in selecting African students became the mainstream practices of U.S. foreign-student exchange programs—which had always been the goal of the AASF's founders and stalwarts.

The assassination of Tom Mboya in 1969 removed a great spirit from the world. Kenya was the poorer for it; during his fifteen years in public life, his vision and his guiding and genuinely collaborative spirit had been a balance to extremism in Kenya, in all its forms. He was also the African with whom Americans had had the most contact and the most sympathy, perhaps because he was so wedded to democratic ideals, capitalism, self-help, and, not least of all, to a love of education. His loss was felt keenly in both countries.

In the half-dozen years between the closing of the African American Students Foundation and Mboya's assassination, Bill Scheinman and Mboya had become even closer. Mboya was the best man at Scheinman's second wedding, and when Mboya wrote his 1963 book, *Freedom and After*, in acknowledging those who helped him he thanked just a handful of people, Scheinman the only American among them.

After Mboya's assassination, Scheinman continued to be close to the Mboya family and to assist them. A self-taught stock analyst, he became licensed as a broker and started a newsletter, *Timings*, for institutional investors. In 1970 he published *Why Most Investors Are Mostly Wrong Most of the Time*, which sold widely and was reissued in 1991. Married and divorced four times, he eventually lived alone in Reno, adopting cowboy garb and wearing his graying hair in a ponytail. After his death in 1999, his ashes were taken to Kenya and buried next to the grave of Tom Mboya on an island in Lake Victoria.

Frank Montero worked with the United Nations as a special assistant to Ambassador Adlai Stevenson in the 1960s, and was also a member of New York City's Commission on Human Rights and took on various tasks for the Democratic National Committee. At the recommendation of Ted Kheel, Montero joined Tishman Realty & Construction as a vice president. Among his projects at Tishman was assuring that appropriate numbers of minority tradesmen were hired for the construction of the World Trade Center towers. Montero died in 1998.

George Houser continued as executive director of the American Committee on Africa through the tumult of the 1960s and 1970s, battles that he recounted in his 1989 book, *No One Can Stop the Rain*. His numerous trips to Africa were supplemented by other missionary adventures abroad, which have continued through his retirement.

Ted Kheel's skills as a labor mediator were called upon by President Lyndon Johnson in national strikes during the late 1960s, and he continued as the mediator for the New York subways and transit

systems into the 1980s. He served as an executive of the Gandhi Society for Human Rights, which solicited funds to underwrite Martin
Luther King, Jr.'s work. The author of several books on mediation,
he established the Kheel Center for Labor-Management Documen-
tation & Archives at Cornell, a labor history archive.

Cora Weiss moved from the AASF into civil rights and peace activism, helping to organize the 1963 March on Washington that featured Martin Luther King, Jr.'s "I have a dream" speech. She, too,
was an officer of the Gandhi Society for Human Rights. She was a
national leader of Women Strike for Peace, which successfully agi-
tated for an end to atmospheric nuclear testing, and the director of a
committee that helped arrange regular exchanges of mail between
American POWs in North Vietnam and their families. In 1972 she
organized a welcoming committee to receive three U.S. pilots released by North Vietnam, and flew to Hanoi to escort them home,
an action for which she was lauded by some people and vilified by
others. She is currently president of the Hague Appeal for Peace and
is a past president of the International Peace Bureau. In 2007, she
initiated the first-ever reunion of the airlift generation alumni in
Nairobi, with Pamela Mboya, which was the genesis of this book.

Acknowledgments

This book could not have been written without the assistance and encouragement of Cora Weiss, former executive director of the African American Students Foundation, who conducted many of the interviews for the project, among them with Harry Belafonte, Harris Wofford, and Olara Otunnu, and has provided guidance throughout the writing process. Ted Kheel, the AASF's former secretary-treasurer, has also been invaluable, and provided access to a grant from the TASK foundation for completion of the manuscript. George Houser, one of the founders of the American Committee on Africa, which gave rise to the AASF, was always helpful. George's, Cora's, and Ted's devotion to the causes of African independence and civil rights has spanned more than five decades and is still continuing. Betsy Kawamura, Elizabeth Omondi, Jane Stanley, and Valerie Anderson aided in the research, and I thank them for their discoveries and diligence. Harriet Shelare did photographic research and in-house editing. Paul Saoke, director of Physicians for Social Responsibility in Nairobi, and Philip Ochieng, Kenya's leading journalist, provided assistance at a critical moment in the project. My thanks also to the staffs of the Martin Luther King, Jr., archives at the Hoover Institution, of the Schomburg Library in Manhattan, and of the General Research Division of the New York Public Library, in whose Wertheim Study I have happily worked on this and many previous books. Assistance also came from Clarence Jones, and from the the archives of the Unitarian Universalist Church, the Amistad Library at Tulane, the Kheel Center Archives at Cornell, and the National Archives, home of the Jackie Robinson Papers. Many colleges and universities responded to a letter from Adelphi University president Robert A. Scott asking them to search their files for information on their East African students, and some found records. Robert Stephens interviewed some graduates in the 1980s for his memoir of the airlifts, whose publication is awaited.

My thanks also to the late Pamela Mboya for information collected on airlift graduates in Kenya, and to her daughter Susan Mboya. Some of the airlift graduates and their children responded to my letters and e-mails, and have sat for interviews; their recollections and insights form an important part of the book, and for them I am grateful.

Nixon scholar Irv Gellman and civil rights and foreign policy scholar James Meriwether were gracious as well as helpful in locating and evaluating materials. Editor Phil Revzin, copyeditor Sara Sarver, and associates at St. Martin's Press provided valuable suggestions and reined in excesses, as did agent Mel Berger. Portions of the manuscript were read by Peter Weiss, Noah Shachtman, James Meriwether, and others who wish to remain anonymous, all of whom made insightful suggestions. I thank them, and all the friends, relatives, colleagues, and airlift graduates who encouraged this project. Whatever errors may remain in the manuscript are mine alone.

—Tom Shachtman, March 2009

Bibliography

This book is based largely on the archives of the African American Students Foundation, which have been in the care of Cora Weiss since the AASF wound down its activities in the 1960s. The files contain letters, telexes, newspaper clippings, proceedings of conferences, internal memos, and many other papers as well as photographs of the activities of the AASF and of senior board members. For instance, the archives contain Jackie Robinson's columns for the *New York Post* on the airlifts, many other newspaper and magazine clippings on the subject, as well as reports on student welfare and student selection by Gordon Hagberg, Albert Sims, and Kenneth D. Luke. Primarily because these AASF papers are currently unindexed and not sorted by categories, this book has not been footnoted. In the future, scholars will be able to access the AASF archive as part of Michigan State University's African Activist Archive Project.

The various speeches and other words of the public figures quoted in the text come from their published papers or other readily available archives. Many can be accessed through the Internet, which has also been a source for information about the airlift graduates. I have listed in the accompanying bibliography texts that have proved particularly useful for understanding the airlifts and their times.

The William X. Scheinman collection of papers at the Hoover Institution is closed to researchers until 2010, and was not consulted.

DOCUMENT COLLECTIONS

The Papers of the African American Students Foundation (New York), in Papers of Cora Weiss. Michigan State University. (in preparation)

The Papers of John F. Kennedy. John F. Kennedy Presidential Library and Museum, Boston, MA.

The Papers of Theodore W. Kheel. Catherwood Library Kheel Center, Cornell University.

The Papers of Martin Luther King, Jr. The Hoover Institution, Stanford University.

The Papers of Jackie Robinson. The National Archives, Bethesda, MD.

BOOKS

Ambrose, Stephen E. *Eisenhower, the President*. New York: Simon & Schuster, 1984.

Branch, Taylor. *Parting the Waters: America in the King Years 1954–63*. New York: Simon & Schuster, 1988.

Bryant, Nick. *The Bystander: John F. Kennedy and the Struggle for Black Equality*. New York: Basic Books, 2006.

Cherny, Robert W., William Issel, and Kieran Walsh Taylor, eds. *American Labor and the Cold War: Grassroots Politics and Postwar Political Culture*. Piscataway, NJ: Rutgers University Press, 2004.

Elkins, Caroline. *Britain's Gulag: The Brutal End of Empire in Kenya*. London: Jonathan Cape, 2005.

Gatheru, R. Mugo. *Child of Two Worlds*. London: Heinemann, 1966.

Goldsworthy, David. *Tom Mboya: The Man Kenya Wanted to Forget*. London: Heinemann, 1982.

Harper, Jim C., II. *Western-Educated Elites in Kenya, 1900–1963: The African American Factor*. London: Routledge, 2005.

Hoffer, Eric. *The Ordeal of Change*. New York: Harper & Row, 1963.

Houser, George M. *No One Can Stop the Rain: Glimpses of Africa's Liberation Struggles*. New York: The Pilgrim Press, 1989.

Immerman, Richard H. *John Foster Dulles: Piety, Pragmatism, and Power in U.S. Foreign Policy*. Wilmington, DE: Scholarly Resources, 1999.

Kariuki, G. C. *The Illusion of Power: Reflections on Fifty Years in Kenya Politics*. Nairobi: Kenway Publications, 2001.

Kenyatta, Jomo. *Facing Mount Kenya: The Tribal Life of the Gikuyu*. New York: Vintage, 1965.

Lewis, David Levering. *King: A Critical Biography*. New York: Praeger, 1970.

Luke, K. D. *Luke's Log*. London: Janus Publishing, 2005.

Maathai, Wangari Muta. *Unbowed: A Memoir*. New York: Knopf, 2006.

Maloba, Wunyabari O. *Mau Mau and Kenya: An Analysis of a Peasant Revolt*. Bloomington: Indiana University Press, 1993.

Mboya, Tom. *The Challenge of Nationhood: A Collection of Speeches and Writings*. London: Heinemann, 1970.

———. *Freedom and After*. Boston: Little, Brown, 1963.

Melanson, Richard A., and David Mayers, eds. *Reevaluating Eisenhower: American Foreign Policy in the Fifties*. Urbana: University of Illinois Press, 1989.

Meriwether, James H. *Proudly We Can Be Africans: Black Americans and Africa, 1935–1961*. Chapel Hill: University of North Carolina Press, 2002.

———. "'A Torrent Overrunning Everything'—Africa and the Eisenhower Administration." In *The Eisenhower Administration, the Third World, and the Globalization of the Cold War*, edited by Kathryn C. Statler and Andrew L. Johns. Lanham, MD: Rowman & Littlefield, 2006.

Murray-Brown, Jeremy. *Kenyatta*. New York: Dutton, 1973.

Nichols, David A. *A Matter of Justice: Eisenhower and the Beginning of the Civil Rights Revolution*. New York: Simon & Schuster, 2007.

Obama, Barack. *Dreams from My Father: A Story of Race and Inheritance*. New York: Three Rivers Press, 2004.

Ogot, Bethwell A. *My Footprints on the Sands of Time*. Victoria, BC: Trafford Publishing, 2003.

Plummer, Brenda Gayle. *Rising Wind: Black Americans and U.S. Foreign Affairs, 1935–1960*. Chapel Hill: University of North Carolina Press, 1996.

———, ed. *Window on Freedom: Race, Civil Rights, and Foreign Affairs, 1945–1988*. Chapel Hill: University of North Carolina Press, 2003.

Poinsett, Alex. *Walking with Presidents: Louis Martin and the Rise of Black Political Power*. Lanham, MD: Rowman & Littlefield, 2000.

Rampersad, Arnold. *Jackie Robinson: A Biography*. New York: Knopf, 1997.

Richards, Yevette. *Maida Springer: Pan-Africanist and International Labor Leader*. Pittsburgh: University of Pittsburgh Press, 2000.

Robinson, Jackie. *I Never Had It Made.* As told to Alfred Duckett. New York: Putnam, 1972.

Roosevelt, Eleanor, and Huston Smith. "What Are We For?" In *The Search for America,* edited by Huston Smith. Englewood Cliffs, NJ: Prentice-Hall, 1959.

Schlesinger, Arthur M., Jr. *Robert Kennedy and His Times.* Boston: Houghton Mifflin, 1978.

Schrecker, Ellen. "Labor and the Cold War: The Legacy of McCarthyism." In *American Labor and the Cold War,* edited by Robert W. Cherny et al. Piscataway, NJ: Rutgers University Press, 2004.

Shelley, Fred M., J. Clark Archer, Fiona M. Davidson, and Stanley D. Brum. *Political Geography of the United States.* New York: Guilford Press, 1996.

Smith, Mansfield Irving. "The East African Airlifts of 1959, 1960 and 1961." Thesis, Syracuse University, 1966.

Stephens, Robert F. "Out of Kenya: An Educational Odyssey." Unpublished manuscript, 2007.

Truman, Harry S. *Memoirs.* Vol. 2, *Years of Trial and Hope.* Garden City: Doubleday, 1956.

Von Eschen, Penny M. *Race Against Empire: Black Americans and Anticolonialism, 1937–1957.* Ithaca: Cornell University Press, 1997.

White, George, Jr. *Holding the Line: Race, Racism, and American Foreign Policy toward Africa, 1953–1961.* Lanham, MD: Rowman & Littlefield, 2005.

Wilford, Hugh. *The Mighty Wurlitzer: How the CIA Played America.* Cambridge: Harvard University Press, 2008.

Wofford, Harris. *Of Kennedys and Kings: Making Sense of the Sixties.* New York: Farrar, Straus and Giroux, 1980.

JOURNAL ARTICLES AND OCCASIONAL PAPERS

Hagberg, Gordon P. "The Rising Demand for International Education." *Annals of the American Academy of Political and Social Science* 335 (May 1961).

Matheson, Alistair. "The Kenyan–U.S. Student Airlift." Unpublished occasional paper, Nairobi, 1986.

Meriwether, James. "'Worth a Lot of Negro Votes': Africa, Black Americans, and the 1960 Vote." *Journal of American History* (January 2009).

Munene, Macharia. "The Civil Rights Movement in the U.S. and the Movement for Kenyan Independence." Paper presented at Martin Luther King, Jr., birthday celebration, U.S. Embassy in Nairobi, January 16, 1997.

———. "United States and Anti-Colonialism in Kenya, 1895–1963." *African Review of Foreign Policy* 1, no. 1 (1999).

Obama, Barack H. (Sr.). "Problems Facing Our Socialism." *East Africa Journal*, July 1965.

Sims, Albert G. "International Education." *The Journal of Higher Education* 38, no. 9 (December 1967).

NEWSPAPER ARTICLES

Awori, Franklin. "Obama Senior: The Untold Story." *East African Standard*, August 11, 2008.

Brooks, David. "Two Earthquakes." *New York Times*, January 4, 2008.

Dobbs, Michael. "Obama Overstates Kennedys' Role in Helping His Father." *Washington Post*, March 30, 2008.

Jacobs, Sally. "A Father's Charm, Absence." *Boston Globe*, September 21, 2008.

Kristof, Nicholas D. "Obama's Kenyan Roots." *New York Times*, February 24, 2008.

Macintyre, Ben, and Paul Orengoh. "Beatings and Abuse Made Barack Obama's Grandfather Loathe the British." *Manchester Guardian*, December 3, 2008.

Merida, Kevin. "The Ghost of a Father." *Washington Post*, December 14, 2007.

Ochieng, Philip. "Discussing Commitment to Humanity." *The Nation* (Kenya), January 3, 2009.

——. "It's About America's Humanity, Not Black Power." *The Nation* (Kenya), November 7, 2008.

Sanders, Edmund. "Obama Clan in Kenya Enjoys Reflected Glory." *Los Angeles Times*, November 22, 2008.

———. "Obama Not Quite His Father's Son." *Los Angeles Times*, July 17, 2008.

Tutu, Desmond. "The Man of Tomorrow." *Washington Post*, November 9, 2008.

Index

WITHDRAWN

24.99   9/17/09